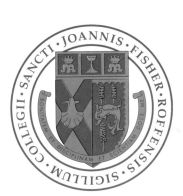

# Responsible Executive Compensation for a New Era of Accountability

Edited by

**Peter T. Chingos**

and

**Contributors from
Mercer Human Resource Consulting, Inc.**

WILEY

**JOHN WILEY & SONS, INC.**

For general information on our other products and services, or technical support, please
contact our Customer Care Department within the United States at 800-762-2974, outside the United States at 317-572-3993 or fax 317-572-4002.

Wiley also publishes its books in a variety of electronic formats. Some content that
appears in print may not be available in electronic books.

For more information about Wiley products, visit our web site at www.wiley.com.

*Library of Congress Cataloging-in-Publication Data*

ISBN 0-471-47431-2 (cloth)

Printed in the United States of America

10  9  8  7  6  5  4  3  2  1

# About the Editor

## PETER T. CHINGOS

Peter T. Chingos is a principal in the New York office of Mercer Human Resource Consulting and a member of the firm's Worldwide Partners Group. For more than 25 years he has consulted with senior management, compensation committees, and boards of directors of leading global corporations on executive compensation and strategic business issues. He is a frequent keynote speaker at professional conferences, writes extensively on all aspects of executive compensation, and is often quoted in the national press. He has appeared before the Internal Revenue Service and the Securities Exchange Commission on a variety of regulatory issues related to compensation. He is a member of the advisory board of the National Association of Stock Plan Professionals and currently teaches basic and advanced courses in executive compensation in the certification program for compensation professionals sponsored by WorldatWork. In 1998 he received WorldatWork's prestigious Keystone Award for outstanding contributions in the areas of compensation and human resource management. He is the editor of *Paying for Performance: A Guide to Compensation Management* (John Wiley & Sons, 2002).

# About the Contributors

## BEVERLY A. BEHAN

Beverly A. Behan is a partner with Mercer Delta Consulting's Corporate Governance Practice, based in New York. She works with chairs of governance committees and CEOs to enhance the effectiveness of their boards of directors. She has worked extensively in the area of board assessment and individual director peer assessment since 1997, when she helped to design and implement a director peer assessment process for an international bank that won international corporate governance awards for innovation in this area. She has been quoted as an expert in corporate governance in the leading business journals.

## MELISSA L. BUREK

Melissa Burek is a principal in Mercer Human Resource Consulting's New York office. She focuses on all aspects of executive compensation and has worked with leading companies and boards of directors on compensation strategy, annual and long-term incentive plan design, tax and accounting issues, and board compensation. She has been responsible for Mercer's "best practices" research among Fortune 100 companies and within the insurance industry. She has worked extensively with manufacturing, insurance, and pharmaceutical companies in assessment and redesign of total compensation programs. Ms. Burek holds BBA and MBA degrees from the University of Michigan.

## K. KELLY CREAN

Kelly Crean is a principal in Mercer Human Resource Consulting's Atlanta office. He consults with clients on equity-based compensation practices, board of director pay, business analysis, and incentive plan design. He is one of the firm's leading consultants on executive pay from the shareholder and institutional perspective. Mr. Crean has written numerous articles on executive compensation and equity-based pay practices for various corporate governance publications. Prior to joining Mercer, he was a senior compensation specialist with Institutional Shareholder Services, the leading proxy and advisor service to institutional investors. He holds BA and MBA degrees from the University of Georgia.

## SUSAN EICHEN

Susan Eichen is a principal in Mercer Human Resource Consulting's New York office and a member of Mercer's Washington Resource Group, which assists Mercer clients and consultants in addressing technical legal and regulatory issues and providing government relations expertise on a wide range of retirement, health, compensation, and other human resource topics. Ms. Eichen specializes in incentive plan design, option valuation, and accounting for compensation arrangements. Her clients include publicly and privately held companies, subsidiaries, and foreign-owned entities in a broad range of industries. She has written extensively on issues in incentive plan design and the impact of accounting rules on compensation policies and practices. A CPA, Ms. Eichen holds an MBA from the Wharton School and a BA from Brown University.

## DIANE L. DOUBLEDAY

Diane Doubleday is a principal in the San Francisco office of Mercer Human Resource Consulting. She specializes in executive compensation and has particular expertise in the design and operation of equity plans. She is a frequent speaker and author on equity compensation and emerging issues affecting executive compensation. She holds an AB and JD from the University of California, Berkeley.

## WILLIAM H. FERGUSON

William H. Ferguson is a principal in Mercer Human Resource Consulting's Los Angeles office, the Performance, Measurement, and Rewards Practice leader for Los Angeles, and a member of the U.S. Practice Leadership Team. He has over 15 years of experience advising executives and boards of directors on creating shareholder value by designing integrated value management, performance measurement, and reward programs. His consulting experience covers a broad range of industries, including high tech, software, real estate, chemicals, and financial services, among others. He received his BA and MS degrees from Stanford University.

## HOWARD J. GOLDEN

Howard J. Golden, JD, is a principal in Mercer Human Resource Consulting's New York office. He specializes in executive compensation design and compliance, the interrelationship of compensation and benefits programs, corporate governance issues, and regulatory matters. Mr. Golden has been a contributing editor for many professional journals, a featured speaker at many national forums, and has testified before Congress. He is quoted often in the national media.

## MICHAEL J. HALLORAN

Mike Halloran is a principal in Mercer Human Resource Consulting's Dallas office and a member of the firm's Worldwide Partners Group. He has consulted on executive compensation and benefit issues for over 25 years, focusing on linking executive compensation to business strategy and enhanced performance for shareholders. He is a frequent speaker on executive compensation issues for Worldat-Work, The Conference Board, and other leading forums. He has a bachelor's degree in mathematics from Northwestern University and an MBA from Northwestern's Kellogg School, specializing in finance and accounting.

## G. STEVEN HARRIS

Steven Harris leads Mercer Human Resource Consulting's executive compensation practice in the southeastern U.S. region and is a member of the firm's Worldwide Partners Group. Based in Atlanta, he has more than 15 years of experience consulting in the business-based design and use of executive equity and cash incentive compensation programs. He is a frequent speaker at business and professional associations on executive compensation and pay-for-performance issues and has provided briefings on executive pay trends to U.S. Senate and House staff as well as to senior officials within the Departments of Treasury and Labor. He holds BA and MA degrees in psychology and an MBA degree from Indiana University.

## SHEPARD LONG

Shepard Long is a principal in Mercer Human Resource Consulting's New York office, where he specializes in executive compensation strategy development, pay-and-performance assessments, and annual and long-term incentive plan design. He also coordinates Mercer's ongoing "best practices" research, which focuses on executive compensation practices at high-performing Fortune 100 companies. He holds an MBA from New York University's Stern School of Business.

## HAIG R. NALBANTIAN

Haig Nalbantian is a member of the firm's Worldwide Partners Group, a founding member of Mercer's Strategy and Metrics group, and co-chair of the company's global R&D Council. He is a labor and organizational economist and has been instrumental in developing Mercer's unique capabilities to measure the economic impact of human capital management. Previously he was on the faculty of economics at New York University and was a research scientist at its C. V. Starr

Center for Applied Economics. He has written extensively on the subject of incentives and organizational performance and has consulted with leading companies across a wide range of industries. Mr. Nalbantian has MA and M.Phil degrees in economics from Columbia University.

## RUSSELL MILLER

Russell Miller is a principal in Mercer Human Resource Consulting's New York office. He consults with senior management and boards of directors on value management, performance management, and compensation issues. The focus of his work is on developing performance measurement systems and compensation programs that are linked to business strategy and drive value creation. Mr. Miller is a frequent speaker on value management and performance measurement. He has a BS degree in finance from the Wharton School of the University of Pennsylvania.

## PETER J. OPPERMANN

Peter J. Oppermann is a principal in Mercer Human Resource Consulting's New York office. He has more than 20 years of consulting experience focusing on executive and board compensation. He has developed executive and management compensation programs for national and international clients in the manufacturing, services, e-commerce, and high-technology sectors. He is a frequent speaker at national and regional seminars on executive and management compensation.

## LEA L. PETERSON

Lea Peterson is the global and U.S. leader of Mercer's Communication Practice and a member of the firm's Worldwide Partners Group. Her responsibilities include setting strategic direction, as well as leading the growth and development of the communication consulting business worldwide. Ms. Peterson has over 25 years of experience in organizational communication for major international corporations. She works with global clients on communication strategies for organizational change and performance enhancement. Her work includes creative problem solving to achieve client business objectives and effective processes to engage internal stakeholders in the execution of complex change. The International Association of Business Communicators has awarded her a Gold Quill eight times for excellence in communications. Prior to joining Mercer in 1984, Ms. Peterson managed employee communication in several major corporations. Ms. Peterson has a BA degree in English from the University of Maryland and an MA degree in English from the University of New Hampshire.

## J. CARLOS RIVERO

Carlos Rivero is a partner in Mercer Delta Consulting's New York office. He works in the areas of organization diagnosis and change, organization culture, and applied research with emphasis on measurement and feedback. Dr. Rivero has published several articles and book chapters on executive team effectiveness, strategic human resources, management development, and corporate governance. He holds an MA and PhD from New York University in Industrial/Organizational Psychology.

## WEI ZHENG

Wei Zheng leads the Performance, Measurement and Rewards Practice in North China. He has worked with a wide range of leading Chinese and U.S. companies spanning many industries. Prior to joining Mercer China, he was with Mercer's Strategy and Metrics group in New York. He is an economist specializing in human capital strategy, performance measures, executive compensation, and financial analysis and was instrumental in developing Mercer's capability to quantify economic effects of human resources management. Mr. Zheng received his PhD in economics from New York University.

# Contents

# Responsible Executive Compensation for a New Era of Accountability

**Peter T. Chingos**

A large organization approached Mercer recently to audit its governance procedures related to executive compensation program design and operation. The organization was confident that the compensation committee was functioning as well as any organization's, but the board wanted assurance that the decisions about compensation programs and the processes used to make those decisions were "above reproach." The board took these extra precautions, in part, to assure stakeholders and avoid media scrutiny.

This example illustrates that the notion of responsible pay—pay that is above reproach—has become inextricably linked with corporate governance and long-term shareholder value creation. It has fueled many companies to action—some more bold than others.

## SPOTLIGHT ON CORPORATE GOVERNANCE

The corporate accounting scandals and executive compensation abuses exposed the pervasive weaknesses in oversight at U.S. companies. Regulators and legislators moved quickly:

The Sarbanes-Oxley Act of 2002 was the first step. It focused on strengthening the role of the audit committee and the independence of the auditor. Among other things, it imposed financial statement certification requirements, prohibited loans to executive officers, and established the Public Company Accounting Oversight Board to regulate the public accounting profession.

The New York Stock Exchange (NYSE), the Nasdaq, and the American Stock Exchange proposed changes in the listing requirements, including a new definition of "independent" director, board and committee membership requirements, and procedures for the compensation and audit committees. The NYSE and the

Nasdaq have issued new final listing standards that require shareholders to approve the adoption or material amendment of any equity plan.

The Securities and Exchange Commission (SEC) is focusing attention on the composition of boards. It has proposed rules to require enhanced disclosure of the director nomination process, including selection criteria and a description of how the board responds to nominations from shareholders. This is the first step in an SEC initiative to give shareholders—in limited circumstances—greater access to the proxy for their own director candidates.

## CHALLENGES TO THE STATUS QUO

Regulators and legislators were not alone in their quick response. The corporate accounting scandals prompted unprecedented media and shareholder scrutiny of governance and executive compensation. Long-standing criticisms of excessive pay levels suddenly acquired new life, sending strong messages to boards that they must alter how they design and implement executive pay programs.

Equity compensation—the principal component in executive pay packages—is at the heart of the issue. In many large public companies, the number of shares set aside for compensation purposes—often exceeding 20 percent of shares outstanding—is at an unsustainable level. With the prolonged economic slump and vastly lower share prices, many options are worthless and have lost their currency as a viable long-term incentive.

Until now, most stock options carried no compensation cost—seen by many as a contributing factor to executive compensation abuse. However, a new accounting standard mandating a P&L charge for stock options seems certain in 2005. What was "free" could now be costly to the company if current stock option grant practices are maintained. This fact raises questions regarding the desirability of awarding stock options and their practicality from the company's cost-benefit standpoint. If the "present value" fixed cost of options is acceptable, is the "perceived value" to the executive consistent with this cost?

## IMPACT OF THESE DEVELOPMENTS

"Responsible pay" encompasses the process for determining pay and the elements and features of the pay program. Both have been affected.

For many boards, the first step in responding to these many outside forces was to change the compensation committee membership to include only independent directors, using the more stringent definitions in the proposed listing requirements. As consultants, we have seen a fairly dramatic change as compensation committees demand direct access—not controlled by management—to outside consultants for advice on executive compensation program design, particularly for the CEO. Committees are holding executive sessions, with no employees or employee-directors present, to discuss executive compensation matters. And under the new listing standards, compensation committees will be charged with conducting an annual evaluation of the CEO's performance. Although a new and often difficult endeavor for many boards, this responsible pay process for determining CEO pay must include a performance assessment that goes beyond meeting financial goals and addresses qualitative matters, such as leadership and relationships with customers, investors, and the board.

Boards also have a keen eye to the stronger influence of shareholders in the decision-making process. In some cases, shareholders express their concerns informally, but often they are resorting to the proxy to express their dissatisfaction with executive compensation matters. Even though these shareholder proposals generally are not binding, boards cannot afford to ignore the popularity of shareholder proposals, such as those asking companies to report options as an expense or to limit severance in change of control situations.

## LESSONS LEARNED FROM THE PAST

By focusing companies on "total shareholder return" in its proxy disclosure reforms of the early 1990s, the SEC gave a strong signal that stock price appreciation is the primary measure of a company's success. Companies, particularly cash-strapped high-tech start-ups, saw stock options as a cost-effective way to align the interests of shareholders and employees. As the 1990s progressed, companies responded to the rising stock market with a higher-growth, higher-risk orientation in long-term incentive plans and stock options increasingly extended down through the management ranks, often to all employees.

As the market soared, total compensation expectations were raised unrealistically. Stock option grant values rose to unprecedented levels, and it was hard to distinguish "mega" grants of several millions of shares from regular grants. The obvious question of whether the underlying performance supported these lofty payouts was seldom addressed.

Today, according to Mercer Human Resource Consulting research, long-term incentives made up mostly of stock options account for about 70 percent of a CEO's pay. In 2002 the median stock option grant was nine times the CEO's salary. Companies are left looking for a responsible pay resolution.

Two things are missing in many executive compensation programs in the United States: balance among elements and accountability for results. A hallmark of a responsible pay program is that there is a balance among the elements: cash and equity, short- and long-term incentives, fixed and variable components. In many companies, the magnitude of equity compensation completely overshadowed the other elements, often making them irrelevant. Companies are now facing the painful process of cutting back their equity programs, often at the same time that salaries are frozen and incentive plans are not paying out because of weak performance.

## PAY FOR PERFORMANCE—A SOLUTION NOW MORE THAN EVER

In order to hold executives accountable for results, the pay programs must be linked effectively to performance. In the bull market, this accountability was lost as share price appreciation occurred even without underlying performance. More than ever before, boards must now take a rigorous approach to ensure that pay reflects performance in a manner that can be understood by all stakeholders and that measures reflect contributions over which employees exercise real control (e.g., return and growth measures, measures of market share, innovation-type measures, customer measures, and measures to manage human capital).

Today we see organizations increasingly responding to shareholder concerns that absolute performance improvement is not enough. Companies must have an eye to relative performance against appropriate external benchmarks as well. The good news is that poor performers will not be rewarded well in a rising market; the better news is that strong performers will be rewarded even if the overall market or their industry sector is suffering. The task does not end with selecting measures. Directors will have to ensure that the targets are appropriate, that the amount of pay delivered for attaining goals is calibrated to the performance level, and that goals are not reset midway through the performance cycle to reward effort rather than results.

For many directors, these will be new and demanding tasks. Strategies to link pay more effectively with performance will not be successful overnight. To describe the process of establishing absolute and relative goals as difficult is an understatement. It is an extraordinarily challenging task, particularly in the volatile economic markets that we have been experiencing in recent years. Nonetheless, boards will have to step up to this challenge.

## LOOKING AHEAD

Corporate governance reform and notions of responsible pay will continue to evolve over the next few years as boards, management, and shareholders become familiar with new processes, different vehicles, and more accountability. Optimists believe that the rebalancing of power among shareholders, management, and the board, along with some painful lessons learned, will keep corporations from making the same executive compensation mistakes in the future that were made in the past. The cynical perspective is that corporate governance reform and rebalancing of executive compensation programs will last only until there is a bull market. For the next few years, the market demand for stronger corporate governance and responsible pay programs will continue to grow. In a stronger economy, the question will be whether the procedural safeguards that are being implemented today will continue to foster responsible pay decisions in the future.

In the end, despite the upheaval in corporate America, we believe that the objective of a responsible pay program has not changed: Pay programs need to be sufficient to attract and retain the best talent to address the individual organization's needs. The structure of the program, particularly incentive plans, should focus participants on the organization's operational and financial priorities. Those, in turn, should be linked to long-term shareholder value creation.

## IN THE CHAPTERS THAT FOLLOW

In an earlier book written by Mercer Human Resource Consulting, *Paying for Performance—A Guide to Compensation Management, 2nd edition* (John Wiley & Sons, 2002), we provided a road map for the design and implementation of an effective pay-for-performance program, focusing on best practices. In this book, we focus on the issues facing companies that accept the need to assess and refine their executive reward strategies in light of what is, in fact, a new era of executive compensation. A few of the hallmarks characterizing well-designed and responsible executive compensation programs include:

- *Business-focused compensation strategy.* A compensation strategy starts with a clear business vision tied to shareholder value creation. The CEO communicates the business goals and road map for achieving short- and long-term success. Senior management then develops financial and nonfinancial operational goals and key decisions that support the vision. The executive compensation strategy, typically created by human resources in partnership with the CEO and board plus finance and legal professionals, begins by addressing such key questions as:

  - Will our strategy generate superior returns for investors?
  - Are we measuring appropriate performance?
  - Do our people know how their decisions impact performance and how to make the right decisions?
  - Are our pay practices fair to both employees and shareholders? Are our incentives really driving business results?

The compensation strategy document relates each element in the pay program to the organization's vision and business strategy, identifies key competitors in attracting and retaining key employees based on where the business is today and where it will be in the future, and articulates the competitive positioning and mix of pay for specific positions and management levels. Incentive compensation vehicles should harmonize with other elements in the pay program but should not duplicate them. Key to any compensation strategy is a commitment to hold management and employees accountable for expected performance.

- *Well-defined compensation components.* Executive compensation consists of an appropriate mix of salary, annual and long-term incentives, and benefits. Base salary reflects core job responsibilities and the relevant external market for these responsibilities. Annual incentives focus on company, team, and individual performance, typically over an annual time frame. Long-term incentives, in the form of equity or cash, focus on corporate and organization performance over a multiyear period.

  Executive compensation positioning—the strategic setting of salary and incentive goals and targets—should be firmly tied to actual and expected performance, taking into consideration various constituencies such as shareholders, employees, and competitor companies. In today's environment, the actual and perceived value of compensation, its cost to the company, and its alignment with shareholder value are issues that must be carefully thought out before implementing changes in the executive compensation program. Targeting pay at above median will no longer be automatic, and targeting premium pay will have to be validated by corresponding financial performance that supports the pay position.

- *Pay and performance validation.* Company management and boards have the responsibility of demonstrating an appropriate relationship between compensation and financial performance. This, as we mentioned above, should not be done in isolation but within the contexts of absolute and relative performance. Drawing on internal human resources, often in conjunction with compensation consultants, senior management determines appropriate peer companies that reflect the marketplace for talent and competition for products and services. These serve as the foundation for pay and performance comparisons. Once an appropriate composite group of companies has been identified, it is then possible to test the degree of stretch for setting incentive targets. This process provides assurance to shareholders and other constituencies that the relationship between pay and corresponding performance is sound. CEOs have found this process to be particularly helpful in managing pay and performance expectations.

- *Executive accountability.* Personal accountability is at the heart of an effective executive compensation program. Although "the numbers tell the story" and numerical targets are either met or not, accountability does not have to mean rigid inflexibility. But there does have to be a clear cause-and-effect relationship between results and rewards. Strong performance should be rewarded;

poor performance should not. Today there is tremendous pressure on getting the measurement system right. Many companies need to rethink how they create value for shareholders and how they translate value creation into understandable and measurable behaviors. This is why the performance assessment process—for the CEO, the board, and management—is so important to the effective implementation of executive compensation programs.

- *Highest standards of governance.* The CEO and the board of directors (typically through the compensation committee) have primary oversight responsibility for approving, reviewing, and communicating the company's executive compensation strategy and pay decisions. As the shareholders' representatives, they have specific responsibilities under federal and state law. Mere compliance with the law is not enough to maintain investor confidence. The recently mandated board self-evaluation process will help assure that boards operate independently of management pressures and within the stated role and scope of their charters. In many companies this will lead to further training and education of directors in better understanding operational and financial processes, greater involvement in assuring executive accountability, and increased oversight of the firm's consulting relationships.

In addressing the issues just outlined, we have taken various approaches in writing the chapters of this book—from the general overview, to the highly technical, to the "hands-on." We begin with how companies create and deliver value since this is the foundation of responsible executive pay practices. Following chapters discuss the accounting and governance issues affecting executive pay and various aspects of assessing the performance of CEOs, boards, and existing executive pay programs. Other chapters focus on executive and board compensation design, communications, and the role of the consultant. Each chapter can be read as a self-contained discussion of a specific topic, with the overall intent being to provide useful information on a broad range of issues related to the current mandate for responsible executive pay.

# Chapter 1

# Creating Value for Shareholders: From Measurement to Management

**William H. Ferguson**

Value, and managing for value, means many things to many people. Since managing for value is the most powerful way to enhance performance and create shareholder value, we need a clear definition of the term. In addition, to make value a day-to-day mind-set, we also need a way to link shareholder value to the everyday decisions that all people make within an organization.

Our link will be the process of managing for value. Managing for value is an organizational mind-set (e.g., information, processes) that helps align decision making with creating shareholder value. It is the foundation on which a pay-for-performance mind-set and shareholder-driven executive compensation design is built. The creation of shareholder value is the ultimate objective of any reward or incentive program design. This objective is particularly important if the program is for the most senior executives. When competing interests are at work, shareholder value creation provides a compass for decision making and design. A clear definition and working knowledge of shareholder value will provide our "true north." Shareholder value is also a compass for good governance. The topics of governance, pay-for-performance and executive compensation, as well as performance measurement, target-setting, reward design, and communication, are subjects for later chapters in this book.

First we will start with a definition of value, and then we will show how a managing-for-value mind-set is the common thread. Only with this common thread can we identify what performance to measure, create reward programs that help strategy execution, and develop other people programs that change behavior and create alignment around the enterprise objectives.

In this chapter we will start the journey, and we will:

- Create a simple, usable definition of value that managers can use every day
- Explain the basic concepts of using the definition as part of managing the business
- Describe how these can be applied every day

By the end, we will see that:

- Value matters
- Value can be managed on a day-to-day basis
- Value creation provides the grounding and line of sight for decisions and management
- Value provides the common thread to align decision makers and key business processes (e.g., reward strategy and performance measurement)
- A managing-for-value mind-set is required for the sustainable, long-term success of an enterprise as well as day-to-day decision making

---

**Illustration**

The working team was conducting an educational session for a broad cross-section of the employee population. This company's value management program had focused on defining a clear corporate objective, establishing aggressive targets, defining a performance measure everyone could understand, and ensuring that everyone knew how each person contributed to making money. As part of the session, the team described how one "unit" of the company's service generated revenue (everyone cheered), generated costs (everyone rubbed their chins), and then created profit (everyone was surprised at how little). The profit margins in this business were very thin, only making hundreds of dollars on tens of thousands of revenue. Then, from the back of the room, a hand went up. One of the most junior employees, just in his first year, observed that if this was the situation, he would reuse that paintbrush more than once, maybe several times. As the group then discussed the costs of this change, everyone quickly figured that in some cases this could be the difference between making money and not.

What did value and managing for value mean for this organization? Engagement and understanding that managing for value has personal relevance for everyone in the company.

## 1.1   WHAT VALUE IS AND WHY IT MATTERS

### (a) Definitions of Value

Our working definition of value will be "market value added." Therefore, an organization's primary objective is to create returns above the value of the owner's investment in the enterprise. From a shareholder (or equity holder) perspective, this return is measured by share price appreciation and dividends over time. For the manager of an enterprise, it represents the economic profit created over time. Economic profits are the returns after covering all expenses and the opportunity costs of the shareholders' investment.

Four primary definitions related to value need to be understood in order to make this a workable concept for management. (See Exhibit 1.1.)

***(i) Market Value***   Depending on the structure of the organization, this value will come through the appreciation of an ownership stake (e.g., share price) and dividends, if paid. From a public market perspective this is defined as market capitalization, or the book value of equity (BV) plus market value added (MVA).[1] (See Exhibit 1.2.)

The book value of equity represents the shareholder investment in the enterprise. Book value of equity and market value of equity are observable from the external market. Therefore, at any point in time, we know the premium (positive MVA) or the discount (negative MVA) that is being applied in the market.

***(ii) Market Value Added***   The MVA is the premium that shareholders put on the value of an enterprise above and beyond the book value of their investment. Management's primary objective is to drive a positive and growing MVA over time. The source of this premium is determined by several factors, including market risk, competitor risk, current performance, expected future performance, and value of intangibles. Since our objective is to maximize this premium, we need to identify each factor's contribution to value and then understand how to manage or influence the factors that have the greatest impact on value. This will be the first critical step in moving from measurement to management.

***(iii) Book Value of Equity***   The book value of equity is the value of the investment in the enterprise by the shareholders as reflected on the accounting statement.

---

[1]Market Value of Equity = Market capitalization *or* Market Value Added + Book Value of Equity
where
      Market Capitalization = Share price × Shares outstanding.

**Exhibit 1.1**   Four Definitions of Value

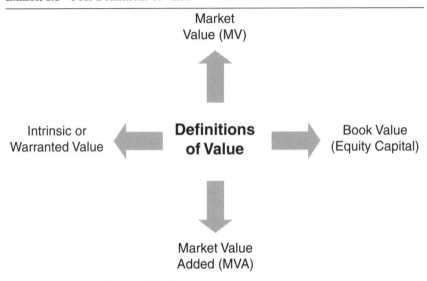

*Source:* Mercer Human Resource Consulting.

**Exhibit 1.2**   Market Value

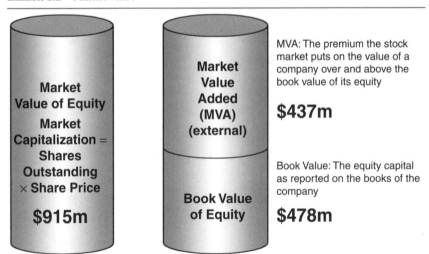

*Source:* Mercer Human Resource Consulting.

---

**Illustration**

During the kickoff of a managing-for-value initiative with a midsize transportation company, a large sample of the senior management was interviewed on various topics surrounding strategic issues, organizational change, and their perspective on specific business processes, programs, and decision making in general. One of the questions asked was "When the CEO says, 'We had a good year,' what does he mean?" Twenty people were interviewed, and there were 20 different interpretations, which resulted in very fragmented focus. Some people were driving for new customers (at any price), others were holding the line on price, and still others were driving new service activities. If there had been the resources or strategy to do all of these things, great, but this business did not have that luxury and needed laserlike focus on broad tactics to succeed.

---

At this point it is important to distinguish the two different sources of capital that an enterprise can use for funding: equity and debt. (See Exhibit 1.3.) Our definition of market value includes equity capital—the money provided by investors. These investors demand a minimum equity capital level of return on their investment. The return required from equity capital is measured from market inputs (a definition of cost of equity follows). The other source of funds is debt. Debt capital investors require an agreed level of return, represented by an interest rate (Kd). This rate of return is determined as one of the conditions for providing the funds. Therefore, this expectation is measured easily.

***(iv) Intrinsic Value and Economic Profit***   At any point in time, the intrinsic value of a company can be derived from the discounted sum of future economic profits. (See Exhibit 1.4.) Discounting the future economic profit (EP) stream puts the value in today's dollars. Using this definition of intrinsic value relies on a forecast of the enterprise's economic profit stream over time, which defines the future returns from the business above the cost of equity $(Ke)^2$.

---

[2]Economic Profit = Net Income – $(Ke \times$ Book Equity)
Net Income = EBIT – Interest Expense – Taxes
$Ke = Rf + (B \times$ Market Risk Premium)

where
$\quad\quad B$ = beta
$\quad\quad$ EBIT = earnings before interest and taxes
$\quad\quad Ke$ = cost of equity
$\quad\quad Rf$ = risk-free rate of return

**Exhibit 1.3**    Enterprise Value: Two Sources of Capital

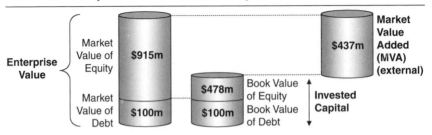

*Source:* Mercer Human Resource Consulting.

Economic profit represents the returns available to the equity investors of the business. In other words, it represents the returns to the investors after paying for the expenses of operating the business (e.g., cost of goods sold, Selling, General & Administration (SG&A), other overhead) and covering the expense for the equity investment. The expense of the equity investment (an opportunity cost) is a per-

**Exhibit 1.4**    Intrinsic Value of Equity

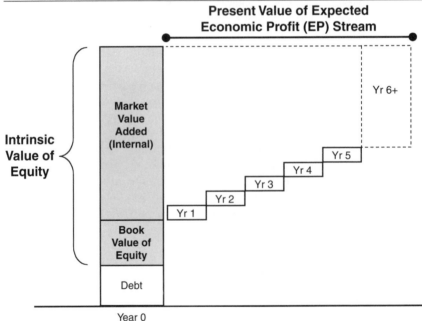

*Source:* Mercer Human Resource Consulting.

centage of the total investment in the business as determined by the cost of equity. *Ke* is the minimum level of return required for the investor to be indifferent between this investment and a risk-free investment.

Combining the concepts of intrinsic value (an internal measure) and market value (an external measure) allows us to understand the shareholders' expectations for performance beyond (or below) current and expected performance. (See Exhibit 1.5.)

## (b) How a Business Creates Value

Let us consider for a moment the messages we can distill from these measures of value, starting with intrinsic value. When intrinsic value is different from market capitalization, this could mean several things:

- Investors do not understand how the business will create value in the future (intrinsic value > market capitalization). There may be a lag in the information or a credibility gap with the current management given past performance.
- Investors may see more risk in the current plan than management acknowledges and therefore will discount the future value (intrinsic value > market capitalization).
- Investors see more opportunity for the business than management (intrinsic value < market capitalization). For example, the investors may view the company's industry as providing good performance and growth opportunities,

**Exhibit 1.5** Shareholder Expectations for Performance

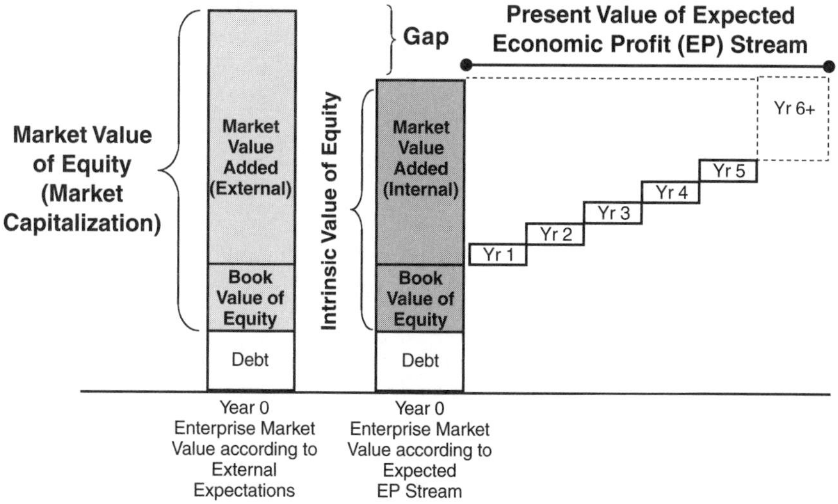

*Source:* Mercer Human Resource Consulting.

and therefore expect more from the enterprise. Or the company has not yet identified the opportunities required to meet shareholder expectations and the gap is real.

- Finally, at any one point in time, the two values may be different, given the volatility introduced by market risk and industry risk. But over time, market capitalization and intrinsic value should converge, so only systematic gaps should be of concern.

Drilling underneath our primary external measure of value (market value added) and our primary internal measure of value (intrinsic value), we then explore how economic profit signals value creation. Very simply, if:

Economic Profit > 0, the business is exceeding the investors' minimum expectations (ROE > $Ke$).

Economic Profit < 0, the business is returning less than the investors' minimum expectations (ROE < $Ke$).

In this characterization we are using $Ke$ to represent the equity investors' minimum level of required returns given the risk of this business (operating risk) and the premium required for making risky vs. risk-free investments (market risk premium). Therefore, if:

Economic Profit over time is > 0, the business is creating value.
Economic Profit over time is < 0, the business is destroying value.

What does a decision maker do with this next level of information? In other words, how do we turn this information into insight and continue the path from measurement to management? Using a characterization of value creation or exceeding minimum returns, we can think about simple implications:

- If Economic Profit is < 0, the immediate and highest priority is to get the economic profit above 0. If this does not happen quickly, any growth in the business will destroy even more value since we will be growing an unprofitable business.
- If Economic Profit is around 0, the priority is much the same, although the business needs to be thinking ahead to prepare for growth and find ways to sustain profitable performance.
- If Economic Profit is > 0, the highest priority is to protect this level of profitability and find ways to grow the enterprise (e.g., invest more to grow a profitable business).

Finally, there are four basic ways that a business will drive value:

1. Grow and/or enter economically profitable elements of the business. This could mean extending profitable products/services into new markets or

adding services to profitable customers. It also could mean entering profitable new markets/products/services/customers.

2. Improve economic cost structure or margins. This might mean lowering costs, rationalizing assets, or investing in new ways to get economies of scale (lower variable costs per unit).

3. Exit unprofitable businesses where there is no possibility of creating economic profit over time and participation in this business does not support value creation in other parts of the business.

4. Reduce the risk on the business relative to competitors, thereby lowering the minimum return required by investors.

## (c) Shareholder and Stakeholder Value

Shareholders are not the only ones with an interest in an enterprise. There are other stakeholders and each has different objectives and a different definition of value. (See Exhibit 1.6.)

For example, customers are looking for the best product or service at the best price. Employees are looking for job satisfaction, rewards, and learning opportunities. Each stakeholder is looking for different things.

Much has been written about the balance between shareholder and stakeholder objectives. However, research has demonstrated that in the long term, those companies that focus on and satisfy shareholder demands are also the ones that outperform

---

**Illustration**

Following a working session with the senior management team of his company, the president sat back and reflected. This company had been started and run by his father. Essentially he had grown up in this family business, which was now part of a public company. The working session had been about defining the value drivers of the business, or how the business made money. After thinking about what he had heard, he mentioned that he saw three things from his team after the day. The analysis and insight had:

1. Confirmed several of the priorities for the business
2. Reprioritized several items (e.g., some of his most important items were now at the bottom of the list)
3. Added some new high-priority action items

What did value mean for this CEO? Clarity, priorities, and consistency.

**Exhibit 1.6**   Shareholder and Stakeholder Value

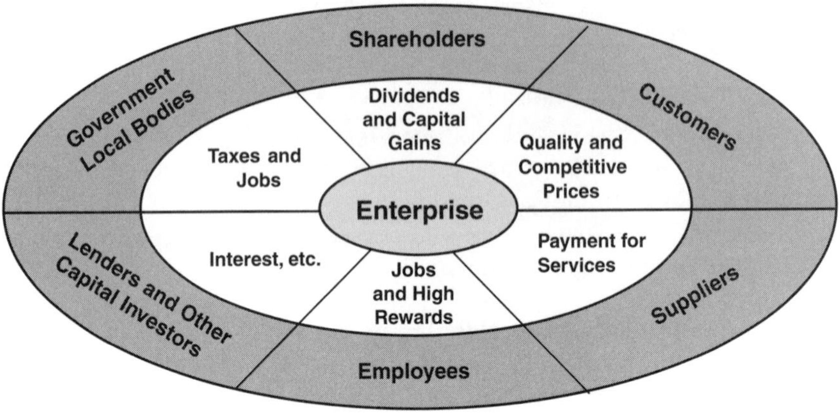

*Source:* Mercer Human Resource Consulting.

on delivering the stakeholder value. The reverse is not true. There are many recent examples, especially in the bull market of the late 1990s, of companies that did little to meet shareholder demands or deliver value for customers or employees, and eventually failed.

## (d) Benefits of Focusing on Shareholder Value

There are two ways to understand how a focus on shareholder value is beneficial. The first is from the mind-set, decision-making, or process perspective. The other perspective is the fiduciary responsibility lens.

A shareholder-value driven mind-set and decision-making process is the foundation of how to manage for value. The benefits of approaching the management of an enterprise with this mind-set are multiple, and all directly relate to the clarity of decision making. Specifically, a shareholder-value driven mind-set includes:

- *Clarity on the enterprise objective:* Ultimately, everyone needs to understand why the enterprise exists, how it makes money, and what their role is in this process. Individuals need to understand how their day-to-day actions affect the overall outcomes of the business. Without this common perspective on the corporate objective, people will work in a fragmented manner (at best) and at cross-purposes (at worst).
- *Use of a common language (e.g., objectives, measures) for decision making:* A value mind-set creates a consistent vocabulary to talk about overall objectives and unite people behind an overall purpose. The common language is powerful since it translates the objective and decisions into words that are meaningful to people in their day-to-day activities.

- *Ability to make trade-offs in resource allocation:* Having one clear way to evaluate decisions avoids competing and unproductive activity.

- *Blueprint for change and ability to identify new opportunities:* The ability of an enterprise to align behind a common objective and provide a common language for success enables the process of spotting new opportunities and empowers people to pursue them.

- *Alignment of key processes:* Each business process needs to send the same signals to people in the enterprise. If creating value is the desired outcome, the reward programs must pay for this outcome, the performance measures must explain the inputs to value creation, promotions must recognize value creators, and training programs need to provide the skills.

## (e) Different Approaches to Estimate Value

There are several different approaches to estimating value. For our purposes we will focus on two of the most common approaches: spot value and discounted cash flow. Other approaches that we will not cover here include the option value method, which includes the risk-adjusted value of potential choice points over time.

*(i) Spot Value*    Spot value is determined using today's results and inputs as a steady-state assumption and projecting the same performance into the future. There

---

**Illustration**

In another company, there had been different objectives between the research & development (R&D) and service sides of the business. The R&D people regularly pursued and allocated existing resources to the development of new technologies and services in response to customer needs. No one would argue with this focus on customer service, even when it took resources away from existing products. The field service people were focused on doing everything they could to improve the customer experience for existing customers. In many cases this required product refinements and redevelopment, especially if the issues were quality related. Here was the rub: new product development vs. customer experience. When the field service people went back to the office to refine current products, resources had been pulled on to other projects. This delayed changes that would benefit and solidify current customer relationships. If this situation did not change, the field service people would have been forced to continually look for new relationships only, since they were unable to respond consistently to the needs of existing customers.

are two ways to think about spot value: based on a market multiple or based on a growth model.

A spot value based on a market multiple can be calculated using a variety of multiples (e.g., market/book value, market/revenue).[3] The approach is particularly useful when:

- Comparably valued companies can be identified and analyzed
- Economic profit is positive
- Detailed plan projections have not been developed

A spot value based on a growth assumption is another approach.[4] For example, let us assume that we have a reasonably accurate estimate that the overall growth in our industry will be a nominal 3 percent per year over the next several years. We then can use this to estimate the future capital base or book value of our enterprise and then, assuming today's level of return on investment, calculate a steady-state cash flow over time. Once again, in this case, economic profit must be positive, and there is no further detailed information on future prospects (e.g., timing of investments, competitor action, new market entry) so that a steady-state growth assumption is our best available information. In addition, we need reasonably good estimates of the weighted average cost of capital (WACC) and the fade rate in returns. The fade rate is the speed at which returns will converge to the cost of equity capital.

*(ii) Discounted Cash Flow*    A discounted cash flow approach is more detailed. It requires a forecast of multiple years of cash flows before applying a steady-state assumption. The forecast period for the discounted cash flow approach will vary based on the level of information available and the business cycle. For example, a retailer may use a 5- to 7-year forecast cycle in order to capture the specific time period that covers the return on new store investments and refurbishments. On the other hand, a natural resource business (e.g., mining company) could use a 15- to 20-year forecast period to incorporate its knowledge of reserves, utilization of reserves, and future value.

---

[3]*Spot Value—Market Multiple*

2003 EP forecast × market MVA/EP multiple + 2003 beginning BV of equity

[4]*Spot Value—Growth Model*

2003 EP / ($Ke$ – EP growth rate + fade rate ) + 2003 beginning BV of capital

[5]Intrinsic Value = 2003 EP / $(1 + Ke)^1$ + 2004 EP / $(1 + Ke)^2$ + 2005 EP / $(1 + Ke)^3$ + 2006 EP / $(1 + Ke)^4$ + 2007 EP / $(1 + Ke)^5$ + terminal value / $(1 + Ke)^5$ + 2003 beginning BV of equity

Terminal value can be determined as: 2007 EP × (1 + EP growth rate)/($Ke$ – EP growth rate + fade rate)

This approach can utilize either cash flow or economic profit forecasts.[5] The outcomes should be identical for the same assumptions.

Overall, estimating the value of an enterprise is a four-step process. (See Exhibit 1.7.)

## (f) Key Messages

This section has covered several key themes that are the foundation of moving from measurement to management of value:

- A valuation reflects investors' own views of the expected returns over time.
- Shareholder and stakeholder interests are aligned in the long run.
- Book Value is Shareholders' Equity Capital.
- Market Value Added is the difference between the Book Value and the Market Value.
- Intrinsic value (MVA + BV) is the present value of future economic profit.
- By increasing economic profit, we will increase market value added.
- "Managing for value" means aligning market value added with operating decisions, and we can use economic profit to help us.

## 1.2   PRIMARY FORCES THAT AFFECT VALUE CREATION

Three types of primary forces act on an enterprise's ability to create value. A clear understanding of these different forces is the next step in moving from measurement to management. A description of each structural force will provide the next set of clues to the value drivers of the enterprise. The value drivers are the actions

**Exhibit 1.7**   Estimating the Value of an Enterprise

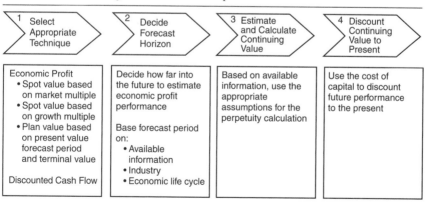

*Source:* Mercer Human Resource Consulting.

or decisions that we will need to focus on to drive market value added. The three primary forces we will focus on are:

Type 1     Sources of share price volatility—market, industry/competitor, business
Type 2     Current performance, expected performance, intangibles
Type 3     Growth vs. returns, elements of the organizational system

The next section gives an overview of how these primary forces support or limit an enterprise's ability to create value.

## (a) Type 1     Sources of Share Price Volatility

So far we have talked about what an enterprise can do to drive market value added directly. These are business-specific value drivers. However, two other factors drive the valuation attributed to any enterprise: industry risk and market risk. In many cases these two elements of secular risk can drive up to half of the movement in share price over time. We will discuss these elements in detail in a later chapter. For our purposes, a working definition of these factors is:

- *Market risk* is how movements in the overall market (e.g., Standard & Poor's 500) act on the enterprise share price. In other words, when the market goes up by 10 percent, does our share price go up by 10 percent, something more, or something less?
- *Industry risk* is similar. When an index of competitor share prices moves, how does our share price react?
- *Business risk* is the remaining volatility. The source of this risk is the reaction to the enterprise's performance and future expectations for that performance.

## (b) Type 2     Performance and Expectations

Characterizing shareholder expectations is our next step to understanding the drivers of market value added and isolating the value drivers of an enterprise. Fundamentally, two elements in the enterprise's control drive market value added: performance and expectations. In order to assign a market value added to an enterprise, shareholders are using all available information to evaluate the:

- Impact of current, or demonstrated, performance
- Expectations for future performance
- Contribution of intangibles (e.g., organizational systems)

An analysis of the contribution of these factors reveals that performance can account for a little over half the market value while intangibles account for the remainder. Intangibles are a significant source of value creation. (See Exhibit 1.8.)

**Exhibit 1.8**    Illustration of Components of Business Value

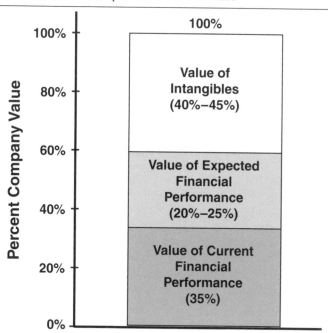

*Source:* Mercer Management Consulting Analysis.

## (c) Type 3    Growth/Return Performance and Intangibles

Performance is measured easily and can be either demonstrated (current) or expected (future). Future performance is only one element of expectations; the other key element is the value of the intangibles, or the organizational system.

The impact of current performance is simply the most recent economic profit performance. The value of expected performance is the extension of current performance into the future. It represents the promise of performance beyond today's results, in other words, value creating growth. The value given to this future performance is a subjective assessment based on the information the enterprise has provided to the market (e.g., new products, new customers, overall business strategy) and the assessment of the competitive landscape (e.g., market growth, competitor response).

Finally, there are the intangibles, or the organizational system. (See Exhibit 1.9.) The organizational system of the business translates strategy into shareholder value. The best performance, without an effective organizational system, will not sustain value-creating performance.

The organizational system is made up of several components:

**Exhibit 1.9**   Intangibles: The Organizational System

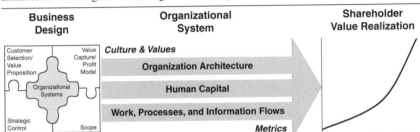

© Mercer Human Resource Consulting and Mercer Management Consulting, 2003.

- *Culture and values:* The grounding of any organizational system is the culture and values, or what the enterprise believes and what it aspires to be. Culture and values are distinct from the climate of the organization, or the environment in which people work. Culture and values are lasting and difficult to change. Climate is an evolving situation. Culture and values are deeply ingrained and, whether spoken or unspoken, are much harder to change. However, despite the qualitative nature of this element, culture and values are key drivers of an enterprise's ability to put strategy into action.
- *Organization architecture:* This is the structure of the enterprise, including roles, responsibilities, and reporting lines. In addition to these formal lines and boxes, there are also key elements of authority and degree of centralization.
- *Human capital:* The most basic definition of human capital is the people and the people programs that an enterprise employs. At its simplest level, this includes how people enter the enterprise, work and develop, and leave the enterprise. In addition to this basic construct, other elements of human capital include feedback, training, and career pathing programs.
- *Work, processes, and information flows:* This broad category includes work flows, how decisions are made, how resources are allocated, technology, and communication.
- *Measures:* This is the language of the enterprise and how it will communicate and translate its strategy into action. Measures highlight what is important and define what is required to succeed. The next chapter talks about the use and development of performance measurement in detail.

## (d) Key Messages

In order ultimately to define the value drivers of a business, we need to begin by understanding the primary forces that affect the enterprise. As we develop an understanding of each type of primary force, we take the next step beyond simply

---

**Illustration**

At the beginning of its efforts to develop a value management mind-set, one of the core strategic objectives of an agricultural company was to eliminate unproductive assets. The various asset management initiatives were viewed as critical to sizing the company appropriately for its markets and future growth. However, an analysis of shareholder expectations demonstrated that asset reductions alone were insufficient to produce market success and meet shareholder expectations. In reality, a balance of objectives was required immediately, not over time as previously thought. The new reality was a change in revenue mix as well as operating margin improvement, in addition to eliminating unproductive assets. Only in combination would the required expectations be realized.

---

measuring value and get closer and closer to understanding the sources of value creation and, therefore, how to drive the creation of market value added.

The Type 1 (sources of shareholder volatility) forces define the contribution of market, industry, and business risk to movements in share price. An understanding of the relative impact of each of these factors will influence our value creation agenda. For example, if market performance is a significant force, we should look at how we can redefine the market we compete in, set new ground rules, and change the economics and nature of competition. If industry risk is the key, then we should be looking at opportunities to drive our competitive positioning within the market in which we compete. Changes to competitive positioning may involve differentiation, pricing, and changes to relative cost structure. Finally, if business risk is the key, then we need to focus our attention on our performance regardless of the actions of others or the context of our industry.

The Type 2 (performance and expectations) forces are the items that help an enterprise change or create markets, industry, or business performance. For example, business performance is driven by actual performance and expectations.

The Type 3 (growth/return performance, intangibles) forces are current performance, expected performance, and intangibles. Both performance and effective organizational systems are required to deliver sustained value creation over time. The organizational system:

- Is generally the most expensive (but also the most valuable) asset the company has
- Is generally the asset that the company knows the least about (e.g., level of investment, productivity, reallocation)

- Can be the most powerful source of strategic control (e.g., sustainable competitive advantage)
- Can be measured and quantified to determine how to better align human capital with business strategy
- Should be viewed as an investment with a required return

Understanding each type of primary force is a critical step on the journey from measurement to management. Building a fact base of measurable, actionable information is key. It is the only way to translate strategy into action.

## 1.3   LINK BETWEEN STRATEGY AND VALUE

Business strategy is the what and how of an enterprise. It is the first step on the path to valued creation. At its simplest level, strategy is the answer to three questions:

1. What product/service are we selling?
2. Whom are we selling it to?
3. How much will we sell it for?

However simple these questions, answering them in a unique way and creating value (i.e., making money) in the process is an ongoing challenge.

### (a) What Is Strategy?

Strategy is defined by the interplay over time of market economics and competitive position. These two basic concepts, originally defined by Michael Porter's research, are the playing field of strategy development.[6]

***(i) Market Economics***   Market economics is the structure, or environment, that each competitor in an industry must understand and address. For example, the airline industry has been characterized by overcapacity, which creates intense pressure on costs and encourages price based competition. Several industry players have tried to change the overall economic opportunity by brand building and switching costs (e.g., frequent flyer programs), but the economic returns still tend to be limited, except for a few cases (e.g., Southwest, Alaska). The basic elements of market economics each act to support (drive up) or limit (drive down) the ability of an enterprise to make money in a specific industry. These factors in-

---

[6]Michael E. Porter, *Competitive Strategy: Techniques for Analyzing Industries and Competitors* (New York: The Free Press, 1980).

clude five primary elements. Each can be further broken down to assess its impact on the profitability of the industry and what will affect it over time.

- *Intensity of competition:* Another way to think about the intensity of direct competition is to consider how many companies are competing for the same customer with the same product. When thinking about how to answer this question, consider that:
  - A large number of competitors will reduce the prices that any one company can charge.
  - Limited differences between products will further intensify the pricing pressures.
  - Switching costs are psychological or economic barriers that make it difficult for a customer to choose a competitor (e.g., shipping costs might make a supplier across the street more attractive than one across the country).
  - Low growth will make it difficult to find new customers or markets.
  - Exit barriers prevent competitors from leaving the industry (e.g., highly specialized equipment with little resale value).
- *Buyer power:* When thinking about buyer power, the other key factor, consider how important the product is to a customer and how much the customer is willing to pay. Then consider:
  - Very few potential customers (e.g., auto manufacturers are the only buyers) will result in significant negotiating power.
  - Product differentiation will be important only if the differences have meaning to the buyer.
  - Low costs to switching will allow buyers to seek the best price.
  - Substitute products make it possible for buyers to find completely different products that meet their needs.
  - Products that result in significant cost improvements or other competitive advantages for buyers will be more important to them and are likely to receive a higher price.

The other three forces are limiting factors, which essentially cap the performance or returns possible from an enterprise. Each acts in its own way:

- *Potential entrants:* Low barriers to entry will lead to a significant increase in competition should an industry be seen as very attractive.
- *Supplier power:* Suppliers with a great deal of bargaining power over the industry will seek to take a share of the profits for themselves.
- *Substitute products:* The availability of other products that may potentially meet customers' needs will limit price increases (customers will weigh the price/benefit trade-off) and increase buyer bargaining power.

Other factors may have a significant influence in how returns play out, but are very dependent on the industry. These include:

- *Government regulation:* Regulations create significant barriers to entry in the utilities industry. Environmental concerns may increase the costs of doing business for manufacturers. International trade policy can open new markets or bring in new competition.
- *Technology:* The use of technology can create product differentiation, reduce costs, and so on. Technical innovation can reduce barriers to entry. Changes in technology may make certain products obsolete or increase the attractiveness of substitutes.
- *Macroeconomic factors:* Competition may become more intense for certain industries during a recession.

Finally, there is a relationship between market economics and profitability and the ability to generate returns over time.

For example, when there is *high*:

- threat of new entrants,
- intensity of competition,
- bargaining power of buyers,
- bargaining power of suppliers, and
- threat of substitutes,

there is downward pressure on profitability and a good chance that the market/industry is economically *unprofitable*.

When there is *low*:

- threat of new entrants,
- intensity of competition,
- bargaining power of buyers,
- bargaining power of suppliers, and
- threat of substitutes,

there is upward pressure/support for profitability and a good chance that the market/industry is economically *profitable*.

**(ii) Competitive Position**    Competitive position generally can be broken down into differentiation and relative economic cost position.

*Differentiation* is how a company offers a unique product or service to customers, and includes several potential sources:

- Establish differentiation which generally results in a price or volume advantage.
- Create new product offerings that can be very broad, full service, or highly specialized.
- Review customer segmentation that will identify a focus on meeting specific customer needs.
- Investigate geographic distribution which can reach customers otherwise overlooked.

*Relative cost/asset position* affects how much money a company can make relative to competitors. A lower cost/asset position will allow a company to receive superior returns even with limited differentiation or, for the same volume, be able to earn higher margins. There are several potential sources:

- Economies of scale: where size may create unique advantages not available to other competitors.
- Technological innovation may create a lower cost structure than competitors.
- Unique access to low-cost supplies.
- Highly efficient operations.

## (b) Strategy's Role in Supporting Value Creation—Business Design

The process of developing a strategy is one step in the business design process. A truly differentiated strategy development approach takes the fundamental elements of market economics and competitive position, and creates a total design based on the insights. Based on the research and experience of my colleagues at Mercer Management Consulting, a robust business design includes:

- *Customer selection and a value proposition:* What high-value customer opportunity is targeted? With what differentiated value proposition?
- *Value capture and profit model:* What profit model is used to capture value? Where does high profit happen? How do we expand there?
- *Scope:* What activities must we perform (vs. others)? What assets must we own (vs. others)?
- *Strategic control:* How can we maximize the sustainability of future cash flows?

Once these four elements of business design are defined, a link is developed to the organizational system and the specific people programs, processes, information, and structure needed to execute the business design.

Strategy and business design play very important roles in the process of value creation. Once the overall objective of the enterprise is defined, the business design provides:

- A road map for change
- The basis for resource allocation
- A way to evaluate success

### (c) Key Messages

Strategy is the what and how of a business. At the level of business design, it is part of creating a unique competitive advantage for an enterprise. Market economics and competitive position are the fundamental building blocks of strategy and business design. In addition, by describing the enterprise in these terms, we develop a "strategic mind-set," even if we are not developing a new strategy.

This is the first step to redefining a strategy and identifying new value-creation opportunities. On a day-to-day basis, it also helps us move from measurement to management. This characterization gives management the context, questions, and insight needed for the best operating decisions. A strategic mind-set is fundamental since it helps people answer four basic questions:

1. How the enterprise "works" today
2. How the enterprise will "work" in the future
3. What the enterprise will do next
4. How the enterprise will make it happen

If decision makers can walk around on a day-to-day basis with cogent responses to these four questions, they will be well grounded for developing a managing-for-value mind-set.

### 1.4    A MANAGING-FOR-VALUE MIND-SET

So far we have measured value, measured movement in share price, and characterized market economics and competition position. Also, at each step we have talked about implications. Now we need to make this information and insight actionable on a day-to-day basis. This is where managing for value plays a role.

Managing for value is a managerial mind-set of translating shareholder objectives into day-to-day decisions. (See Exhibit 1.10.) It is decision making and busi-

**Exhibit 1.10**   Managing for Value: A Managerial Mind-Set

*Source:* Mercer Human Resource Consulting.

ness processes working together to achieve the corporate objective and execute the business strategy. Performance measures are the language of a managing-for-value mind-set.

In other words, managing for value is:

- A way of thinking
  - The primary objective of any business is to maximize the equity value it creates for the shareholders.
  - Shareholder value can be managed on a "day-to-day" basis by the managers and all employees of the business.
- A decision-making process
  - Decisions must address the long-term economic trade-offs between returns and growth.
  - The decision-making process must include the identification and evaluation of alternatives.
  - The best decisions create the most long-term equity value for the business, thereby maximizing market value added.
- A way of managing
  - The building block business processes of strategy development, resource allocation, performance measurement, performance management, and rewards must be aligned and integrated.

A managing-for-value mind-set is also something that exists on the level of the individual, not just the enterprise. Individuals with this mind-set understand:

- How their decisions and day-to-day actions contribute to the value creation of the enterprise.
- What drives the value of the enterprise and how the enterprise makes money.
- How to systematically recognize new value-creation opportunities and allocate resources accordingly.

Whether at the coal-face or on the shop floor, it means understanding the part one person plays in making money for the enterprise.

The process of developing a managing-for-value mind-set is a journey from awareness to accountability. (See Exhibit 1.11.) It is not a single communication, training session, mandate, or initiative. It is a change process that becomes an on-going part of the enterprise's cultural fabric.

The first steps on this journey are varied, but usually start with measurement of value and an understanding of the enterprise's objective. This is a data-driven approach. Other enterprises might decide to start with a broad education and training program given how their culture responds to change. Each enterprise is unique, and so is every managing-for-value program.

The transition to awareness begins when information evolves into insight. Insight then can lead to impact. Once the people of the enterprise see that they have

---

**Illustration**

For one organization, the process of identifying new opportunities really went to the shop floor. In this beverage company, technology had been a significant driver of improvements over time and particularly when it came to throughput. The enterprise had continued to invest in new high-speed and customizable machinery to respond to increased demand and the ever-increasing variety of packaging in the market. However, no one had given any thought how to leverage the improvement in the precision of fill-levels in the new equipment over time. It used to be that you overfilled by 10 ml to ensure that you matched your stated size; now you only needed to over-fill by 3 ml. Over a year, and hundreds of thousands of liters of production, this made a significant difference in raw material costs. Just imagine the extra bottles or cans that could be filled with this additional volume. Who spotted this opportunity? The second-shift canning line supervisor who had just been through a quick introduction to a managing-for-value initiative and a new performance measure for the enterprise.

**Exhibit 1.11**    Illustration of Developing a Managing-for-Value Mind-Set

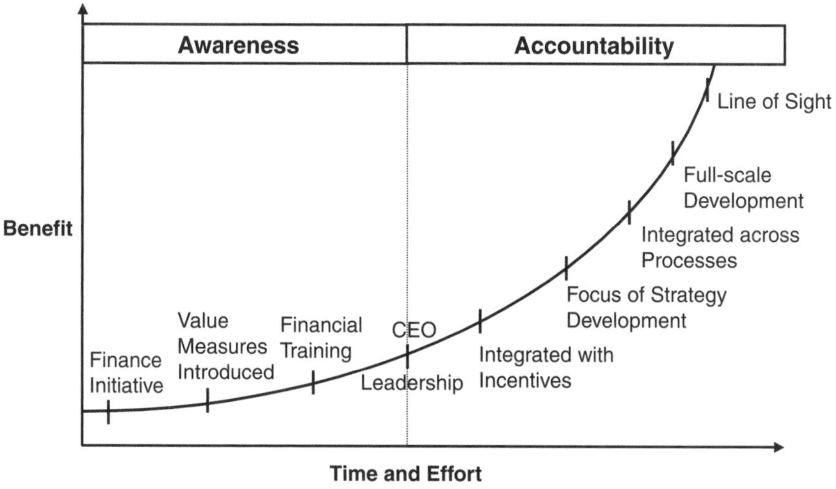

*Source:* Mercer Human Resource Consulting.

the ability to affect the results, the process of institutionalization has begun. Key processes are aligned, information is shared, rewards are linked to value-creating actions, and decision makers begin systematically to identify new opportunities for value creation.

## (a) Key Messages

Managing for value is a mind-set that links day-to-day operating decisions with shareholder value. Managing for value is not a new performance measure, a new strategy, or a new business management process, although each of these plays a role. Managing for value is about creating alignment and consistent signals. It is different for every enterprise. Finally, managing for value is a journey, not an initiative.

## 1.5   VALUE DRIVERS

There are many definitions of value drivers. However, if we are using value drivers in the context of a managing-for-value effort, they must fulfill several specific roles, including:

- Provide an insight on opportunities for value creation and facilitate the ongoing strategy development process
- Help prioritize resource allocation and decision making

So far we have talked about Type 1, 2, and 3 external forces. At some level these are value drivers since they help an enterprise diagnose and focus on key priorities and sources of value creation (e.g., impact of growth vs. returns, what shareholders expect, how we organize). At this level, these drivers are actionable only by senior leadership and on a large scale. It is true that everyone participates, but only a few are responsible. For our purposes, value drivers must be the language of the masses.

Value drivers can be thought of as:

- "Input" factors with a significant influence upon a company's value
- A way to tell the story of the strategy
- Actionable leverage points
- Unique customer propositions
  — Serving specific customer segments
  — Providing certain products/services
  — Bundling of products/services into a "customer solution"
  — Serving specific geographical areas
- Differentiated business processes
  — Streamlined process
  — Focus on core processes
  — Organizational development

In other words, value drivers are the operating behaviors and financial results that have the most impact on creating shareholder value. A clear definition of the value drivers highlights the most important day-to-day decisions for managers, thereby improving line of sight. Knowledge of value drivers helps individuals:

- Answer the question "What do I do differently today?"
- Understand their role in creating value.
- Make high-level business strategy actionable.
- Identify metrics that have a demonstrated and meaningful link to the eventual creation of shareholder value. Once identified, they can be incorporated into incentive plans, strengthening the link between shareholder and employee experience.
- Provide a foundation for evaluating the current business strategy and identifying new opportunities for value creation.

Through identifying the financial, operating, and activity-related drivers of value creation, we bring the shareholder value objective into the daily life and decisions of the people who run the business. Add this up across all of the individuals and all of the roles, and the impact is across the total business.

**Illustration**

During a working session, the senior management team was reviewing the product profitability across the business portfolio. To date, they had operated under the working assumption that the enterprise needed more and more high gross margin products. This was the path to growth. As we reviewed the outcomes of the analysis, they discovered that a high gross margin did not imply a high product profit. In many cases, the opposite was actually true. It was only when they drilled underneath the highest-level forces (e.g., growth vs. returns) that they understood the real drivers were speed of new market penetration and level of rework. What did value and managing for value mean for this organization? A new mind-set on how to create value and the need for a new strategy.

One way to develop and then represent this continuum is through a combination of financial and value chain analysis. We can develop a picture that creates a link between managers of the business and shareholder value. This is the analysis that brings shareholder value to the shop floor and gives people something different to do on Monday. (See Exhibit 1.12.)

Defining the value drivers of an enterprise is a critical step in:

- Understanding how the business makes money
- Creating a common language for value creation

**Exhibit 1.12**   Financial and Value Chain Continuum

| | | | | Example "Unit" Performance Measures |
|---|---|---|---|---|
| Economic Profit | NOPAT | Revenue | Revenue Growth | • Revenue per Salesperson against Budget<br>• Revenue per full time equivalent |
| | | COGS | Operating Margin | • Quality Variance from Specifications<br>• Cost per Barrel to Dump and Fill |
| | | Selling, General & Administration Expense | | |
| | − | Other Charges | | |
| | Capital | Working Capital | Capital Efficiency | • Inventory Turnover (Days)<br>• Cost of Capital<br>• Output per Equipment Hour/Rated Output per Equipment Hour |
| | | Fixed Assets | | |
| | | Other Capital | | |

*Source:* Mercer Human Resource Consulting.

- Establishing a link between individuals and shareholder value
- Providing information to allow individuals to spot new opportunities to create value

## (a) Key Messages

Value drivers are the engine of managing for value and focusing on value as the overall objective. They are the last step in moving from measurement to management. Without this last step, our process of measurement would be like laying the cable down the neighborhood streets and not connecting any of the houses to it. Value drivers are the "last mile" of shareholder value and a managing-for-value mind-set. Value drivers are also dynamic. As strategies, markets, and competitors change, so will the value drivers. This makes identifying value drivers a core skill.

## 1.6   CONCLUDING THOUGHTS

Through this chapter we have developed a detailed understanding of what value means, how to measure it, and the insight we can gain from knowing this information. The detailed definitions and measurement create the awareness we need to start our managing-for-value journey. Our awareness works through three major areas:

1. Measurement of value creation (market value, intrinsic value)
2. Sources of value creation (Type 1, 2, 3 external forces)
3. Value drivers (financial, operating, activity drivers)

The use of performance measures as part of this system is critical and will be covered in the next chapter. This information is the foundation for the accountability each enterprise must develop. This information provides the foundation to move from insight to impact, and from measurement to management. A managing-for-value mind-set drives us down this path. It is the foundation of creating alignment in mind-set, decision making, and business processes. From here we can work to align our people processes and programs in a way that adds additional value to the enterprise and becomes a source of value creation through the intangible value included by investors in every market value added.

Remember, the journey is not just the steps; it is a lifelong pursuit.

## 1.7   CASE STUDY: GLOBAL FINANCIAL INSTITUTION—CREATING THE FUTURE BY MANAGING FOR VALUE

FinCo is a global brand name with millions of customers and a presence in multiple countries around the world. At the time it realized it needed to improve its value creation capabilities, it was a highly valued company and a leader in the global growth of financial services.

At this point, there was an important reevaluation taking place. Despite an outstanding performance track record and historical share price performance, the new chief executive officer (CEO) believed it should go much higher. Very soon after reporting the largest profits of any institution at that time, the new CEO delivered his message: "This result does not guarantee our success, it is a reflection of our efforts to date. We need to find ways to create value in the future, or others will step in and create it for our investors."

FinCo's challenge was to create a strategy that augmented their evolution, but also instilled a style of managing that focused on shareholder value. The new CEO reflected further, "We had a strong enterprise and culture. These served as the foundation as we looked to leverage the company's strengths. The whole process of change was called Managing for Value (MFV)."

Overall, FinCo wanted to create and communicate a broad strategy throughout the company. It also wanted to clearly establish what it meant to work with and at this company. In order to get the process started at FinCo, it created a pilot program and ran a trial with selected executives. The program was highly customized to match the strategy and culture of FinCo and translate MFV from concept into actionable steps for a worldwide audience.

For FinCo, MFV meant two things:

1.   Thinking about everything in the organization in terms of shareholder value
2.   Beginning to measure everything from an economic value perspective

The message needed to be simple, and it was not about fixing the business—it was about driving it to new heights. In other words, it was essential that the corporate "brain" was wired in a common way.

The tailoring of MFV for FinCo was the critical step. Several key initiatives were launched to create this customized approach, including:

*   Working with trainers in each of the company's major business units, a modified MFV message was developed to incorporate into ongoing training
*   Delivering a significant number of local sessions around the world to communicate an ongoing message to middle management
*   Creating an MFV booklet that took the imperatives of the program and put them in easy-to-understand language about what it means in day-to-day practice; a major application of this booklet is small, local working team meetings and brainstorming sessions
*   Developing a training/introduction program for new hires around the world

In addition, the messages of MFV needed to be integrated into other key processes in order to align the day-to-day workings of the organization with the overall objective. This required changes to the reward programs as well as performance measurement and planning systems.

After all of these initial changes, and a year into the process, FinCo is still at the beginning of the journey. The destination has been identified, real progress has been made, and new opportunities are emerging. Many of these new opportunities are only apparent given the MFV mind-set. It is a continuous, dynamic process.

Overall, individuals embraced the concept. The key group of middle managers understand the enterprise objective, have a common language of success, and understand what they do, and need to do, to add value to the business. The strongest outcome has been how it has focused the company on what needed to be done. It created focus, and that is critical in a global, decentralized, and diverse organization.

# Chapter 2

# Performance Measurement: How Companies Deliver Value

**Russell Miller**

A well-designed performance measurement system can be a powerful tool to help drive long-term stock price appreciation and deliver superior value to shareholders. It also can be used in incentive compensation planning to translate strategic goals into objective and understandable behaviors by relating day-to-day operations with the company's strategic plan. In this chapter we discuss how companies establish a "value creation objective" and how performance measurement is used to track and drive success against the value creation goal. We highlight the key elements of an effective performance system, alert the reader to potential pitfalls, and describe how goals and measures can be aligned with management processes.

## 2.1 VALUE CREATION OBJECTIVE

In order to get started, it is important to understand where we are today and why our stock price is where it is. Once we understand our starting point, then we can begin to determine how to grow from there.

### (a) Understanding Investor Expectations

In publicly traded companies, we need to start with the company's shareholders. The shareholders are the group that the company ultimately needs to deliver value to, and therefore it is critical that we understand their expectations. Shareholders' expectations of a company's performance are reflected in the company's market valuation. Specifically, the market value of equity (i.e., stock price × number of shares outstanding) reflects the value shareholders place on the company. Said another way, the stock price represents (or is equal to) the discounted present value of the future stream of cash flows to be generated by the company. For example, the only reason investors would pay $20 for a share of company stock today is because they expect to get back in return at least $20 in future cash flows (on a present value basis).

By applying this methodology to a company's stock price, we can determine what shareholders are expecting in terms of future performance and resulting cash flow. For example, a company with a $20 stock price would require a stream of future cash flows to justify the price. (See Exhibit 2.1.) The cash flow can be used to pay out dividends or to reinvest in the business; in either case, the value will be returned to the shareholders in the long run. And, while cash flow is what shareholders are looking for over time, other measures may be considered in the near or intermediate term as an indicator of potential cash flows over the long term.

Ultimately, a company's market valuation is a function of the combination of shareholders' expectations of performance and meeting those expectations over time.

### (b) Determining the Value Creation Objective

Building off of shareholders' expectations and combining it with the company's internal projections, the company needs to determine its value creation objective. The company's value creation objective establishes the standard by which all decisions and results should be evaluated. For example, if a company determines that its value creation objective is to achieve 15 percent long-term sustained average annual shareholder returns, then all decisions need to be judged relative to this goal.

Since performance can be translated into shareholder value, different levels of performance represent different values. (See Exhibit 2.2.) Establishing a benchmark, or baseline, represented by current levels of performance will help to set

**Exhibit 2.1**   Shareholder Expectations of Company Performance

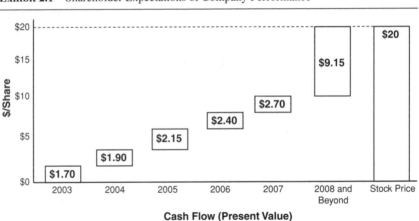

Cash Flow (Present Value)

**Exhibit 2.2**   Setting the Value Creation Objective

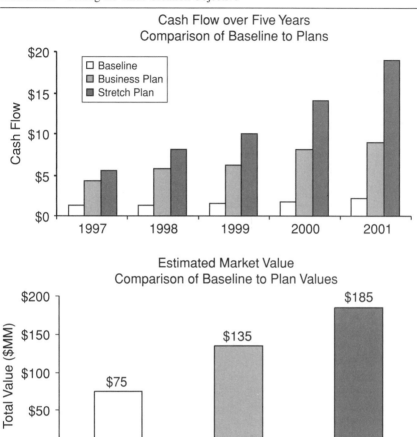

target, or business plan, and stretch plan goals. These performance levels then can be translated into a company's market value objectives. So, setting the value creation objective is a critical first step in this performance measurement process.

## 2.2   PERFORMANCE MEASUREMENT SYSTEM

Translating a company's value creation objective into a framework for decision making makes the goal actionable as opposed to conceptual. Asking a management team to double the stock price over the next five years may be a reasonable goal, but it is not necessarily clear what it needs to do to achieve that goal. However, asking the team to improve return on capital from 10 to 15 percent provides a framework for making decisions on different business issues, from growing revenue to controlling expenses to investing capital.

A performance measurement system is a powerful translation tool. By identifying the key measures of performance that guide progress toward achievement of the value creation goal, managers have a basis for decision making to help achieve the goal.

### (a) Performance Measurement as a Decision-Making Framework

The performance measurement system can be used as a decision-making framework in several areas, including:

- Incentive compensation and total reward decisions
- Strategic decisions (e.g., acquisitions and divestitures)
- Capital investment decisions
- Communication on progress toward goals both internally to employees and externally to shareholders, customers, and other stakeholders

Effective performance measurement provides the critical link between day-to-day strategic operating decisions and creating shareholder value. Specifically, the performance measurement system provides key input into making value-creating business decisions (e.g., should we raise prices to increase margins, or should we maintain or lower prices to increase market share?). At the same time, the performance measurement system provides the output of results that shareholders are looking for relative to their expectations.

In the end, in order for a performance measurement system to be effective, it must:

- Align the interests of employees and shareholders
- Reflect the economics of the business
- Match the culture and capabilities of the company

### (b) Performance Measurement as a Competitive Advantage

When used as a tool to help drive business results, an effective performance measurement system provides a company with a competitive advantage by

- Communicating how to create shareholder value by identifying the key measures on which to focus
- Communicating internal performance expectations required to meet and exceed shareholder expectations

- Providing a sound framework for making decisions
- Signaling how we are doing along the way
- Providing a basis for variable pay decisions
- Producing behavioral change over time

## (c) Components of a Performance Measurement System

There are several key components to be determined in developing an effective performance measurement system, including:

- *Performance measure selection:* the measure(s) to be used as the indicator of success
- *Goal-setting:* the desired level of performance on the selected measures (see Section 2.5)
- *Linkage:* the organizational unit (department, business unit, corporate) to which the measure applies
- *Time horizon:* the time period over which performance is measured
- *Corporate processes:* the processes that capture the measure

Getting each component right is critical for having a performance measurement system that truly helps drive business results. Next we discuss the key factors to consider for each of these components.

## 2.3   SELECTING PERFORMANCE MEASURES

In selecting the performance measure(s) for the performance measurement system, several questions must be answered:

- What measure(s) most closely align with shareholder value?
- What measure or set of measures best capture the economics of the business?
- What measure(s) best reflect the company's business strategy?
- What is the right balance between financial, operational, and nonfinancial/ strategic measures?
- What measures are understandable and measurable within our company?
- How can the measure(s) be defined to minimize gaming?

## (a) Applying Selection Criteria

Multiple inputs are required in order to answer these questions.

*(i) Alignment*   Each company needs to determine what measures have the strongest correlation with shareholder value. Given that shareholder value is the present value of shareholders' expectations of future performance, each company needs to understand what performance matters most to shareholders. Are shareholders currently focused on revenue growth, earnings improvement, returns, or some other measure as they form their expectations for performance and ultimately long-term cash flow generation to determine the company's market value?

Through a combination of quantitative analysis, analyzing the relationship between operating performance measures and shareholder value for the company and industry over time, and qualitative analysis through discussions with investors, each company can identify those measures that most closely align with shareholder value.

*(ii) Understanding*   To be an effective management tool, the performance measurement system needs to be understandable. Each company must determine the appropriate balance between accuracy of the measure(s) and complexity. Typically, as a measure becomes more accurate in correlating with shareholder value and aligning with the economics of the business, it also becomes more complex to understand. (See Exhibit 2.3.) For example, revenue is a relatively simple measure that is widely understood; however, it ignores much of the business results of the company, such as expenses and investments, and as a result, on its own, revenue typically does not correlate strongly with value creation (with the exception of earlier-stage companies to be discussed). A measure like cash flow return on investment (CFROI) captures many aspects of the business and often strongly

**Exhibit 2.3**   Accuracy versus Complexity

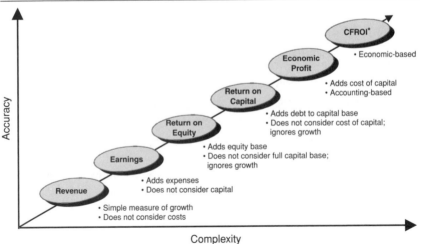

*Cash flow return on investment

correlates with value, but is much more complex than revenue and would require significant training to educate employees.

*(iii) Fit*   Although it is critical to ensure that the measure meets the first two objectives of aligning with value and being understandable, if the measure does not fit with the company's strategy, culture, or industry, then ultimately it will fail as a tool to help drive performance. This step often requires both a quantitative and a qualitative assessment of the measures and their fit with the company. Considerations of shifts in strategy, pace of change, and ability to capture the required information all need to be factored in when determining the performance measurement system going forward.

Two other criteria to consider in selecting the appropriate performance measure(s) for a company are:

1. Measures that capture controllable operating results of the company and are relatively independent of changes in external market conditions (e.g., operating profit, operating cash flow). Note, however, that this objective needs to be balanced with the understanding that shareholders are subject to changes in external conditions.
2. Measures that provide employees with direct line of sight (e.g., revenue growth, customer satisfaction) in terms of what they can do to positively influence results on the measure (unlike measures based on stock price).

## (b) Assessing Performance Measures

Among the various types of performance measures, financial measures are most commonly used since they are objective, quantifiable, and typically have a direct link to shareholder value. Financial measures usually are taken from the accounting statements and conform to generally accepted accounting principles (GAAP) or are a modified version of these GAAP measures, where adjustments are made better to reflect the economics of the business.

Revenue is certainly a key measure of growth; however, it does not tell anything about how much money a company is earning or give any information about the investment required to generate the revenue. Earnings-based measures, such as net income and earnings per share (EPS), provide more information in that they combine revenue with expenses; however, these measures do not reflect how much capital is used in the business. Return measures, such as return on assets (ROA) and return on equity (ROE), address this issue but potentially understate and distort the true amount of capital by using GAAP book figures based on initial purchase prices and GAAP-based depreciation. Although each of these concerns can be addressed by adding more measures or by adjusting the definition of the measure, going down this path needs to be balanced with the inherent added complexity that will result.

In considering which measure(s) to use for a company, it is helpful to keep in mind that, historically, companies that achieve both top-line revenue growth and bottom-line return on capital deliver superior value to shareholders. (See Exhibit 2.4.) And while one may want to focus on one or the other, given the company's strategy or stage of development, one should not do it inadvertently by the measure(s) selected for the performance measurement system. For example, return on capital (ROC) may be the best measure, given the company's strategy, industry, and shareholder expectations; however, an exclusive focus on ROC can result in decisions that stifle growth over time. A company may spend more time trying to manage expenses and minimize investments to drive up ROC and not do the things necessary to grow the business, which is vital for long-term sustainable value creation.

As mentioned, there are cases in which focusing on either growth or returns exclusively is appropriate. Emphasizing growth over returns might make sense for a start-up company in a high-growth emerging industry, where early market share is critical to future success. An emphasis on returns over growth might make sense in restructurings or turnaround situations and in declining industries where there is limited opportunity for top line growth. However, in both cases, the singular focus on either growth or returns is for a finite period of time, and once the company transitions out of that stage of business, the measure needs to be reevaluated to ensure that it is highly correlated with long-term cash generation.

In addition to financial measures, companies need to determine if nonfinancial strategic measures are required to capture performance appropriately. Examples

**Exhibit 2.4**    Growth and Returns to Deliver Superior Shareholder Value

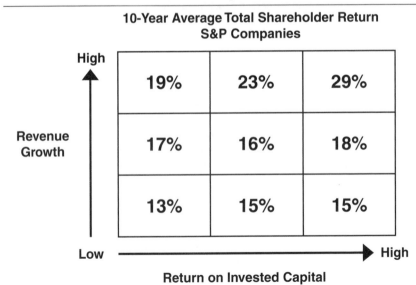

**10-Year Average Total Shareholder Return S&P Companies**

| Revenue Growth | | | |
|---|---|---|---|
| High | 19% | 23% | 29% |
| | 17% | 16% | 18% |
| Low | 13% | 15% | 15% |

Return on Invested Capital (Low → High)

of strategic measures are product development, market share, customer satisfaction, and milestone measures such as project completion (e.g., building a plant or implementing a new information technology system). Oftentimes these measures, in combination with key financial measures, provide managers with the full story of what is critical to long-term success and value creation.

## (c) Company and Industry Characteristics Impact Performance Measure Selection

In determining the appropriate measure(s) for a company, it is critical to consider the company and industry stage of development, since they are key drivers of shareholder expectations. Specifically, in the early stages of a company's development, shareholders are less concerned with near-term financial results and are more focused on key milestones that the company must achieve in order to position itself for future success. Following the early stage, shareholders begin to shift their attention from milestones to revenue as an indicator that the early successes are translating into business results. And finally, once a company has established itself as a revenue-generating business, shareholders shift to focusing on profitability, wanting to see actual returns on their initial investment, while continuing to see growth over time.

    Each company must determine what stage of business it is in and how the performance measures should be selected to balance shareholder expectations at each stage. Often companies are not distinctly in one stage or another but are in multiple stages across their business, and the measures selected need to reflect this balance. Exhibit 2.5 provides general guidelines to consider.

    In addition to stage of development, the degree of capital intensity affects performance measure selection. Among highly capital-intensive businesses, measuring earnings without any recognition of the capital investment required results in an incomplete picture of results. It is like watching a baseball game and knowing how many hits each team has but not knowing how many runs each has scored. One

**Exhibit 2.5**   Performance Measures for Different Stages of Business

| Pre-Revenue Stage | Revenue Stage | Profitability Stage |
|---|---|---|
| Time Line → | | |
| **Development Measures** | **Growth Measures** | **Income Measures** |
| • Brand-building measures | • Customer growth | • Customer profitability |
| • Infrastructure development milestones | • Revenue growth | • Operating cash flow |
| | • Market share | • Return on capital |

> **Measures should focus on the key value-creating activities.**

may have an idea of how each team is performing but one does not know who is winning. In order to get a full picture of performance for capital-intensive businesses, some measure of returns is required. (See Exhibit 2.6.)

## (d) Defining and Adjusting Performance Measures

Once the performance measure(s) is selected, defining it appropriately is a key detail to make the measure effective. In determining the specific definition of the measure, one needs to ask whether the standard definition meets one's needs (e.g., accounting-based measure defined according to GAAP), or if some adjustments would make the measure more effective as a decision-making tool. Questions to ask are:

- Will the adjustment have a material impact on the results?
- Is the adjustment meaningful to employees?
- Is the adjustment consistent with treatment of other adjustments?
- Do the adjustments enhance the strategic fit of the measure?
- Will the adjustments reinforce the desired behaviors?
- Is there adequate information to capture the adjustments?
- Is the added complexity of making the adjustment worth the gain?

In the end, the real question is whether employees make better decisions because of the measure and the adjustment to the measure. The measure's definition can have a profound impact on decision making and the link to shareholder value. For example, a manufacturing company decides that ROA is going to be a key measure in its performance measurement system. When defining ROA, the company chooses to define assets based on their net book value after accumulated depreciation (return on net assets, or RONA). Although this definition may be reasonable in many cases, in this situation—the company has a mix of older and newer plants, all of which are

**Exhibit 2.6**   Degree of Capital Intensity

|  | Capital Intensity | |
|---|---|---|
|  | Low<br>Company A | High<br>Company B |
| Revenue | $1,500 | $2,200 |
| Expenses | $1,200 | $1,800 |
| Earnings | $300 | $400 |
| Capital | $1,500 | $4,000 |
| Return on Capital | 20% | 10% |

fully functioning—this definition can lead to value-destroying decisions. Since the older plants have a significantly lower asset base (due to the years of accumulated depreciation), the ROA for the older plants is relatively high. As a result, a manager may decide to stop building new plants because they are dragging down returns. In reality, the returns on the older and newer plants may be compared more appropriately on a gross book value basis (return on gross assets, or ROGA) rather than on net book value (RONA). Clearly defining a measure will help ensure that the measure used yields the most meaningful results. (See Exhibit 2.7.)

## (e) Performance Measurement Pitfalls

There are three basic types of pitfalls to avoid when building the performance measurement system:

1.  *Wrong measure:* There is a disconnect between the measure and shareholder value.
2.  *Right measure, wrong goal:* There is a disconnect between the measurement goal and shareholder expectations.
3.  *Right measure, wrong behavior:* There is a disconnect between the measure and operating decisions.

*(i) Pitfall 1: Wrong Measure*   In this situation, a company effectively communicates the measure, and employees understand it and focus on making decisions to deliver positive results on the measure. However, the performance achieved does not result in value creation since the measure is not aligned with shareholder value. As a result, the value creation potential for the company is minimized.

For example, a company determines that revenue is not appropriate, given that it ignores expenses and profitability; the company identifies EPS as the key measure to focus on and clearly communicates the measure to employees. Employees focus decisions on increasing EPS and make investments in the business to grow EPS. However, given that the company is capital intensive, measuring return on capital is the most critical driver of shareholder value; EPS does not fully recognize capital invested in the business. As a result, the investments grow EPS but the return on those investments is below the company's cost of capital, and as a result the investments destroy value while increasing EPS.

*(ii) Pitfall 2: Right Measure, Wrong Goal*   A company properly identifies the performance measures that correlate with shareholder value, sets goals on the measure, and communicates these goals to employees. However, the goals are not aligned with shareholder expectations. As a result, the company achieves its goals but the goals are below shareholder expectations, resulting in value destruction.

For example, a company establishes an EPS goal of 12 percent growth per year; however, shareholder expectations would suggest EPS growth of 15 percent

**Exhibit 2.7**    Definition of Measure and Impact on Decision Making

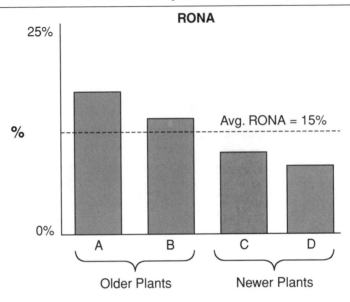

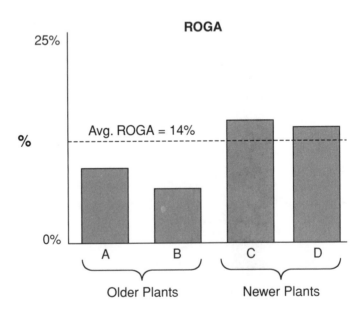

per year is required to justify the current stock price. As a result, business decisions are based on achieving 12 percent growth, and management is rewarded for success against this objective; however, it fails to meet shareholder expectations, and as a result the stock price goes down.

*(iii) Pitfall 3: Right Measure, Wrong Behavior*   The measures and goals are appropriately determined; however, employees do not know how to focus their efforts to achieve success on the measure. As a result, the performance measurement system does not provide a framework for decision making, and there is no change in employee behavior and no improvement in value creation.

Companies often spend significant time and resources in determining the appropriate performance measures and goals and then send out a memo, e-mail, or brochure detailing the new performance measurement system. Although this approach allows the company to "check the box" regarding communication, it does not allow for effective implementation and understanding by employees. In order for the measure to be effective as a framework for decision making, employees not only have to understand how the measure is defined but they also have to have an in-depth understanding of how their day-to-day business decisions link with success on the measure.

Even if the communication is thorough, the measure itself can be too complex to be used as a guide for decision making. Measures with so many adjustments that only the chief financial officer can calculate the outcome likely will fail as a management tool for the broader population.

## (f) Overcoming Barriers and Obstacles to Success

*(i) Senior Management Buy-in*   As with any initiative, there are going to be roadblocks that must be overcome in order to achieve success. The most obvious and important step is to obtain senior management buy-in and commitment early on in the process. Without senior management on board, one may be working toward goals that are not in sync with senior management's goals. For example, through a thorough measurement selection process it may be determined that the measure should shift from a focus on EPS to a focus on cash flow, but when the CEO discusses performance, the first thing mentioned continues to be EPS. At best, one will be sending mixed messages about EPS and cash flow, and at worst one will be sending a very clear message that EPS is what really matters and cash flow was simply part of an intellectual exercise that is not relevant to the company.

*(ii) Balancing the "Perfect" Measure with the "Right" Measure*   Another barrier to overcome is the tendency to want to make the measure "perfect." If one is going to take on an initiative to determine the best measure for the company, it is only natural to want to find the most accurate measure possible. However, in doing so, one typically will find that a number of adjustments must be made

to recognize the unique characteristics of the business that the accounting numbers do not accurately reflect. Although adjusting for significant items is appropriate in many cases, the measure should not become a "black box" where performance information goes in and the measure comes out and no one has any idea what happens in between. The "right" measure is not always the "perfect" measure, but it is the best measure to achieve the ultimate objective of driving shareholder value.

*(iii) Communication*    As mentioned earlier, communication is a major contributor to success. Effective communication, including training sessions, workshops, town hall meetings, and progress updates, can require a significant investment, and often it is difficult to demonstrate their return on investment in advance. However, without communication the measurement system often becomes just another means of keeping score but does not change behavior or decision making. (See Chapter 13.)

*(iv) Integration*    Another obstacle is not integrating the performance measures into all management processes. For example, if the measure is determined to be return on equity (ROE) and ROE is used for the incentive plan, then the start of an integrated approach exists. However, if resource allocation and investment decisions are made based on a discounted cash flow analysis and financial results are reported to the board based on EPS, then multiple measures potentially send conflicting signals to managers.

## (g) Best Practices for Selecting Performance Measures

Given all of the factors to consider in selecting performance measures for the company, it is helpful to have a list of best practices to apply to the process. Although each of these seven factors needs to be tailored to a particular organization, together they form a foundation on which to get started.

1. Ensure that the measure is linked to shareholder value creation.
2. Determine the measure that best aligns with the company's strategy and reflects operating performance.
3. Emphasize objective, quantitative measures.
4. Balance growth and returns.
5. Provide a clear line of sight for managers' day-to-day decisions and how their decisions affect results as indicated by the measure.
6. Determine the measure that will enable employees to generate insights into the business and assist them in evaluating alternatives.
7. Define the measure so it is understandable to employees (i.e., keep it as simple as possible).

## 2.4   BUILDING A PERFORMANCE MEASUREMENT SYSTEM

After all that discussion on performance measures, what else can possibly need to be done to have a performance measurement system? Although selecting the performance measures is arguably the most difficult and critical step in the process, several other aspects of the performance measurement system need to be determined; to recap, they are:

- *Goal setting:* The desired level of performance on the selected measures
- *Linkage:* The organizational unit (department, business unit, corporate) to which the measure applies
- *Time horizon:* The time period over which performance is measured
- *Corporate processes:* The processes that capture the measure

### (a) Linkage

Where to measure results is a key question when determining performance. The level of measurement needs to be driven by the company's strategy and how value is created within the business.

Did a business unit have a great year if the business unit exceeded all its goals but the company as a whole missed its goals (or vice versa)? If a company has multiple business units that operate independently (the corporation is more of a holding company), then an emphasis on business unit measurement is going to be most appropriate. In a company with interdependent businesses with significant collaboration among the units, measurement at the corporate level would make more sense. Ultimately, each company needs to determine where its value-creating platforms are: at the business unit level or at the corporate level. (See Exhibit 2.8.)

In addition, the organization level at which performance can be impacted should be considered when determining the appropriate level of measurement. For example, corporate performance would be the indicator of success for corporate executives, whereas a business unit president may measure success based on a combination of corporate and unit results.

### (b) Time Horizon

The time frame over which performance is measured needs to fit the business and the company's current situation. Although annual measurement and multiyear (e.g., three years) measurements are the most common and are appropriate in many cases, one still needs to determine if they are right for the company.

Industry dynamics play a big part in determining the appropriate time frame. For example, measuring product development in a pharmaceutical company requires a significantly longer time period than measuring product development in

**Exhibit 2.8**   Focus on Corporate versus Business Unit Measures

| Characteristics Favoring Use of Corporate Measures | Characteristics Favoring Use of Business Unit Measures |
|---|---|
| • Significant corporate management/control of business units | • Business unit develops own strategic plan with little corporate coordination |
| • Business units interdependent because of shared resources/integrative strategies | • Significant differences in business unit strategies/key success factors |
| • Encourages collaboration among business units | • Little interdependence; business units do not sell or transfer products to other company operations |
| • Significant mobility of talent across business units | • Little mobility of talent across business units |
| • Supports one-company culture | • Need to support strong business unit cultures/values |

an apparel company. Both need to lead to sales and profits, but the time required to bring the product to market is vastly different.

Also, each company's financial situation will impact the time frame for measurement. In a turnaround situation, typically a window of opportunity exists in which to try to turn the company around before bankruptcy or liquidation is required. In these cases, measuring performance for the next year may be irrelevant if the turnaround has to occur in the next 6 months or the next 18 months.

## (c) Corporate Processes

The final piece of the performance measurement puzzle is to integrate the performance measures into all corporate processes throughout the organization, including:

- Incentive compensation
- Strategic investment decisions
- Day-to-day resource allocation
- Annual and long-range planning
- Financial reporting
- Internal and external communications

This step, while easy to outline, typically is one of the most difficult to implement effectively. Each of these processes has a long history of how it is done within each company, and the "owner" of each process needs to adopt the new measurement system. Integrating the performance measures into all of these processes will take time, not only to get the measures incorporated but to have people focus on the measure for making decisions. For example, a company that historically has made resource allocation decisions based on contribution to EPS decides to use returns above the cost of capital as the basis for decisions going forward. This change will require a significant mind-set shift and will take time to achieve.

## 2.5  GOAL SETTING

Even though determining the "right" measures is important for success, value creation will not result if the goals on the measure are not set properly. Although predicting the future is impossible, there are ways to develop goals that are sound and grounded in the information that is available.

### (a) Consider Multiple Perspectives

Since we cannot predict the future, we need to use all of the information we have available to us to develop appropriate goals. Information to consider when developing goals should not be limited to a company's budget or last year's results, but should be a combination of internal and external inputs, including:

*Internal Considerations*

- Company annual budget and long-range plan
- Company historical performance (last year and prior years)
- Company prior year goals

*External Considerations*

- Peer group historical performance
- Broad market historical performance
- Shareholder expectations for company
- Shareholder expectations for peer companies

Combining each of these perspectives provides a basis for determining the appropriate goal for the company. (See Exhibit 2.9.)

After analyzing each of these factors, a company needs to decide whether the goal will be stated as an internal absolute target (e.g., EPS growth of 15 percent) or relative to an external benchmark (e.g., EPS growth at the 75th percentile of the industry peer group). Using an internal absolute target provides a clearly defined goal that employees can rally around and can track over time, whereas a relative measure is somewhat of a moving target and one never really knows where one might end up. In addition, an internal target provides the opportunity

Exhibit 2.9    Considering Multiple Perspectives

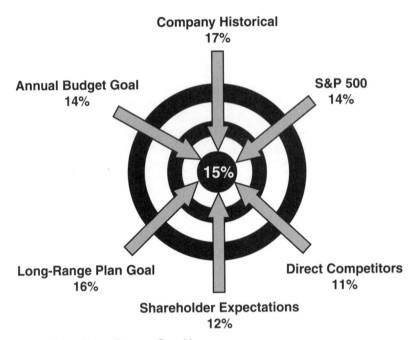

# Earnings per Share (EPS) Growth Rates

*Source:* Mercer Human Resource Consulting.

to recognize company-specific factors in setting the target, but also may promote gaming by those setting the target if their performance will be evaluated relative to the target.

An external goal tied to an industry benchmark avoids the need to try to predict the future and allows any market and industry shifts to be captured in the relative measurement process. However, in order to have an effective benchmark, there needs to be a relevant group of companies with the required information available to analyze. In addition, an external goal can lead to superior relative performance but poor absolute performance. Is it good performance when earnings go down by 5 percent but the industry benchmark decreased by 10 percent?

If an internal absolute goal is used, a combination of top-down and bottom-up goal setting should be used to ensure that the goal is meeting corporate requirements while also providing for a goal that is achievable at the operating level. If goals are set based only on top-down corporate needs, there is potential for a disconnect between corporate needs and what a business unit can deliver. Balancing these two perspectives provides for challenging yet attainable goals; otherwise one runs the risk of having goals that are perceived to be unachievable as opposed to stretch. As a result, the goals become meaningless because employees think they cannot win right from the start.

### (b) Checklist for Goal Setting

Here is a simple checklist to keep in mind for goal setting:

☐ Integrate top-down corporate objectives with bottom-up business unit perspectives.
☐ Compare annual and long-term goals to industry and market performance.
☐ Set attainable stretch goals linked to meeting or exceeding shareholder expectations.

## 2.6 FROM PERFORMANCE MEASUREMENT TO PERFORMANCE MANAGEMENT

In order for the performance measurement system to help drive value creation, it needs to be understandable and actionable. Performance measurement is the transactional science of data analysis and goal setting; performance management is the transformational art of changing behaviors and shifting the way people make decisions.

### (a) Keys to Shifting from Measurement to Management

Shifting from measurement to management requires:

- *Communication:* Clear communication of the measure and the goal
- *Motivation:* A reason for an individual to change behavior
- *Control:* The ability for an individual to have some degree of control over the outcome
- *Understanding:* Understanding what is being asked and what to do to effect the outcome positively

Just because something is being measured does not mean that people will make different decisions. For purposes of changing employee behaviors, the final goal should be alignment with shareholder value creation. Achieving shareholder alignment is critical; if a company successfully completes all of the steps outlined in this chapter but does not achieve alignment with shareholders, then everyone may have changed his behavior and may be using the performance measurement system as a decision-making tool, but the decisions are not creating value.

## (b) Translating Performance Measures into Operating Decisions

In talking about changing behaviors and providing a decision-making framework, it would be helpful to be able to translate performance measures into operating decisions. This process can be applied to any measure for any company, but the outcome of the process must be tailored to each specific company.

If we consider it from the perspective that every decision that is made has an impact on business results, then we can reverse the order and start with the business results and track back to the decisions that drove the outcome. For example, if a company determines that cash flow is its key measure, then we can decompose cash flow into its component parts to track back to the discrete decisions that drive cash flow results. (See Exhibit 2.10.)

## (c) Measurement without Management or Management without Measurement

Each one is ineffective without the other. Having a measurement system without the management attributes discussed will result in an after-the-fact set of information that only tells us how we did and nothing about what we should be doing. Conversely, management without measurement may provide for an overall sense of what we are trying to do but does not provide the required information to make the appropriate decisions. For example, if the goal is to grow profits of existing customers, it may be clear what is being asked but it is not clear how to achieve the goal without measurement information regarding current customer profitability, customer buying patterns, and the like.

Neither performance measurement or performance management is effective in driving value without being aligned with shareholder expectations. For example, a company determined that the key measure was operating income by product. It clearly communicated the measure and goal, and management was able to make

**Exhibit 2.10**   Translating Performance Measures into Operating Decisions

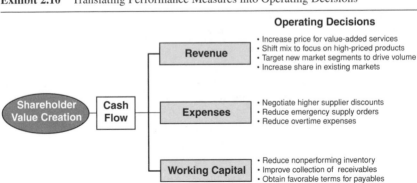

effective decisions to improve product profitability. However, when the goals were achieved, there was surprise that shareholder value did not improve as a result of the increase in product profitability. On deeper analysis, it became clear that, given the highly capital-intensive nature of the business, it was not operating income by product that was important but rather return on investment by product that drove shareholder value.

### (d) Achieving a Mind-Set Shift

Changing the way employees make decisions and achieving a mind-set shift can sound like a daunting and even insurmountable task. But in reality, all it really requires is getting people to think about the trade-offs between various courses of action in the context of the performance measurement system. And the trade-offs amount to determining the appropriate balance between short-term and long-term results on revenue, expenses, assets, and liabilities.

For example, managers are accustomed to thinking about how to improve profitability by increasing revenues and decreasing expenses through their operating decisions. However, managers often are not asked to think about how their operating decisions have an impact on assets and the associated cost of carrying those assets (through debt or equity financing). The result can lead to poor working capital management and overinvestment in plant, property, and equipment. As such, a manager's decisions may improve profitability but destroy value because there was not full consideration of the trade-offs between revenue, expenses, assets, and liabilities.

Achieving the desired mind-set shift requires senior management leadership and commitment, ongoing communication and education, and an integration of the performance measures into all of the corporate processes (incentive compensation, investment and resource allocation decisions, and planning and reporting).

## 2.7 CONCLUSION

All companies work hard to deliver long-term value to shareholders. There are many ways to do this, and there are many potential pitfalls along the way. Performance measurement in conjunction with other management and financial strategies can be an effective tool to help steer a company toward its goals. Applying a methodical approach to developing the performance measurement system and transforming it into a performance management system will help provide a company with a competitive advantage and position it for success in delivering superior returns to shareholders.

# Chapter 3

# Assessing Executive Pay Programs

**Melissa L. Burek and Shepard Long**

## 3.1 OBJECTIVES OF AN EXECUTIVE PAY ASSESSMENT

An executive pay program should be (1) responsible to shareholders, (2) competitive, so that it properly motivates and retains key executive talent, (3) effective at supporting and driving company success, and (4) compliant with relevant regulations. By periodically conducting an assessment of the total executive compensation program, companies can test the degree to which their pay program meets the above objectives. The assessment also will identify aspects of the program that need to be modified to meet these objectives and help guide the redesign process. Assessing executive pay programs has always been an important exercise for companies; however, the need to do so is becoming more acute in today's rapidly changing economic, legislative, and shareholder environment.

Assessing the pay program allows a company to test the pay and performance relationship on a retrospective basis to determine if executive rewards and compensation costs are commensurate with the level of company performance. A comparison of the company's salary levels, incentive opportunities, and equity use with market practice also will provide a benchmark of the degree to which the program is competitive. These external analyses will test the degree to which the pay program is "responsible" to both shareholders and executives.

A review of the program framework, including plan design, performance measurement, and incentive vehicles also serves as a test for alignment with the company's internal business strategies, organization culture, and compensation philosophy. As companies make strategic decisions to enter or exit businesses, shift operational priorities to cost control, growth, or quality improvement, and respond to the changing economic environment, the compensation program cannot get left behind or run counter to company priorities. Program design must support and reinforce company-specific priorities.

Compensation practices and incentive plan provisions also need to be reviewed to ensure they comply with government regulations, the tax code, accounting rules, and stock exchange requirements. As corporate governance issues come to the front burner, pay programs must hold up against investor, shareholder, and public scrutiny.

To summarize, executive pay program assessments should be conducted to ensure:

- Alignment with performance
- Market competitiveness
- Support of business strategy
- Fit with company culture and compensation philosophy
- Compliance with relevant regulations and governing entities
- Identification of program components requiring redesign
- Cost efficient, motivational, and responsible pay practices with respect to shareholders and executives

### (a) Holistic Program Review

Various work steps should be completed in any pay program assessment. A certain analysis or step should not be ignored simply because a problem has been identified with one particular program component only. For example, if the bonus plan is viewed as being ineffective or global stock option practices are believed to be noncompetitive, other key analyses should not necessarily be abandoned.

Exhibit 3.1 lists some key questions that human resources (HR) and compensation staff should consider before beginning a review.

Having a clear understanding of these issues will help guide the timing, resources, overall direction of the review, as well as the degree to which each part of the assessment should be emphasized over others.

## 3.2  EVALUATING CURRENT PROGRAM UNDERSTANDING

The first step of an overall executive pay program assessment is testing the degree to which the current compensation program and philosophy are understood and considered to be effective by program participants, as well as the degree to which changes are desired. This is done most often through individual interviews, focus groups, and surveys.

The objective is to obtain feedback on elements of the compensation program that are well understood, influence behavior, and drive performance, as well as those that are not effective. Obtaining this input is important because it often identifies problems, new ideas, or insights on program effectiveness that HR or senior company management were not aware of. It also may reveal viewpoints or perceptions contrary to those assumed to be true.

**Exhibit 3.1**   Key Questions to Consider

| Compensation Program Assessment Consideration | Sample Answers |
| --- | --- |
| Why is the assessment being conducted? | • Formal biannual review<br>• Consecutive years of declining performance and unusually high executive turnover<br>• Poor corporate governance rating<br>• Merger<br>• Request of compensation committee |
| Who is driving the assessment? | • CEO<br>• Compensation committee<br>• Business unit leaders<br>• Human resources |
| What are the objectives and required end products of the review? | • Report to compensation committee on competitiveness of current program design and competitive gaps<br>• Identification of plan redesign areas for required shareholder approval<br>• A new global long-term incentive plan design |

Obtaining executive feedback helps guide future plan design and promotes buy-in and commitment to program changes. A potential drawback in soliciting such input is that false expectations and/or anxieties may develop with respect to pay levels or program changes. The purpose of obtaining such information should be explained clearly to participants. Providing discussion topics in advance may contribute to effective information gathering, but should be balanced with the need for spontaneous gut-reaction responses.

These broad topics should be discussed when obtaining feedback, with tailoring as needed for any special program areas:

• Business environment
• Company performance and business strategy
• Financial planning process and performance measurement
• Competitive market for executive talent and business
• Compensation strategy
• Pay/performance relationship
• Overall pay program—strengths and weaknesses

— Salary management program

— Annual incentive plan design

— Long-term incentive plan design

• Role of benefits and perquisites

• Corporate governance issues and the role of the compensation committee

## (a) Executive Interviews

One-on-one interviews with executives are typically the most effective method of obtaining feedback for program participants. Executives are more candid and generally forthcoming in these individual discussions. The interviewer needs to make sure that questions are open-ended and not biased or leading in any way.

The executives interviewed should include any senior "policy/operating" committee members, as well as a cross-section of key senior corporate executives (e.g., chief financial officer [CFO], general counsel, top HR) and top sector/business unit executives. If a company has numerous business units, it may also be preferable to include the appropriate unit heads. Interviewing 8 to 12 executives usually is sufficient, but if a company has a significant executive population outside the United States (or potential global compensation issues), a subsection of geographic locations also should be represented. Some companies may choose to go below the most senior executive group to include participants in certain compensation programs (e.g., stock option participants but not long-term incentive plan [LTIP] participants).

Executive interviews are conducted most often by a third party who compiles all feedback into areas of consensus and disagreement. Company representatives may participate in interviews with the outside party, but executives tend to be more candid and open when a company representative is not present.

## (b) Executive Focus Groups

Focus groups are efficient when the goal is to obtain feedback from a larger or more diverse group of executives. Often comments made in focus groups elicit a reaction from other participants, and an exchange of ideas takes place that otherwise would not occur in an interview. Drawbacks to focus groups are that some members may not be comfortable expressing opinions that do not represent the norm, and that sessions can be dominated by outspoken individuals. (This may not be as likely to occur with a senior executive group.)

Generally, focus groups should include executives from various business units (including corporate staff) and geographies. Executives who participate in different pay programs, as well as supervisors and their subordinates, should not be put in the same group. Discussions should be structured so that conversation does not stray to less relevant topics, while at the same time allowing for thorough explanation of key points. An outside party trained in conducting focus groups should be used. If company representatives participate, one benefit is that company information can be clarified as necessary, but participants may be inhibited from sharing honest views and perceptions.

## (c) Surveys

Surveys are a less labor-intensive way to obtain feedback from a broad participant base. Surveys ensure the uniformity of questions for which data is gathered, yet feedback is more limited, particularly if the questionnaire is multiple choice. While the depth of information gleaned is not nearly as great, surveys can be used effectively as a supplement to individual interviews and/or focus groups. Surveys also are useful in tracking the degree of change in responses over time or after program changes have been implemented.

When choosing a particular approach, consider the purpose for which the information is being gathered. Also, it is important to manage expectations so that executives are not necessarily expecting significant changes in pay levels or programs.

## (d) Board of Directors/Compensation Committee

Obtaining the views of the compensation committee of the board of directors is extremely important, particularly given the committee's increased responsibility in the current governance climate. Compared to executive feedback, input from directors typically will be more strategic and directional in terms of plan design or company pay practices. Such input is informative and often enlightening for senior executives. And while it will help guide future program design, initial involvement by the compensation committee also will encourage support and commitment to the review process and any changes that may be recommended as a result.

## 3.3   VALIDATION OF COMPENSATION STRATEGY

The second step in assessing the executive pay program is to validate the company's current compensation strategy. The executive compensation strategy should clearly define and articulate overarching principles that drive program design and influence daily compensation decisions. It should reflect the philosophy and objectives of the compensation committee, the chief executive officer (CEO), and senior executives, and fit with the organization's culture. Key elements of the strategy are disclosed annually in the compensation committee report of the company's proxy statement, and it is the committee's and management's responsibility to shareholders to adhere to the strategy.

A pay strategy should address:

- Definition of the competitive market and/or defined peer group
- Target pay position for various components of pay
- Target total pay mix (fixed vs. variable; short-term vs. long-term)
- Desired relationship between performance achievement and earned pay
- Emphasis on equity, shareholder value creation, and executive stock ownership
- Compliance with key legislative, tax, and accounting regulations
- Non-U.S. executive compensation philosophy (if different)

Validating a compensation strategy may involve different things depending on the degree to which a strategy is currently in place and its appropriateness. These questions should be considered as a company begins its review:

- Is a formal compensation strategy currently in place?
- Is the current strategy well defined and well understood by executives?
- Are current pay practices aligned with the compensation strategy, or do they conflict?
- Does the strategy reflect the current thinking, objectives, and direction of the overall program?

In validating the compensation strategy, the end result should be an affirmative answer to these questions. Strategy validation may involve minimal changes for some companies, and it may involve developing a new strategy for others. But without a sound strategy, the effectiveness of a company's pay plans and practices cannot be determined.

## (a) Key Elements of a Compensation Strategy

*(i) Definition of Competitive Market*   For senior executives (including the top-five "Named Executive Officers" whose compensation must be disclosed in public company proxy statements), companies typically construct a "peer group" of public companies against which to benchmark pay levels and performance. Most companies use at least one peer group that represents the competitive market for executive talent and business, and this is most frequently an industry peer group. This primary peer group should reflect companies whose size typically ranges from one-half to two times the revenue or asset size of the company. (Company size and base salary levels are highly correlated at the senior executive level.)

Depending on the company's needs, some companies may choose to use a defined peer group from a published index (e.g., Standard & Poor's Property &

Casualty Insurance Index), a high-performing peer group (selected using total shareholder return, earnings per share, or growth criteria), a cyclical company peer group or other cross-industry group, often as a secondary peer group. For example, an insurance company may use a primary peer group of other insurers to benchmark its executive pay practices, but also use a secondary, high-performing financial services peer group to track pay trends for its most senior executive group, where the competitive market extends beyond insurance companies.

(There are various criteria to selecting peer groups, depending on the objective. Some companies may want to use comparator companies that they compete with for investor dollars; others may want to use a peer group for relative performance measurement in an incentive plan. Chapter 9 addresses this topic in greater detail and describes statistical approaches to developing a peer group.)

Below the senior executive group, the competitive market often is more broadly defined. For example, the competitive market may be defined as the financial services industry, the retail industry, or durable goods manufacturers, within an appropriate company size range. If there are multiple business units in discrete businesses, each may require a different competitive market. Also, for staff or corporate positions, the market often is defined even more broadly to include general industry.

The key is to have a defined pay market for executive positions and to use this market consistently to benchmark pay practices so that compensation strategy and resulting pay levels are credible and market based.

*(ii) Target Pay Position*    Companies should have a desired "target" pay position for the executive population for target (or "meets expectations") performance results. The target position may differ by component (base, bonus long-term incentives), but is typically consistent for the executive group. It will reflect the emphasis on fixed vs. variable compensation and the degree to which the company wishes to have a premium or below-average pay position vs. market (e.g., salaries targeted below median, incentives targeted at the 65th percentile). Among many factors, a company's risk/reward profile, degree of cyclicality, and growth stage may all impact its desired pay position.

*(iii) Target Pay Mix*    Related to the target pay position, companies also should determine what portion of target total compensation should be fixed (i.e., base salary) and what portion should be variable (i.e., linked to short- and long-term performance). The cash versus equity mix also should be considered. For example, in financial services companies, annual incentives typically are emphasized to a greater degree than in other industries.

*(iv) Pay and Performance Relationship*    In addition to target pay position, a company must determine what level of performance is required to earn target

compensation as well as above- or below-target compensation. For example, one company may require above-average performance to earn target compensation, which is positioned at the market median, while another company may require average performance to earn target compensation, which is positioned at the market 60th percentile. Clearly, the first company has a more performance-oriented pay program.

A very common approach is to pay at the market median for median performance, with significant leverage for performance that significantly exceeds expectations and to pay below the median for below-median performance.

**(v) Role of Equity Compensation**   Compensation strategies also should contemplate the degree to which equity-based compensation and incentives will be emphasized. The objective of all public companies is to create shareholder value, yet companies differ in the degree to which the pay system is linked directly to equity. The company's stock ownership culture is also a factor that impacts use of equity (see Chapter 8).

**(vi) Non-U.S. Executive Compensation**   At the senior executive level, most global organizations have a consistent compensation strategy for all executives, both within and outside the United States. The program framework, use of equity, and pay/performance expectations generally are consistent. Targeted cash compensation (base plus bonus) position often is consistent, and the equity program is usually based on U.S. practices and "exported" globally. This practice can result in different competitive total pay positions across different countries or geographies, but the overriding principle is to keep program design consistent, so that executives are treated comparably and can relocate more easily to different countries. This approach may change over time, but the important factor is to define the strategy and articulate it in advance.

## 3.4   PAY LEVELS: COMPETITIVENESS AND ALIGNMENT WITH COMPENSATION STRATEGY

When companies undertake an assessment of their compensation program, the most common thing that comes to mind is an analysis of pay levels. Competitiveness of pay is very important, but it should not be analyzed in isolation, given that it is highly interrelated to the method of pay delivery and the corresponding value derived from performance results. Pay opportunities need to be competitive with the market because their impact is far reaching in terms of motivating, attracting, and retaining executives, driving appropriate short- and long-term business decisions, supporting team success and corporate goals, developing human capital, and managing personnel costs.

Pay levels are also an area of great interest and sensitivity to executives. Careful attention must be given to maintaining a market-based program and communicating the competitive position of the program, the alignment with the company's strategy, and the linkage between performance results and earned compensation.

## (a) Benchmarking Mechanics

To assess pay levels, companies periodically should benchmark compensation for a sample of executive positions. If done annually, benchmarking should include approximately 20 percent of executive positions. If done less frequently, then benchmarking 25 to 40 percent of executive positions is usually appropriate. The benchmark positions should encompass different functional groups and business units, as well as various position levels (e.g., different pay grade or bands).

These components of a company's pay program should be analyzed to the extent that market data is available:

| *Actual Pay* | *Target Pay* |
| --- | --- |
| Base salary | Base salary |
| Actual (recent) bonus paid | Target bonus opportunity |
| Actual annual cash compensation | Target annual cash compensation |
| Actual long-term incentive awards[1,2] | Target long-term incentive opportunity[2] |
| Actual total direction compensation | Target total direct compensation |

[1] Long-term incentive awards made over the past one to three years should be valued to develop an "average" long-term incentive value.

[2] Most often valued on a present value basis; an alternative methodology is to analyze actual equity "gains" realized (and/or actual long-term incentive plan payments made) over a specific time period.

Sources of benchmark data include peer company proxy statements, published survey data, custom survey data, and proprietary databases.

## (b) Benchmarking Guidelines

To develop credible market data, these guidelines represent good rules of thumb:

- Use three to five market data points to develop a market consensus for each benchmark position

- Obtain various market reference points (i.e., 25th percentile, median, 75th percentile) to the extent they are relevant to the company's pay practices or strategy (e.g., if company has a 75th percentile pay strategy, 75th percentile market data may be most relevant)
- Select market data based on the similarity of position scope, responsibilities, and reporting structure for each benchmark position
- Use data that represent the defined competitive market for the company and/ or each position (e.g., the appropriate asset/revenue scope size, specific industry, and/or public peer group)
- Make adjustments to market data if company position responsibilities are greater or less than those for the market position
- Eliminate outliers
- Ensure that long-term incentive data is valued on a consistent basis among various survey sources (e.g., Black-Scholes value, grant value, adjustments for vesting or forfeitures, target awards vs. actual payouts, present value of equity awards vs. in-the-money equity value)

## (c) Analysis of Benchmarking Results

Once competitive market data are compiled for each position and pay component, the variance between the company's pay levels and market pay levels can be analyzed. Individual position pay variances within +/– 10 percent of "market" generally indicate that the pay level is competitive. For a group of positions, average variances of +/– 5 percent are considered to be competitive with the appropriate market reference point (i.e., 25th, 50th, or 75th percentile).

Examining data for individual positions and/or a group of positions (i.e., a business unit or corporate function) will help identify market pay gaps or internal discrepancies and areas where market-based pay adjustments may need to be made. To assess the company's overall pay structure, however, market data should be analyzed by relevant executive groups (i.e., executive pay grade, title, or whatever basis is appropriate for the organization). A key objective is to assess, on average, the degree to which executive salary bands and target incentive guidelines are competitive with market practice for each executive group. The basis for this evaluation is the compensation strategy and the company's desired pay position; in other words, is the market position of the company's pay structure (for base, bonus, long-term incentives, and total compensation) reflective of its compensation strategy and desired pay position? The company's targeted pay mix also can be tested against market norms.

Finally, companies can use market data to determine the appropriateness of their pay and performance relationship, particularly with respect to annual cash compensation (base plus bonus) and the extent to which it reflects the company's compensation strategy (see next section).

To summarize, a competitive analysis of executive pay levels serves multiple purposes in the overall executive pay program assessment:

- It compares actual pay levels vs. market and identifies competitive gaps.
- It evaluates the alignment of the executive pay structure with the company's compensation strategy.
- It helps evaluate the pay and performance relationship and degree to which it reflects the company's strategy.
- It identifies where change is necessary in either the pay program or the compensation strategy.
- It provides a market basis to help guide the development of such changes.

These objectives are described in more detail in Exhibit 3.2.

**Exhibit 3.2**  Key Objectives

| Pay Comparison | Objective/Findings Used to |
|---|---|
| Individual position pay levels vs. market<br>• Positions may be grouped by business unit, function, etc. | Identify competitive pay gaps and any need for market-based adjustments<br><br>Identify internal discrepancies in pay practices |
| Target pay structure vs. market<br>• By executive pay group, classification, etc. | Evaluate competitiveness of company's executive pay structure (salary bands, incentive award guidelines)<br><br>Determine if pay structure is aligned/consistent with compensation strategy<br>  • Target pay position<br>  • Pay mix<br><br>Identify required changes in pay structure or compensation strategy and guide development of changes |
| Actual pay levels and corresponding performance vs. market | Assist in evaluation of company's pay and performance relationship and extent to which it reflects that articulated in the compensation strategy |

## 3.5 PAY AND PERFORMANCE RELATIONSHIP

One of the most important aspects of any executive pay program assessment involves the relationship between pay and performance. While it is certainly important for executive pay levels to be competitive and aligned with a company's business strategy, it is perhaps even more important that they be properly aligned with actual business results.

If a company is consistently a top-quartile performer relative to its peers, but delivers pay at the industry median, are its executives being fairly compensated? Or does the company risk losing its key executives to another firm that is willing to pay top dollar for star performers? Conversely, if a company's performance consistently trails the broader market, but executive pay is routinely pegged at the market median, are the company's compensation dollars being spent appropriately?

Assessing the relationship between pay and performance is critical to evaluating any executive pay program and to ensuring that executives' financial interests have been appropriately aligned with those of the company's true owners—the shareholders.

### (a) Direction versus Precision

When assessing the pay and performance relationship, it is unrealistic to expect (or even strive for) aerospace precision. Instead, it is more important to assess whether the relationship between pay and performance is directionally correct. If a company's pay levels are well above median, has it delivered performance that would support relatively high compensation? And if a company's performance has lagged its peers, have executive pay levels been impacted accordingly?

Exhibit 3.3 shows the target relationship between executive pay and company performance. In the second and third quadrants, pay is aligned with performance, while in the first and fourth quadrant, pay and performance are misaligned.

### (b) Performance Measures

The first question that must be answered when assessing the relationship between pay and performance is: What do we mean by performance? Because the ultimate goal of any company is to increase shareholder value, it is almost always appropriate to use total shareholder return as a key performance measure. However, TSR is not the only measure that is appropriate for pay and performance comparisons.

Depending on a company's specific circumstances, other measures can be just as appropriate, and in some cases even more illuminating. Examples of other possible measures include internal financial measures such as revenue, operating income, or net income, as well as non-financial measures such as customer satisfaction, quality, or market share. If a measure is not directly related to stock price,

**Exhibit 3.3**   Relationship between Pay and Performance

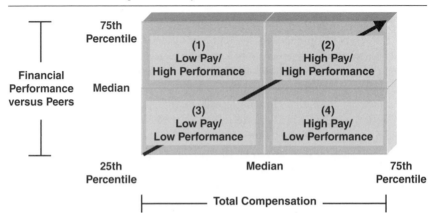

---

**Illustration**

A company in the manufacturing industry was meeting its internal financial goals year after year and had regularly been rewarding executives with annual bonus payments that were at or above target. At the same time, the company's share price was fairly flat while the overall market continued to rise.

At the request of the company's board of directors, management reevaluated its prior 10 years' financial results on a relative (as opposed to absolute) basis. Despite having met or exceeded their absolute financial targets each year, the company was surprised to find that its overall performance was in the bottom quartile relative to a group of industry peers.

Although the exercise did not specifically address the relationship between pay and performance, it points out the problems with relying on absolute measures to evaluate success. Each year the company achieved its internal goals. And each year the company fell behind the competition. Had the company used relative performance measures to test the degree of "stretch" in its annual goals or to validate its achievements against the broader market, it would have quickly discovered that absolute performance measures can be extremely misleading.

however, it should be highly correlated with increases in shareholder value and directly related to the company's overall business strategy.

While many companies prefer to use *absolute* performance measures for incentive plan purposes and internal goal-setting, absolute measures shed little light on the relationship between executive pay and company performance. To properly assess this relationship, both pay and performance must be evaluated on a *relative* basis.

## (c) Performance Periods

Another key question when evaluating the relationship between pay and performance is: What is the appropriate measurement period? The short answer is: It depends.

One should generally try to align the performance period with the compensation period. This means that we should not look at 10-year shareholder return figures to assess the appropriateness of last year's bonus, and we should not look at a company's most recent quarterly results to determine if historical stock option grant practices have been reasonable.

Because pay and performance comparisons require relative performance data, and competitor financial information is available only on an annual or quarterly basis, most companies default to using fixed performance periods that typically correspond to each company's fiscal year. If we keep in mind that the goal of a pay-and-performance analysis is to test for directional correctness, the convenience of using fiscal year data generally outweighs any problems associated with using point-to-point (as opposed to rolling) calculations and slightly misaligned performance periods (e.g., peer company fiscal years may not all end on the same date, or even in the same quarter).

*(i) Base Salary*   Base salaries are the one element of executive compensation that generally are not benchmarked against performance. Instead, they are considered "fixed" compensation that is based on the complexity, scope, and overall responsibilities of the job. Performance has a direct impact on "variable" compensation elements such as annual bonus payments and long-term incentives, but is generally not as highly correlated with base salary levels.

Of course, just because executive salaries typically are not benchmarked against performance does not mean that they cannot or should not be benchmarked. In many cases, the measure that is most highly correlated with executive salary levels is company size (typically measured by revenue or assets), with the CFO of a $10 billion company typically commanding a higher salary than the CFO of a $1 billion company in the same industry. (As a rough rule of thumb, a doubling of annual revenue tends to translate to a 20 percent salary increase for otherwise comparable positions.)

Although a number of other factors also impact executive salary levels (i.e., tenure, individual performance, internal equity, and multinational or global responsibilities), company performance is usually not a significant part of the equation.

***(ii) Total Annual Compensation***    Total annual compensation (TAC) typically includes base salary plus any additional payments from the company's annual bonus program, regardless of whether those bonus payments are delivered in the form of cash or stock. Because TAC represents pay for a specific year, it is appropriate to compare TAC and company performance to that of a specific group of peer companies over that same one-year period. If the pay and performance relationship is strong, top-performing companies will have higher levels of TAC and poor performers will have relatively low TAC.

For public companies, the required compensation data are readily available in annual proxy statements, which must disclose the compensation of the company's top five executives (the Named Executive Officers). After analyzing how the target company's compensation compares to peers, one can then analyze the company's performance vs. those same peer companies, using a combination of stock price and internal financial measures.

***(iii) Long-Term Incentives***    TAC can be benchmarked against one-year company performance easily, but long-term incentives (stock options, restricted stock, and other long-term awards) are not as straightforward. The guiding principle is to attempt to match the performance period to the compensation period. Unfortunately, there is often no clearly defined compensation period for long-term incentive (LTI) awards.

Most stock options have a 10-year term but can be exercised at any time once they are vested. Restricted stock may vest ratably over four years at one company, but cliff vest after five years at another. And some companies may have intermediate-term plans with clearly defined multiyear performance periods. Clearly, there is no one "compensation period" that covers all of these possibilities.

A second complication regarding long-term incentives is how to value them (the "pay" portion of the pay-and-performance analysis). If Company A gives its CEO 100,000 stock options, and Company B gives its CEO 50,000 stock options, 25,000 restricted shares, and an opportunity to earn an additional $500,000 or more in cash based on performance over the next three years, which CEO received more "pay"? Depending on each company's stock price at the time of grant and actual performance in the future, a compelling case can likely be made for either one.

The most common way to value long-term incentives is to calculate the estimated present value of the award at the time it is granted. For stock options, this calculation requires using an option pricing model (e.g., the Black-Scholes model), which in turn requires assumptions regarding the expected life of the option, future volatility of the stock, dividend yield, and the risk-free interest rate. The result is a theoretical value of the award that may or may not be similar to what the executive ultimately receives. If the stock price increases significantly, actual gains may be much higher. And if the stock price remains flat or decreases, the executive will receive nothing.

Most companies use some variation of this estimated present value approach when benchmarking long-term incentive levels against the broader market, because they want to ensure that they are delivering a competitive long-term incentive opportunity that is aligned with their target pay strategy. Present values also can be used to evaluate the relationship between pay and performance, under the theory that higher-performing companies can and should provide their executives with higher long-term incentive opportunities.

Another way to value long-term incentives for pay-and-performance comparisons is to focus not on estimated values at the time of grant but rather on paper gains over a specific time period.

"Paper gains" refers to the current market value of all stock awards, plus the spread (the difference between the current market price and the original exercise price) on any option grants. For example, by looking at paper gains to date on all LTI awards (for the target company and the peer companies) over the last three years, and comparing those gains to each company's stock price performance over that same three-year period, we can determine if the value executives are receiving from LTI awards is in line with actual company performance.

Although such calculations still represent a snapshot of LTI values that may or not be similar to what an executive ultimately receives, and can give an incomplete picture of the true economic value of stock options (especially if they have eight or nine years remaining before expiration), a paper gains analysis can help level the playing field for LTI and performance comparisons across companies.

## 3.6 PAY PRACTICES

Compensation benchmarking and pay-and-performance analyses are designed to help companies determine how much they should be paying their executives. Benchmarking pay practices helps companies answer an equally important question—not how much, but how?

"Pay practices" is a general term that encompasses a wide variety of issues, such as eligibility and participation in various compensation programs, incentive plan measures, equity usage, equity ownership, and potential shareholder dilution due to equity compensation programs. These and other key practices all should be reviewed regularly, as part of the overall executive compensation program assessment, to ensure that they are:

- Aligned with the company's compensation philosophy and business strategies
- Competitive with peer company or broader market practices
- Meeting the needs of executives in terms of appropriate motivation

When benchmarking pay practices, it is important to keep in mind that just because a particular practice is "competitive" from a market perspective, it is not necessarily right for every company. It is important that practices be appropriate for the organization in question, even if they are unusual by industry or "market" standards. For example, if a company has made a commitment to employee stock ownership at all levels of the organization, it may make annual stock option or restricted stock grants to all employees, even though "competitive" practice might be to limit such grants to employees making $100,000 per year or more.

On the other hand, investors and shareholders also will be making determinations based on the degree of a company's alignment with market practice. Consider again a company that makes annual equity grants to all of its employees. This approach may be aligned with its internal compensation philosophy, yet through benchmarking the company may discover that the cost of those grants results in a 5 percent reduction in EPS per year. In contrast, its closest rival makes annual equity grants that result in a 2 percent reduction in EPS.

The company will need to decide, as will shareholders, if the real and perceived benefits of broad employee stock ownership outweigh the cost of the reduction in EPS. By benchmarking pay practices against both internal and external standards, companies can begin to arm themselves with the data required to make informed decisions.

The remainder of this section discusses specific pay practices that all companies should review as part of the overall executive compensation program assessment.

## (a) Annual Incentives

Benchmark data regarding annual incentive levels for top executives is readily available in annual proxy statements, but benchmark data on annual incentive practices can be more difficult to find.

For annual incentive plans, public companies are not required to disclose how many total executives are eligible for the bonus program, how the bonus pool is calculated, and (other than for their top five officers) the size of individual bonus awards. Some of this information may be contained in the compensation committee report in the annual proxy statement, but the level of detail provided varies from company to company. If the bonus plan has been approved by shareholders, the plan document will be publicly available, but it still may not provide enough information to thoroughly benchmark plan design practices.

Given these potential gaps, publicly disclosed peer company data often must be supplemented with survey data that address these topics more specifically. Many consulting firms conduct periodic surveys of executive pay practices, including "custom" surveys on behalf of clients that target a specific group of peer companies instead of a broader market sample.

*(i) Eligibility*    A fundamental aspect of any executive bonus program is eligibility—how many individuals should have an opportunity to earn a bonus each year? Mercer Human Resource Consulting's most recent *Survey of Best Practices in Executive Compensation* found that executive bonus programs typically extend to individuals or annual salaries above $100,000. (Broad-based bonus programs extend much further into the organization, often to all employees.) When it comes to eligibility, however, companies must balance external market data with what makes sense internally, given the company's organizational structure, compensation strategy (including emphasis on short-term incentives), other incentive programs in place, cost, and any other unique business issues.

*(ii) Funding*    Companies can use a variety of different funding approaches to determine the overall size of the bonus pool. With a goal-attainment approach, the company establishes target, threshold, and maximum performance levels in advance, along with corresponding individual awards for each level. If the company achieves target performance, the total bonus pool will be the sum of the individual award targets.

An alternate funding approach is formula-based, in which the total bonus pool will be a predetermined percentage of some financial measure (i.e., 3 percent of net income, 5 percent of operating income). Such formulas can use a fixed percentage across the board or a sliding scale in which the percentage changes at different performance levels.

Finally, some companies fund their annual incentive plan on a purely discretionary basis. Although they may use some variation of a goal-attainment or formula-based approach to guide their thinking, the ultimate funding is based on a discretionary retroactive assessment of a variety of factors.

*(iii) Performance Mix*    "Performance mix" refers to the various organizational levels at which performance is measured. It is often a key design decision for companies and reflects a company's philosophy on the relative importance of overall team performance and accountability vs. unit and individual performance. Some companies prefer to reward all senior executives based on overall corporate results; others base a portion or even all of the award on unit or individual performance, especially if the executive is responsible for a specific profit center. The former approach can help foster an all-for-one mentality among the company's senior executive team, while the latter provides greater line of sight between an executive's day-to-day management decisions and his or her ultimate bonus award.

The most common approach is a blend of corporate, unit, and individual performance. Performance assessments typically are discrete funding components or used to allocate incentive monies that have been funded on an overall corporate basis.

*(iv) Performance Measures*   Performance measures are the specific criteria on which incentive plan payments are based. Many companies will use at least two measures for executive incentive plan purposes, often with the goal of balancing a bottom-line measure (i.e., net income or EPS) with a top-line measure (such as revenue growth) or a quality of earnings measure (i.e., ROE). Other companies may use more sophisticated measures of "economic" (as opposed to accounting) profit that incorporate the cost of capital used by the business.

When a company measures performance at both the corporate and the business unit level, it may use different measures for each (e.g., net income at the corporate level but operating income at the unit level). If that is the case, however, the company must make sure that the unit-level measures do not conflict with those of the larger organization. The same also holds for both individual performance measures and nonfinancial performance measures (i.e., quality or customer satisfaction), which should be specific, quantifiable goals that directly support overall company objectives.

Pay practices benchmarking can help reveal which performance measures are most common in a particular industry or peer group, but the measures a company uses must make sense from a business strategy perspective. Measures should be clearly understood by participating executives, who in turn should have the ability to impact the results. If not measuring share price directly, performance measures should at least be highly correlated with (and, it is hoped, lead directly to) long-term shareholder value creation.

*(v) Leverage*   "Leverage" refers to the variability of bonus awards when performance either exceeds or falls short of target or meets-expectations performance. In a highly leveraged plan, executives might be able to earn two or three times their target award if performance is outstanding and may not receive any bonus at all if performance is below a certain threshold. In a less-leveraged plan, bonus payments will cluster in a more narrow range, such as 50 percent to 150 percent of target.

Exhibit 3.4 illustrates two different leverage models. Company A pays executives a small bonus when performance is well below target, with payments increasing on a straight-line basis as performance improves. Company B has a much higher threshold before any bonus is paid, and bonus payments increase more rapidly when performance exceeds the specified target. In this example, Company B has the more highly leveraged program—executives have a greater risk of receiving no bonus, but will receive a greater reward if performance is above target.

*(vi) Payment Methods*   Historically, the most conventional approach has been to pay annual incentive awards in cash at the end of the performance period. However, it is becoming increasingly common for companies to pay a portion of the award in equity, especially at senior executive levels. This can be accomplished by paying a portion of the award in the form of restricted stock that will vest over

**Exhibit 3.4** Sample Leverage Models

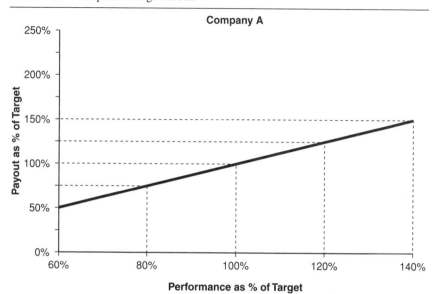

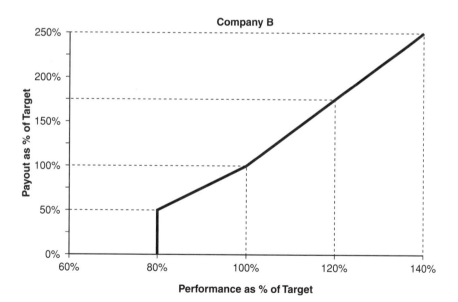

several years or by allowing executives to voluntarily exchange cash payments for equity (stock or stock options), often at a favorable exchange ratio.

Many companies also link annual bonus payments to a deferred compensation program, which can be either mandatory (a fixed portion of all bonus payments is automatically deferred to a future date) or voluntarily (to allow executives to better manage their personal tax liabilities).

## (b) Long-term Incentives

In 2003, the Financial Accounting Standards Board (FASB) announced plans to require U.S. companies to include the "fair value" of all equity compensation awards as an expense on their annual income statements. As a result, long-term incentive practices are drawing much closer scrutiny as companies struggle to balance the accounting cost of various awards with the perceived value received by employees and executives. In many cases, companies are rethinking their long-term incentive programs and changing many of their long-standing LTI practices.

From a benchmarking perspective, publicly disclosed data regarding LTI practices is much more readily available than for annual incentive practices. In addition to disclosing all LTI awards to the top five executive officers (in proxy statement disclosures), companies must disclose how many shares they grant on an aggregate basis each year, the total number of awards they have outstanding and available for future grant, the weighted-average exercise price of outstanding options, and the hypothetical impact of fair value accounting on their overall EPS (in the financial statements in their annual 10-K reports). A company can undertake a number of analyses to test how its LTI program compares to peers or the broader market.

***(i) Eligibility***   Eligibility for long-term incentive programs often is more selective than eligibility for annual incentive programs, but can vary widely by company and by program. According to Mercer's most recent *Survey of Best Practices in Executive Compensation,* stock option eligibility typically extends to the $80,000 to 100,000 salary level, long-term performance plans to executives making $200,000 per year or more, and restricted stock eligibility is even more limited.

It is important to note that these figures all predate FASB's tentative decision to require fair value accounting for all equity-based compensation. As companies begin to recognize stock options as a compensation expense, most likely many will limit stock option eligibility and broaden participation in other long-term vehicles, such as restricted stock.

***(ii) Annual Share Usage***   "Annual share usage" (sometimes called "run rate" or "burn rate") refers to the total number of shares a company grants to its employees each year in the form of stock options, restricted stock, and other equity-based LTI awards. Typically it is expressed as percentage of total shares outstanding to reflect how much of the total value of the company is being distributed or allocated to employees in the form of equity-based compensation each year.

According to Mercer's database of 350 U.S. industrial and service companies, median share usage in 2002 was 1.9 percent, but this figure can vary considerably based on industry (technology companies generally have higher share usage than manufacturing companies) and overall market capitalization (larger market cap companies may have lower run rates than smaller companies).

When benchmarking annual share usage, one must be cognizant that companies may differ in how they reward executives, and therefore run rates may vary. For example, a company that uses all restricted stock should have a much lower run rate than a company that uses all stock options, because more options are required to deliver a comparable award present value. Program eligibility and compensation strategies also will influence run rates. There is also increasing external pressure from institutions, shareholders, and others to manage run rates (and equity dilution) more closely than in the past. At the present time, run rates much greater than 2 percent of common shares outstanding are being more closely scrutinized.

*(iii) Total Potential Dilution*   When a company grants a share of stock to an executive, it dilutes the ownership of all other shareholders, who now own a slightly smaller percentage of the overall company. Total potential dilution provides an estimate of the dilutive impact of all outstanding (unexercised) stock option grants, plus any additional shares that the company has available to grant in the future from any incentive plans. Sometimes called "overhang," it is typically expressed as a percentage of total shares outstanding.

When benchmarking total potential dilution, it is important to understand the specific methodology being used. Some companies will count outstanding stock options but exclude restricted stock, and some will add the numerator to the denominator before calculating the dilution percentage. Such differences must be understood clearly to ensure that all benchmarking comparisons are made on an apples-to-apples basis.

In Mercer's 350-company database, median dilution is approximately 15 percent, and can range from 10 to 20 percent or higher. In the past, 10 percent dilution was considered a red flag. In recent years, with increased use of options and a downward-trading market, 15 percent dilution may be considered a red flag. Companies must evaluate their dilution in light of industry norms or peer group practices, and also must consider their compensation strategy, stock price performance, and which programs or "practices" have led to their dilution. Often companies must reevaluate plan design due to the level of their dilution. Investors and shareholders are sensitive to unusually high dilution, and benchmarking helps determine if a company's dilution is "unusually" high.

*(iv) Award (Incentive Vehicle) Mix*   "Award mix" describes how a company weights the different compensation vehicles (e.g., stock options, restricted stock,

performance shares, and performance cash plan) within its LTI program. In general, the mix should be aligned with the company's overall compensation strategy, which will guide how much the company wishes to emphasizes stock price appreciation and shareholder value creation vs. other measures of long-term financial or operational success.

At various performance levels, award mix can have a substantial impact on how much value executives ultimately receive. If a company's stock price is rising, an award mix that places a greater emphasis on stock options likely will deliver more value than a more balanced mix of stock options and full-value shares. Conversely, if a company's stock price is falling, an all-options program will deliver no value whatsoever (because the options will be underwater), while a more diversified program still can deliver at least some value to executives. By introducing restricted stock into the award mix, companies can promote retention of key executives and provide a hedge against falling stock prices.

By benchmarking its LTI practices, a company can determine how much of its program is linked to absolute stock price (in the form of restricted or unrestricted shares), stock price appreciation (e.g., stock options), and non-stock price measures, and how that mix compares to both its competitors and its stated compensation philosophy.

***(v) Stock Ownership Guidelines and Holding Requirements***    A final area that public companies should review as part of an overall program assessment is executive stock ownership and holding guidelines. In today's corporate governance environment, many institutions look favorably on companies that have demonstrated a commitment to high levels of executive stock ownership. Strong guidelines expressed as either a fixed number of shares or as a multiple of base salary (i.e., 5 × salary for a CEO, 3 × salary for other senior executives) can send a powerful message regarding a company's commitment to executive stock ownership and linking executives' interests to those of the shareholders.

Things that may impact the "right" level of ownership for a company include the amount of compensation and benefit programs that are delivered, awarded, or denominated in company stock and the company's general compensation strategy. For example, a company that uses a great deal of restricted stock strongly facilitates executive ownership regardless of the company's stock price performance. On the other hand, a company that uses all options, and whose stock has been flat for three years, may not wish to strictly enforce stringent ownership guidelines. Instead, holding requirements (of net shares upon exercise) may be more appropriate.

## 3.7  REGULATORY REQUIREMENTS

Another important component of any executive compensation program assessment is evaluating the degree to which the company complies with various governmental and stock exchange rules and regulations. For example, Section 162(m) of the Internal Revenue Code (IRC) states that any compensation paid to top-five officers in excess of $1 million per year must be "performance-based" in order to be deductible for tax purposes. If a company's compensation strategy and long-term incentive award mix place even a moderate emphasis on service-based restricted stock, which does not qualify under IRC Section 162(m), it may well exceed this $1 million limit and forfeit its tax deduction on the excess compensation. The company then will have to decide which goal is more important, qualifying compensation as performance-based under Section 162(m) or encouraging executive retention with service-based restricted stock.

Other regulatory issues that should be assessed on a regular basis include shareholder approval of equity compensation plans (required by both the Nasdaq and the New York Stock Exchange), compliance with the various provisions of the Sarbanes-Oxley Act, and other Securities and Exchange Commission (SEC) disclosure requirements. All of these issues are explored in more detail in Chapters 4 and 6.

## 3.8 COMMUNICATION

While SEC rules govern what a company must disclose about its compensation programs in its annual proxy statement and 10-K filings, a thorough assessment of an executive compensation program also should include a review of any other communication materials the company distributes to participating executives (see Chapter 13). The communication materials should clearly explain how the various plans work, what performance will be measured, and how success will be rewarded. When compensation plans do not appear to be driving the desired behavior, poor internal communication and lack of understanding are often to blame.

# Chapter 4

# Corporate Governance Issues Affecting Executive Compensation

## Howard J. Golden

This chapter addresses selected corporate governance issues in the executive compensation area.* This discussion focuses on the role of the board of directors and corporate management as fiduciaries, the impact of proposed new governance standards, and the effect of the new requirements on board processes and executive compensation disclosure.

The information in this chapter is current as of the date of writing and is provided by Mercer in its capacity as a consultant in the area of executive compensation. Matter of a legal nature should be reviewed by appropriate counsel. In addition, as the area is changing rapidly, practitioners should make themselves aware of the latest developments.

## 4.1  INTRODUCTION

The area of corporate governance as it affects board determination of executive compensation changed for the foreseeable future on December 2, 2001, when Enron Corporation declared bankruptcy. As a result of investigations arising from the bankruptcy of Enron and other corporations, the compensation community, legislators, and regulators recognized that considerable attention had to be given to corporate governance matters.

Management and directors again became aware of their responsibilities to shareholders, and to the investing public, with respect to discharge of their duties.

*The author wishes to thank Mark A. Borges and Neil M. Grossman of Mercer Human Resource Consulting for their thorough and thoughtful peer reviews of this chapter.

In addition, the specific events of the corporate world led to two separate but overlapping attempts to regulate management and board behavior:

1. The Sarbanes-Oxley Act, eventually enacted on July 30, 2002, created a number of obligations with respect to companies with reporting obligations under the Federal Securities Laws.

2. Major stock exchanges in the United States began to revise their listing standards, using the listing requirements as a vehicle for increased matters of corporate governance.

Each of these developments will be discussed in some detail in this chapter.

The area of best practices in corporate governance continues to change. Although significant changes have arisen as a result of the work of the regulators, it is expected that over the next few years there will evolve a complete set of appropriate practices by boards and management with respect to corporate governance. The standard for compliance is expected to be raised as the years go by.

## 4.2 ROLE OF THE BOARD AND MANAGEMENT AS FIDUCIARIES

Historically, the board of directors was envisaged in the corporate structure as the representative of the shareholder group. In concept, the shareholders delegate to the board certain actions on behalf of the shareholders, and the shareholders may require of the board remedies or penalties for dereliction of duty. While the board appoints the management of the corporation, management too, historically, has increasingly acted as a corporate fiduciary on behalf of the shareholders.

Board obligations and activities are primarily a matter of state corporate law. However, Congress also has, pursuant to its power to legislate under the Commerce Clause of the United States Constitution, enacted a considerable amount of legislation affecting the conduct of corporate boards and management. For example, the federal securities laws, among other things:

1. Require the disclosure of specific information about the board and management to a corporation's shareholders
2. Require the reporting by the board and executives of transactions in securities of the employer
3. Limit the trading by corporate "insiders" with respect to employer securities
4. Prescribe civil and criminal penalties for violations of the securities laws

In a similar manner, a major law affecting the regulation of employee benefit plans, the Employee Retirement Income Security Act (ERISA) of 1974, as amended, requires that corporations and those administering plans act as fiduciaries on behalf of plan participants in a manner that reflects a form of federal fiduciary common law. The relationship between federal and state laws in this area is complex, but in the case of state securities laws, federal laws always apply and state securities laws may be preempted in certain cases.

## 4.3   SARBANES-OXLEY ACT OF 2002

The Sarbanes-Oxley Act (SOA), enacted on July 30, 2002 as Public Law 107-204, contains 11 titles, comprising sections numbered from 1 to 1007. Here we explore a number of specific provisions of the statute in order to show the law's effect on corporate governance in regard to executive pay.

### (a) Accelerated Insider Reporting

For companies with a class of equity securities registered under the Securities Exchange Act of 1934 (generally, those traded on a U.S. stock exchange and certain other corporations), the law in effect before the SOA generally required officers, directors, and more than 10 percent shareholders (known for this purpose as insiders) to report trades in employer equity securities to the Securities Exchange Commission (SEC) by the tenth day of the month following the month in which the transaction occurred. To enhance the availability of this information to investors, Congress decided to accelerate the reporting deadline for insider trades.

Accordingly, section 16(a) of the Securities Exchange Act, as amended by Section 403(a) of the SOA, requires that a transaction by an insider involving employer equity securities must be filed with the SEC before the end of the second business day following the date on which the transaction has occurred. The act further specifies that, no later than July 30, 2003, these change in ownership reports by an insider must be filed electronically, and the SEC must provide each such statement on a publicly accessible Internet site not later than the end of the business day following that filing. In addition, the issuer of the security (i.e., the corporation) must provide the statement filed with the SEC on its corporate web site (if a corporate web site is maintained) not later than the end of the business day following the filing. Note that the two-day filing requirement took effect August 29, 2002, and the rules relating to electronic filing and posting on company web sites became effective June 30, 2003. The SEC has issued regulations implementing these provisions.

*Regulations and Interpretation:* See SEC Release No. 34-46421, containing final rules, effective August 29, 2002, on ownership reports and trading by officers, directors and principal security holders. See also SEC Release No. 33-8230, providing final rules on mandated electronic filing and web site posting for SEC forms 3, 4, and 5 (the reports implementing the requirements under section 16(a)).

## (b) CEO/CFO Certifications

A new requirement applies to annual and quarterly reports that must be filed with the SEC. Under Section 302(a) of the SOA, the chief executive officer (CEO) and the chief financial officer (CFO) of a corporation filing reports under the Exchange Act must each certify that: (1) the signing officer has reviewed the report; (2) based on the officer's knowledge, the report does not contain any untrue statement of a material fact or omit to state a material fact necessary in order to make the statements made not misleading; and (3) based on such officer's knowledge, the financial statements and other financial information included in the report fairly present in all material respects the financial condition and results of operations of the issuer as of and for the periods presented in the report. In addition, the certifying officers must stipulate that (1) they are responsible for establishing and maintaining internal controls, (2) they have designed the internal controls to properly reflect material information, (3) they have evaluated the controls, and (4) they have disclosed to the issuers, auditors, and the audit committee of the board of directors all significant deficiencies in the design or operation of the internal controls. This certification requirement also became effective August 29, 2002, and the SEC has issued regulations implementing the provision.

*Regulations and Interpretation:* See SEC Release 33-8124, adopting final rules, effective August 29, 2002, on the certification of the disclosure in companies' quarterly and annual reports. SEC Release 33-8212, issued March 21, 2003, proposed changes to the rules, which were adopted on May 27, 2003.

Note: Corporate officers are also subject to criminal penalties for failure to certify periodic financial reports filed with the SEC. See Section 906 of the SOA.

## (c) Loan Prohibition

An important feature of executive compensation has been the ability to provide loans to executive officers and directors. Traditionally, the loans have been used by the recipients to exercise stock options or otherwise purchase employer securities; and loans also have been used to enable the purchase of a house or other personal items. Section 402(a) of the SOA adds new Section 13(k) to the Securities Exchange Act of 1934 to prohibit personal loans to executive officers and directors of companies subject to the reporting requirements of the act (generally publicly traded companies). On or after July 30, 2002, it is unlawful for any issuer, directly or indirectly, including through any subsidiary, to extend or maintain credit, to arrange for the extension of credit, or to renew an extension of credit, in the form of a personal loan, to or for any director or executive officer of the company. Loans in effect as of the effective date of the prohibition are not subject to the prohibition, provided that there is no material modification to any term of such loan or extension of credit, or any renewal of the extension of credit on or after July 30, 2002. The loan prohibition is self-executing, and the SEC has not issued guidance on the provision.

The loan prohibition has raised a number of questions that have been addressed by various law firms in the absence of SEC guidance. Any transaction that may involve the use of loans, directly or indirectly, for the executive officer or director group (including cashless exercise of options, signing bonuses that must be paid back on termination, use of company credit cards, split-dollar life insurance, and other matters) should be reviewed with legal counsel.

*Regulations and Interpretation:* In the absence of SEC guidance, a group of 25 law firms issued a document on October 15, 2002 that discusses a variety of interpretative issues arising in connection with Section 402. The document reaches a consensus on many issues, frequently finding that the statute's prohibition on loans or extensions of credit does not or should not apply.

## (d) Disclosing Existence of Code of Ethics

Section 406(a) of the SOA requires the SEC to issue rules mandating that each company subject to the Securities Exchange Act of 1934 disclose whether or not the company has adopted a code of ethics for senior financial officers. The code must be applicable to the company's principal financial officer and controller and principal accounting officer, or persons performing similar functions. If the company has not adopted a code of ethics, it must disclose the reason for not doing so. Under regulations issued by the SEC, the company also must disclose promptly any change in, or waver of, the code of ethics for senior financial officers. Section 406(b) of the SOA requires this disclosure to be made on Form 8-K, filed with the SEC. Dissemination of the disclosure must be made on the Internet or by other electronic means.

For the purpose of this requirement, the term "code of ethics" means standards that are reasonably necessary to promote:

- Honest and ethical conduct, including the ethical handling of actual or apparent conflicts of interest between personal and professional relationships
- Full, fair, accurate, timely, and understandable disclosure in the periodic reports required to be filed by the company
- Compliance with applicable governmental rules and regulations

This provision took effect on January 26, 2003. The SEC has issued regulations implementing the provision.

*Regulations and Interpretation:* See SEC Release No. 33-8177, effective March 3, 2003, containing final rules with respect to the business code of ethics.

Companies must comply with the code of ethics disclosure requirements in their annual reports for fiscal years ending on or after July 15, 2003.

## (e) Relations with Auditors

The SEC is also required to prescribe rules, under Section 303 of the SOA, to prohibit improper influence on the conduct of audits by company directors or officers. Section 303 makes it unlawful for an officer or director of a company, or any other person acting under the direction of an officer or director, to take any action to fraudulently influence, coerce, manipulate, or mislead an independent public or certified accountant engaged in the performance of an audit of the financial statements of that company for the purpose of rendering the financial statements materially misleading. This provision took effect on January 26, 2003, and the SEC has issued regulations implementing the provision.

*Regulations and Interpretation:* SEC final rules have been adopted. See SEC Release No. 34-47890 containing rules with an effective date of June 27, 2003.

## (f) Use of Non-GAAP Financial Information

Another provision affects reporting of financial information in accordance with generally accepted accounting principles (GAAP). The SOA, in Section 401(b), also requires the SEC to issue regulations providing that pro forma financial information included in any report filed with the Securities and Exchange Commission pursuant to the federal securities laws, or in any public disclosure or press or other release, must be presented in a manner that does not contain an untrue statement of a material fact or omit to state a material fact necessary in order to make the pro forma financial information not misleading. In addition, the presentation must reconcile the pro forma financial information with the financial condition and results of operations of the company under generally accepted accounting principles. This provision was effective January 26, 2003 and the SEC has issued regulations implementing the requirement.

*Regulations and Interpretation:* See SEC Release No. 33-8176, adopting final rules effective March 28, 2003, on conditions for use of non-GAAP financial measures. See also Release No. 33-8216, effective March 28, 2003.

## (g) Other Matters

The preceding requirements directly affect issues relating to the payment of executive compensation. In addition, the SOA contains a number of other requirements affecting corporate governance, including:

- The Public Company Accounting Oversight Board is established to regulate the accounting practices of public accounting firms (effective April 26, 2003).

- Auditors must meet specific independence requirements (effective January 26, 2003); rules effective April 25, 2003.
- Audit committees of the board of directors must meet specific requirements (effective April 26, 2003); rules effective April 25, 2003.
- Chief executive officers and chief financial officers must disgorge inappropriate profits upon the restatement of financials.
- Unfit officers and directors must be barred from participation in officer and director positions.
- Trading in employer securities by executive officers and directors must be prohibited during pension blackouts (effective January 26, 2003).
- Off–balance-sheet arrangements in special-purpose entities must be specially disclosed (effective January 26, 2003); rules effective April 7, 2003.
- A report on internal controls must be filed annually. See Release No. 33-8238, effective August 14, 2003. The release contains extended effective dates.
- The audit committee must contain one or more financial experts, as defined in SEC regulations (effective January 26, 2003); rules effective March 3, 2003.
- Material financial changes in the financial or operating condition of a company filing disclosures with the SEC must be disclosed (in real time) in plain English; rules effective March 28, 2003.

## 4.4   STOCK EXCHANGE LISTING REQUIREMENTS

### (a) Introduction

As part of the complex movement involving regulation of the corporate governance area, the major stock exchanges and the Nasdaq proposed to amend their listing requirements to introduce additional obligations relating to corporate governance. In order to be listed on a stock exchange (or to be quoted on the Nasdaq), a company must comply with these listing requirements; as a result, the listing requirements are a convenient method of introducing corporate governance obligations.

Amendments to the New York Stock Exchange (NYSE) and the Nasdaq Exchange rules were approved by the SEC on November 4, 2003, and the rules are now in final form. The effective date of the NYSE rules is discussed in the following sections (see Release No. 34-48745).[1]

---

[1] Note that the NYSE listing standard requiring shareholder approval of most equity compensation plans became effective June 30, 2003. The new standard also prohibits discretionary broker voting of street name shares in connection with the approval of these plans. These matters are discussed in the following sections. The Nasdaq also had made final that portion of its proposals dealing with shareholder approval of equity compensation plans.

This section discusses the rules of the NYSE. Those rules are detailed and comprehensive, and reflect extensive corporate obligations in the governance area. In addition, the principles underlying the NYSE rules are generally reflective of the rules of the other exchanges as they are being developed.

The proposed changes in the NYSE's listing standards originally arose as a result of the work of a committee set up by the exchange (the New York Stock Exchange Corporate Accountability and Listing Standards Committee), which issued its report in March of 2002. The proposals were submitted to the SEC in August of 2002. The SEC issued for public comment the specific proposal dealing with shareholder approval of equity plans in October 2002. On April 4, 2003, the NYSE submitted a comprehensive amendment and restatement of its proposed listing standards to the SEC, and the SEC published the restated proposals for comment on April 11, 2003 (see SEC Release No. 34-47672). As pointed out previously, final approval of the rules (other than those relating to shareholder approval of equity plans) occurred on November 4, 2003. Except for the rules relating to shareholder approval of equity plans (which became effective June 30, 2003), companies have until the earlier of (1) their first annual meeting after January 15, 2004, or (2) October 31, 2004, to comply with the final rules. Certain transitional rules are provided for classified boards, foreign private issuers, companies listing in connection with an initial public offering, and companies listing upon transfer from another stock market.

## (b) Independent Directors

The NYSE rules require that independent directors must compose the majority of the board of directors (Rule 1).

Note that no director will qualify as "independent" unless the board of directors affirmatively determines that the director has no material relationship with a listed company. (This relationship may be either direct or as a partner, shareholder, or officer of an organization that has a relationship with the company.) A company must disclose its determinations as to whether its directors are independent (Rule 2(a)).

According to the commentary to the rule, the basis for a board determination that a relationship is not material must be disclosed in the company's annual proxy statement or, if the company does not file an annual proxy statement, in the company's annual report on Form 10-K filed with the SEC. In this regard, a board may adopt and disclose categorical standards to assist it in making determinations of independence and may make a general disclosure if a director meets these standards. Any determination of independence for a director who does not meet these standards must be specifically explained. A company must disclose any standard it adopts. It may then make the general statement that the independent directors meet the standards set by the board without detailing particular aspects of the immaterial relationships between individual directors and the company. In the event that a director with a business or other relationship that does not fit within the disclosed standards is determined to be independent, a board must disclose the basis for its determination in the manner described previously.

In addition, the following rules apply in order to exclude from board membership persons who have had recent relationships with the company (Rule 2(b)):

- A director who receives more than $100,000 per year in direct compensation from the listed company, other than director and committee fees and pension or other forms of deferred compensation for prior service (provided such compensation is not contingent in any way on continued service), is not independent until three years after he or she ceases to receive more than $100,000 per year in such compensation. According to the commentary, compensation received by a director for former service as an interim chairman or CEO does not need to be considered as a factor by a board in determining independence under this test.

- A director who is affiliated with or employed by a present or former internal or external auditor of the company is not "independent" until three years after the end of the affiliation or the employment or auditing relationship.

- A director who is employed as an executive officer of another company where any of the listed company's present executives serve on that company's compensation committee is not "independent" until three years after the end of such service of the employment relationship.

- A director who is an executive officer or an employee of a company that makes payments to, or receives payments from, the listed company for property or services in an amount which, in any single fiscal year, exceeds the greater of $1 million, or 2 percent of such other company's consolidated gross revenues, is not "independent" until three years after falling below such threshold.

- Directors with immediate family members in the foregoing categories may also be subject to the cooling off provisions for purposes of determining independence (Rule 2(b)).

- Transition Rule. In order to facilitate a smooth transition to the new independence standards, the NYSE will phase in the "look-back" provisions by applying only a one-year look-back for the first year after adoption of these new standards. The three-year look-backs provided for in Rule 2(b) will begin to apply only on and after November 4, 2004.

Note that a specific feature of the independence requirement is that nonmanagement directors must meet at regularly scheduled executive sessions without management (Rule 3). These directors may designate as a director to chair such meetings. Such a director is often referred to as a "lead director." The name of the person chairing the meeting or the method of designating the director who chairs the meeting must be disclosed in the proxy statement. The company also must disclose a method for interested parties to communicate directly with the presiding director or with the nonmanagement directors as a group.

## (c) Required Committees

In the NYSE rules, the board of directors must establish and maintain at least three committees: (1) a compensation committee, (2) an audit committee, and (3) a nominating/corporate governance committee. The following treatment pays particular attention to the compensation committee, although summaries of the requirements for the audit committee and the nominating/corporate governance committee also appear.

### (i) Compensation Committee   A compensation committee is required, and it must be composed entirely of independent directors (Rule 5(a)).

The compensation committee must have a written charter that addresses:

- The committee's purpose and responsibilities—which, at minimum, must be to have direct responsibility to:
  - Review and approve corporate goals and objectives relevant to CEO compensation, evaluate the CEO's performance in light of those goals and objectives, and, either as a committee or together with the other independent directors (as directed by the board), determine and approve the CEO's compensation level based on this evaluation; and
  - Make recommendations to the board with respect to non-CEO compensation, incentive-compensation plans, and equity-based plans; and
  - Produce a compensation committee report on executive compensation as required by the SEC to be included in the company's annual proxy statement or annual report on Form 10-K filed with the SEC.
- The committee's obligation to evaluate annually the committee's performance

The commentary states that, in determining the long-term incentive component of CEO compensation, the committee should consider the company's performance and relative shareholder return, the value of similar incentive awards to CEOs at comparable companies, and the awards given to the listed company's CEO in past years. The compensation committee is not precluded from approving awards (with or without ratification of the board) as may be required to comply with applicable tax laws (i.e., Section 162(m) of the Internal Revenue Code).

The commentary also points out that compensation committee charters should also address administrative matters, such as member qualifications, the appointment and removal of members, and the committee structure and operations, including the authority of the committee to delegate its responsibilities to subcommittees and the committee reporting to the board.

The commentary also provides that if a compensation consultant is to assist in the evaluation of director or senior executive compensation, the compensation committee charter must give that committee sole authority to hire and terminate the consultant and approve the consultant's fees and other retention items. This provision has created a restructuring in the nature of the relationship among executive compensation consultants, management, and the board, since the compensation committee must retain the person or firm who serves as the consultant regarding the compensation of directors and senior executive officers. It is generally interpreted that this provision does not preclude management retaining its own compensation consultant. Many also hold the opinion that the same compensation consultant may perform services for both the management and the compensation committee, if the consultant is retained by the compensation committee and if matters of director and senior executive compensation are reserved to the purview of the compensation committee.

Boards may allocate the responsibilities of the compensation committee to committees of their own determination, provided that the committees are composed entirely of independent directors. Any such committee must have a published committee charter.

The commentary also adds that nothing in the rule should be construed as precluding discussion of CEO compensation with the board generally, as it is not the intent of this standard to impair communication among members of the board.

***(ii) Audit Committee***    The audit committee is required to satisfy the requirements of the SEC rules for audit committees under the SOA—Rule 10A-3 under the Exchange Act (Rule 6).

The audit committee must have a minimum of three members (Rule 7(a)).

Each member of the audit committee is required to be "financially literate" (as determined by the board in its business judgment) or to become financially literate within a reasonable period of time after appointment to the committee. At least one member of the audit committee is required to have accounting or related financial management expertise (as determined by the board in its business judgment) (Commentary to Rule 7(a)). A person who satisfies the definition of an "audit committee financial expert" under SEC rules will be considered to have accounting or related financial management expertise for purposes of the new standard.

The audit committee also must have a written charter (Rule 7(c)). The committee's charter must address:

- The committee's purpose—which, at minimum, must be to:
  — Assist board oversight of (1) the integrity of the company's financial statements, (2) the company's compliance with legal and regulatory requirements, (3) the independent auditor's qualifications and independence, and (4) the performance of the company's internal audit function and independent auditors; and

— Prepare an audit committee report as required by the SEC to be included in the company's annual proxy statement.
- An annual performance evaluation of the audit committee; and
- The duties and responsibilities of the committee—which, at a minimum, must include those described in Rule 10A-3 of the Exchange Act such as having sole authority to hire and terminate any registered public accounting firm for the company; establish procedures for the receipt and treatment of complaints on accounting, internal accounting controls, or auditing matters; obtain assistance from outside legal, accounting, or other advisors; and receive appropriate funding. The duties and responsibilities of the committee also include:
  — Reviewing the independent auditor's report on internal quality control procedures.
  — Discussing the company's financial statements, and the section in financial reports on management discussion and analysis with management and the independent auditor.
  — Discussing press releases on earnings, as well as financial information and earnings guidance provided to analysts and rating agencies.
  — Discussing policies with respect to risk assessment and risk management.
  — Meeting separately, periodically, with management, the internal auditors, and the independent auditors.
  — Reviewing with the independent auditors any audit problems or difficulties and management's response.
  — Setting clear hiring policies for employees or former employees of the independent auditors.
  — Reporting regularly to the board of directors.
- The internal audit function that a company is required to maintain must provide management and the audit committee with ongoing assessments of the company's risk management processes and system of internal control (Rule 7(d)).

***(iii) Nominating/Corporate Governance Committee***   A nominating/ corporate committee is required and must consist entirely of independent directors (Rule 4(a)).

Again, a written charter is required. In the case of the nominating/corporate governance committee, the written charter must address:

- The committee's purpose and responsibilities, which, at minimum, must be to:
  — Identify individuals qualified to become board members, consistent with criteria approved by the board
  — Select, or recommend that the board select, the director nominees for the next annual meeting of shareholders
  — Develop and recommend to the board a set of corporate governance principles applicable to the corporation

- Oversight of the evaluation of the board and management
- An annual performance evaluation of the committee (Rule 4(b))

The commentary to the rule states that the nominating/corporate governance committee charter should also address these items:

- Committee member qualifications
- Committee member appointment and removal
- Committee structure and operations (including authority to delegate to subcommittees)
- Committee reporting to the board

In addition, the commentary states that charter should give the nominating/corporate governance committee sole authority to retain and terminate any search firm to be used to identify director candidates, including the sole authority to approve the search firm's fees and other retention terms.

## (d) Shareholder Approval of Equity Plans

In a major effort to increase shareholder control over equity compensation plans, the NYSE had proposed that all equity compensation plans, and any material revisions to the terms of such plans (including for this purpose the repricing of existing options), must be subject to shareholder approval. This provision has become final and is effective June 30, 2003 (Rule 8). The discussion in this section is based on the SEC description of the new rule.

An "equity compensation plan" is a plan or other arrangement that provides for the delivery of equity securities (either newly issued or treasury shares) of the listed company to any employee, director, or other service provider as compensation for services. Even a compensatory grant of options or other equity securities that is not made under a plan is, nonetheless, an "equity compensation plan" for these purposes.

However, the following plans are not "equity compensation plans," even if the brokerage and other costs of the plan are paid for by the listed company:

- Plans that are made available to shareholders generally, such as a typical dividend reinvestment plan
- Plans that merely allow employees, directors, or other service providers to elect to buy shares on the open market or from the listed company for their current fair market value, regardless of whether:
  - the shares are delivered immediately or on a deferred basis or
  - the payments for the shares are made directly or by giving up compensation that is otherwise due (e.g., through payroll deductions)

Other exemptions are discussed in the following sections.

***(i) Definitions of Material Revision*** A material revision of a plan includes, but is not limited to, a revision that does any of the following:

- Materially increases the number of shares available under the plan (other than an increase solely to reflect a corporate transaction such as a reorganization).

  — If a plan contains a formula for automatic increases in the shares available (sometimes called an evergreen formula) or for automatic grants pursuant to a formula, each such increase or grant will be considered a revision requiring shareholder approval *unless* the plan has a term of not more than 10 years. This type of plan (regardless of its term) is referred to below as a formula plan. Examples of automatic grants pursuant to a formula are annual grants to directors of restricted stock having a certain dollar value and "matching contributions," whereby stock is credited to a participant's account based on the amount of compensation the participant elects to defer.

  — If a plan contains no limit on the number of shares available and is not a formula plan, then each grant under the plan will require separate shareholder approval regardless of whether the plan has a term of not more than 10 years. This type of plan is referred to as a discretionary plan. A requirement that grants be made out of treasury shares or repurchased shares will not, in itself, be considered a limit or preestablished formula so as to prevent a plan from being considered a discretionary plan.

- Expands the types of awards available under the plan.
- Materially expands the class of persons eligible to participate in the plan.
- Materially extends the term of the plan.
- Materially changes the method of determining the exercise price of options under the plan.

An amendment is not considered a "material revision" if it curtails, rather than expands, the scope of the plan.

In addition, if a plan contains a provision that prohibits a repricing of options, any revision that deletes or limits the scope of such provision is considered a material revision. If a plan does not contain a provision that specifically permits repricing of options, the plan will be considered as prohibiting repricing, and any actual repricing of the options will be considered a material revision, even if the plan itself is not revised. This consideration will not apply to a repricing through an exchange offer that commenced before June 30, 2003.

"Repricing" means any of the following or any other action that has the same effect:

- Lowering the strike price of an option after it is granted.
- Any other action that is treated as a repricing under GAAP.
- Canceling an option at a time when its strike price exceeds the fair market value of the underlying stock, in exchange for another option, restricted stock, or other equity, unless the cancellation and exchange occur in connection with a merger, acquisition, spin-off, or other similar corporate transaction.

*(ii) Exemptions*    The new listing standard does not require shareholder approval of employment inducement awards; certain grants, plans, and amendments in the context of mergers and acquisitions; and certain specific types of plans, all to be described. However, these exempt grants, plans, and amendments may be made only with the approval of the company's independent compensation committee or the approval of a majority of the company's independent directors. Companies also must notify the NYSE in writing when they use one of these exemptions. A discussion of these exemptions follows.

- **Employment Inducement Award**    This award is a grant of options or other equity-based compensation as a material inducement to a person or persons being hired by the listed company or any of its subsidiaries, or being rehired following a bona fide period of interruption of employment. Inducement awards include grants to new employees in connection with a merger or ac-quisition. Promptly following a grant of any inducement award in reliance on this exemption, the company must disclose in a press release the material terms of the award, including the recipient(s) of the award and the number of shares involved.[*]
- **Corporate Acquisitions and Mergers**
  1.  Shareholder approval generally will not be required to convert, replace, or adjust outstanding options or other equity compensation awards to reflect an acquisition or merger transaction.
  2.  In addition, shares available under certain plans acquired in corporate ac-quisitions and mergers may be used for certain posttransaction grants without further shareholder approval.

  This latter exemption applies to situations where a party that is not a NYSE listed company following the transaction has shares available for grant under preexisting plans that were previously approved by shareholders. (A plan adopted in contemplation of the merger or acquisition transaction would not be considered "preexisting" for purposes of this exemption.) Shares available

---

[*] Q&A-25 of the questions and answers released by the NYSE on Dec. 16, 2003 states that the press release and notice requirements do not apply to a grant from a *shareholder-approved* plan to a newly hired employee as an inducement to employment.

under such a preexisting plan may be used for posttransaction grants of options and other awards with respect to equity of the entity that is the listed company after the transaction, either under the preexisting plan or another plan, without further shareholder approval, so long as three additional conditions are met:

1. The number of shares available for grants is appropriately adjusted to reflect the transaction.

2. The time during which those shares are available is not extended beyond the period when they would have been available under the preexisting plan, absent the transaction.

3. The options and other awards are not granted to individuals who were employed, immediately before the transaction, by the posttransaction listed company or entities that were subsidiaries immediately before the transaction.

• **Plans Exempt from the Shareholder Approval Requirement**   These types of plans (and material revisions thereto) are exempt from the shareholder approval requirement:

1. *Qualified plans* intended to meet the requirements of Section 401(a) of the Internal Revenue Code (IRC) (e.g., employee stock ownership plans).

2. *Statutory employee stock purchase plans* intended to meet the requirements of Section 423 of the IRC.

3. "Parallel excess plans," as defined below

   Note, however, that Section 423 of the IRC requires shareholder approval for the implementation of a plan seeking the status of a Section 423 plan, and it is often considered good practice to put the establishment of a plan described in Section 401(a) of the IRC before the shareholders for approval.

   The term "parallel excess plan" means a plan that is a "pension plan" within the meaning of ERISA that is designed to work in parallel with a plan intended to be qualified under IRC Section 401(a) to provide benefits that exceed the limits set forth in IRC Sections 402(g) (which limits an employee's annual pretax contributions to a 401(k) plan), 401(a)(17) (which limits the amount of an employee's compensation that can be taken into account for plan purposes), and/or IRC 415 (which limits the contributions and benefits under qualified plans).

   A plan will not be considered a parallel excess plan unless (1) it covers all or substantially all employees of an employer who are participants in the related qualified plan whose annual compensation is in excess of the limit of IRC Section 401(a)(17); (2) its terms are substantially the same as the qualified plan that it parallels except for the elimination of the limits described in the preceding sentence and the limitation described in clause (3); and (3) no participant receives employer equity contributions under the plan in excess of 25 percent of the participant's cash compensation.

***(iii) Transition Rules***   The standard also provides for transition rules. Except as provided below, a plan that was adopted before June 30, 2003, will not be subject to shareholder approval unless and until it is materially revised. In the case of a discretionary plan, whether previously approved by shareholders or not, additional grants may be made after June 30, 2003 without further shareholder approval only for a limited transition period, defined below, and then only in a manner consistent with past practice. In applying this rule, if a plan can be separated into a discretionary plan portion and a portion that is not discretionary, the nondiscretionary portion of the plan can continue to be used separately, under the appropriate transition rule. Similarly, in the case of a formula plan that either has not previously been approved by shareholders or does not have a term of 10 years or less, additional grants may be made after the June 30, 2003 date without further shareholder approval only for a limited transition period.

The limited transition period just described will end upon the first to occur of:

- The listed company's next annual meeting at which directors are elected that occurs more than 180 days after June 30, 2003
- June 30, 2004
- The expiration of the plan

A shareholder-approved formula plan may continue to be used after the end of the transition period if it is amended to provide for a term of 10 years or less from the date of its original adoption or, if later, the date of its most recent shareholder approval. Such an amendment may be made before or after June 30, 2003, and would not itself be considered a "material revision" requiring shareholder approval. In addition, a formula plan may continue to be used, without shareholder approval, if the grants after the effective date of this listing standard are made only from the shares available immediately before June 30, 2003—in other words, based on formulaic increases that occurred prior to the effective date.

The transition rules are complex but most will ultimately phase out. It is expected that companies will reach a level of best practice wherein shareholder approval is sought even though covered by a technical transition rule.

Note that on December 16, 2003, the NYSE issued a list of frequently-asked questions on the rules requiring shareholder approval of equity compensation plans. The questions cover the definition of an equity compensation plan, transition issues, material revisions, formula plans, and exemptions.

***(iv) Broker Voting***   The new listing standard also provides that the NYSE will preclude its member organizations from giving a proxy to vote on equity-compensation plans unless the beneficial owner of the shares has given voting instructions. This is codified in NYSE Rule 452. Amended Rule 452 will be effective for any meeting of shareholders that occurs on or after the 90th day following the date of the SEC order approving the rule change. The NYSE will establish a working group to advise with respect to the need for, and design of, mechanisms to facilitate implementation of the proposal that brokers may not vote on equity compensation plans presented to shareholders without instructions from the beneficial owners. This will not delay the effectiveness of the broker-may-not-vote proposal.

## (e) Corporate Governance Guidelines

The NYSE rules also require listed companies to adopt and disclose their corporate governance guidelines (Rule 9). Each listed company's web site must include its corporate governance guidelines, the charters of its most important committees (including at least the audit, compensation, and nominating committees) and the company's code of business conduct and ethics (see Section 4.4(f)). Each company's annual report must state that the foregoing information is available on its web site and that the information is available in print to any shareholder who requests it.

These subjects must be addressed in the corporate governance guidelines:

- *Director qualifications standard:* At a minimum, the independence requirements should be addressed. In addition, companies may also address other substantive qualification requirements, including policies limiting the number of boards on which a director may sit, and director tenure, retirement, and succession.
- *Director responsibilities:* The guidelines should clearly articulate what is expected from a director, including basic duties and responsibilities with respect to attendance at board meetings and advance review of meeting materials.
- *Director access to management, and, as necessary and appropriate, independent advisors.*
- *Director compensation:* These guidelines should include general principles for determining the form and amount of director compensation and for reviewing those principles, as appropriate.
- *Director orientation and continuing education.*
- *Management succession:* These guidelines should include policies and principles for CEO selection and performance review, as well as policies regarding succession in the event of an emergency or the retirement of the CEO.
- *Annual performance evaluation of the board:* The board should conduct a self-evaluation at least annually to determine whether it and its committees are functioning effectively. (See Chapter 12 for a discussion of the board assessment process.)

## (f) Code of Business Conduct and Ethics

Under the NYSE listing requirements, companies are required to adopt and disclose a code of business conduct and ethics for directors, officers, and employees. Companies also are required to disclose promptly any waver of the code for directors or executive officers (Rule 10).

Although the rule points out that each company may determine its own policies, all listed companies are expected to address the most important topics, including:

- *Conflicts of interest.*
- *Corporate opportunities:* This issue involves prohibition of employees, officers, and directors from benefiting personally through the use of a corporate position, using corporate property, information, or position for personal gain, and competing with the company.
- *Confidentiality.*
- *Fair dealing:* This area includes a prohibition that no employee should take unfair advantage through manipulation, concealment, abuse of privileged information, misrepresentation of material facts, or any other unfair dealing practice.
- *Protection and property and proper use of company assets.*
- *Compliance with laws, rules, and regulations (including insider trading laws).*
- *Encouraging the reporting of any illegal or unethical behavior.*

The commentary points out that the code of business conduct and ethics must require that any waiver of the code for executive officers and directors may be made only by the board or a board committee and must be disclosed promptly to shareholders. In addition, each code of business conduct and ethics must contain compliance standards and procedures that will facilitate the effective operation of the code.

## (g) Other Matters

In addition to the preceding requirements, the rules require each listed company's CEO to certify to the NYSE each year that he or she is not aware of any violation by the company of NYSE corporate governance listing standards. The certification must be disclosed in the annual report to shareholders. In addition, each listed company CEO must promptly notify the NYSE after any executive officer of the listed company becomes aware of any material noncompliance with any applicable provisions of the corporate governance listing requirements (Rule 12).

A further requirement is that listed foreign private issuers must disclose any significant ways in which their corporate governance practices differ from those followed by domestic companies under the NYSE listing standards (Rule 11).

Finally, the NYSE is permitted to issue a public reprimand letter to any listed company that violates a NYSE listing standard (Rule 13).

## 4.5  EFFECT ON COMPENSATION COMMITTEE PROCEDURES

### (a) Relations with Management

Obviously, the combination of the Sarbanes-Oxley Act and the new stock exchange listing requirements have effected a revolution in the requirements of corporate governance that reaches beyond the traditional corporate fiduciary requirements. An important consideration for each board committee is to consider its relationship with management and to be specific in its practice as to when it will receive or accept recommendations from the CEO and senior management as to specific matters within the committee's jurisdiction. We expect this area of clarification to continue to evolve over the next 6 to 18 months.

### (b) CEO Evaluation

Specific procedures should be developed for CEO evaluation. These issues are discussed in Chapter 5.

### (c) Committee Self-Assessment

In addition, specific procedures should exist for committee self-assessment, at least annually. These issues are discussed in Chapter 12.

### (d) Relationship to Board

A further important and evolving matter is the relationship of each board committee of the compensation to the full board. For example, are all committee acts subject to approval by the board of directors, or will the committee be the exclusive authority in certain matters? These issues can affect the traditional fiduciary standards relating to the responsibility of the board. Again, these issues will become clearer over the next few years.

### (e) Director Compensation

Obviously, care must be taken to be aware of the scope of committee authority and board practices with respect to determining the amount paid for directors' compensation. (See Chapter 11.) It remains to be seen whether the compensation committee, or the nominating/governance committee, or both, will have such authority. It is expected that intense scrutiny of this area will be forthcoming over the next few years.

## 4.6   CONCLUSION: THE MOVING TARGET

Boards and board committees always have been generally aware of their fiduciary obligations. In the revolutionary area in which we find ourselves, however, it becomes apparent that there are considerable additional obligations and duties of care for boards and committees. Apart from the voluminous statutory and regulatory changes suggested in this chapter, boards and committees have become aware of shareholder optics requiring an honest and efficient presentation of all transactions. In particular, the compensation committee report and the audit committee report in the proxy statement will be held to a high level of scrutiny. Care should be taken to review the increasing number of "corporate governance reform" proposals. Organizations, such as The National Association of Corporate Directors, The Conference Board Commission on Public Trust and Private Enterprise, The Business Roundtable, and The Financial Economists Roundtable have proposed views that seek to become the new best practices.

This is a very exciting time to be involved with executive pay. The incorporation of the new corporate governance standards into the consciousness of boards, committees shareholders, and the public makes possible an increasingly satisfactory relationship among these constituencies as the nature of executive pay continues to develop.

# Chapter 5

# CEO Evaluation: Navigating a New Relationship with the Board

J. Carlos Rivero, Mercer Delta Consulting

## 5.1 INTRODUCTION AND OBJECTIVES

Never in recent memory has chief executive officer (CEO) performance been the subject of such intense scrutiny or broad concern. In the wake of some appalling corporate scandals and a general decline in company performance, shareholders, employees, analysts, journalists, and politicians are all looking for someone to blame—and the CEO is the easiest and most obvious target. In addition, increasingly independent and empowered boards are moving faster than ever to remove CEOs who do not seem to be getting the job done. In this harsh and often unforgiving environment, a serious process for assessing CEO performance is no longer a "nice to do"; it has clearly become a "must have."

Every segment of society is demanding greater CEO accountability. We are seeing a fundamental change that is more than just a passing, post-Enron fad; this trend has been building steadily for the past decade. Even before Enron, Tyco, WorldCom, and other scandals made headlines, statistics were giving CEOs good reason to worry. The career of an average CEO has shortened in the past six years from 9.5 to 7.3 years, and one-third of current exits from the post are the result of dismissal. CEOs are now three times more likely to be fired for the same level of stock performance than they were in 1980.[1]

A CEO who misses the opportunity to engage the board on this topic runs a very real risk of being blindsided by serious problems. When Gilbert Amelio was forced out as CEO of Apple Computer in 1997, he told interviewers that his dismissal had come as a total surprise. He added, "Not a single Board member felt comfortable telling me I was in trouble. CEOs really want feedback about how

---

[1]J.A. Sonnenfeld and Rakesh Khurana, "Manager's Journal: Fishing for CEOs in Your Own Backyard," *Wall Street Journal*, July 30, 2002.

we're doing and what we can do to improve."[2] This plaintive cry of an unseated CEO captures the purpose of an effective CEO evaluation process perfectly.

The process of formally evaluating a CEO needs to be done carefully and deliberately. Each company makes different tactical choices based on its history and culture, market, board/CEO relationship, and strategy. There are almost as many varieties of CEO evaluations as there are companies that use them. Nevertheless, whether building a new process or revising an existing one, the CEO and board need to raise and address a range of key questions:

- *Why are we engaging in this evaluation?* Will the process be used solely to determine appropriate compensation given the CEO's past performance? To what extent will it also be used for developmental purposes—to provide feedback that helps the CEO align his or her future actions with the board's expectations and company's strategic objectives?
- *What will be measured in the evaluation?* Are the company's bottom-line financial metrics sufficient to capture the depth and breadth of the CEO's impact? To what degree will the process include other aspects of performance, such as personal impact, quality of strategic thought, operational leadership, and so on?
- *Who will be involved in the evaluation process?* Should the process be limited to just the CEO and compensation committee, or does it make sense to seek input from a wider range of stakeholders (e.g., executive team, lead outside director, full board, critical customers)?
- *How and when will the evaluation be implemented?* What are the specific steps in the process? When will performance feedback be given and how frequently?

The choices made in each of these areas are important for ensuring that the evaluation process meets the needs of the company and its CEO at a specific point in time. At the same time, the CEO needs to bear in mind how fragile the process can be—without ongoing cooperation between the board and the CEO, supportive decisions, and openness to feedback on the part of the CEO, the best-designed evaluation process will be undermined.

The goal of this chapter is to facilitate the development of an effective evaluation process by:

- Providing an overview of the major issues in CEO evaluations
- Discussing some of the options available to CEOs and their boards of directors and introducing concepts and ideas that provide a way of looking at the options
- Providing examples of what companies currently are doing to evaluate their CEOs

[2]"Behind the Scenes at One CEO's Performance Review." *Wall Street Journal,* April 27, 1998.

* Providing both practices and principles that help a CEO determine how his or her current process stacks up


## 5.2   MANDATE FOR MORE THOROUGH AND DISCIPLINED CEO EVALUATION

CEO evaluations are a fact of life in most American corporations. Recent surveys by Korn Ferry and the American Society of Corporate Secretaries revealed that out of all large companies, three in every four formally evaluate their CEOs each year—and that number is on the rise.[3] The widespread use of CEO evaluations stems in part from the increasing scrutiny of corporate governance practices by shareholders, regulators, the financial community, and the business press. Primarily, though, the use of these evaluations arises from a genuine interest in ensuring that a CEO's actions and decisions drive company performance and increase shareholder value.

For these reasons and others, overseeing the CEO's performance is no longer optional for the board. As stated in the TIAA-CREF Policy Statement on Corporate Governance:

> Ensuring continuity of strong leadership is a primary and exclusive responsibility of the Board of Directors. Accordingly, evaluation of a corporation's chief executive officer is critical. A clear understanding between the Board and the CEO regarding the corporation's expected performance and how that performance will be measured is very important.[4]

This mandate is echoed by many other corporate governance watchdogs and policy groups, including the California Public Employees' Retirement System (CalPERS), the National Association of Corporate Directors, and the Council of Institutional Investors. It also is being reinforced through litigation. In a review of recent court cases published in *Liability of Corporate Officers,* one of the six primary roles for which directors can be held legally accountable is "overseeing the performance of management by setting objectives and measuring actual results against those objectives."[5]

Since the evaluation of the CEO is, more or less, a foregone conclusion, why does it continue to garner such attention? The short answer is, as the saying goes, "The devil is in the details." The board and CEO have wide discretion in deciding not only how the evaluation will be done and who will participate in it but indeed

---

[3]Korn/Ferry International, 28th *Annual Board of Directors Survey,* New York, New York, 2001. American Society of Corporate Secretaries, *Current Best Practices, Third Study,* 2001.
[4]Teachers Insurance and Annuity Association—College Retirement Equities Fund (TIAA-CREF), *TIAA-CREF Policy Statement on Corporate Governance,* 1997.
[5]D. Bailey, and W. Knepper (eds.) *Liability of Corporate Officers* (Lexis Law Publishing, 2000).

even in how CEO performance will be defined and measured. As we outline in the coming pages, there is a vast array of options at the board's and CEO's disposal. The challenge is designing the right evaluation process for the CEO's roles and responsibilities in the context of the company's business strategy.

## 5.3   CLARIFYING THE PURPOSE OF THE PROCESS

A first step in designing an effective CEO evaluation process, not surprisingly, is establishing clear objectives for the process. Consistent with performance appraisal processes at other levels of the organization, a CEO evaluation process can serve two related but distinct objectives:

1.   To help the board collect and interpret the data required to judge the CEO's past performance. This is the basis for critical decisions such as compensation or continuation in a particular role.
2.   To help the CEO and board establish a clearer focus on the company's future direction by specifying a set of strategic objectives at the start of the evaluation process. This goal-setting aspect of CEO evaluation also can serve the ongoing leadership development of the chief executive, with the board providing feedback on the areas where personal development is needed.

Thus, CEO evaluations can be backward-facing, focusing on accountability and rewards for past performance, and/or forward-facing, focusing on future objectives and whether the CEO has the vision, strategy, and personal capabilities to achieve those objectives (see Exhibit 5.1). Adding the future view turns the process into something much more robust than a mere accounting exercise. That perspective requires the board to assess the degree of fit between the CEO's leadership qualities and the demands imposed by the organization's strategic objectives.

Although these evaluation objectives are clearly distinct, in practice often they are bundled into the same process. Time constraints may force the board to evaluate the CEO's performance over the previous year while simultaneously making compensation decisions, setting next year's targets, and discussing specific areas for improvement—often in a single board meeting. In addition, the board and CEO may recognize the conceptual distinction between these objectives without seeing it as important in practical terms.

However, when the two objectives are not clearly separated, neither gets served very well. Without clearly delineated processes, one objective may receive a disproportionate amount of attention relative to the other. When this happens, usually the review of past performance for the purposes of compensation dominates the conversation. Because it is far more tangible and focused on objective (or at least predetermined) metrics, the compensation review tends to be more straightforward

**Exhibit 5.1**   Objectives of the CEO Evaluation Process

| PAST YEAR: BACKWARD-FACING | COMING YEAR: FORWARD-FACING |
|---|---|
| **OBJECTIVES** • Organization Performance  • CEO Compensation | **CEO Evaluation** • CEO Capability  • CEO Development/ Replacement |
| **MEASURES** • Goal Accomplishment  • Quantitative Measures | • Vision/Strategy  • Qualitative Indicators |

© Mercer Delta Consulting LLC, 2003.

and to produce less emotional or defensive reactions than discussions of the CEO's behavior and developmental needs.

When time is short, CEOs and boards may dispense with developmental discussions altogether, using the compensation review to set the CEO's future objectives. This approach is likely to overemphasize "what" the CEO is expected to achieve (e.g., increased revenue from cross-business collaboration) relative to "how" the CEO is expected to behave (e.g., giving more attention to developing future leaders). Such is the status and power of the CEO role that without a board committed to providing formal developmental feedback, the chief executive may rarely be exposed to candid, detailed perspectives about his or her behavior and personal impact.

At Honeywell, separate meetings focusing on past and future performance ensure adequate attention to each evaluation objective. In mid-January, the CEO sends the board an assessment of his or her past performance as well as a plan for the coming year, including personal leadership objectives. As follow-up, the January board meeting is largely devoted to discussion of the coming year's objectives, while the February meeting focuses on the CEO's performance over the past year. Whether these two objectives are served through separate meetings is less of an issue than the fact that ultimately both are served. For instance, at the Target Corporation, a company with a reputation for excellence in corporate governance, both evaluation objectives are well served in a single meeting because of the board's and CEO's commitment to a detailed review of past performance as well as an open discussion of future performance expectations and developmental needs.[6]

[6]J. A. Conger, E. E. Lawler III, and D. L. Finegold, "CEO Appraisal: Holding Leadership Accountable" *Organizational Dynamics,* Vol. 27, Issue 1 (Summer, 1998).

## 5.4    DEFINING PERFORMANCE DIMENSIONS AND MEASURES

A defining element of any evaluation process, whether for compensation decisions, goal-setting, or developmental feedback, is the set of performance dimensions to be evaluated. These form the basis of the measures, objectives, and targets
used in the process. Among all of the decisions that need to be made throughout
the process, this is probably the most challenging as it raises the complex issue of
the relationship among the CEO's actions, effectiveness as a leader, and corporate
performance.

A useful distinction is to consider how effectively the CEO *behaves* as a leader
and the organizational *impact* of his or her actions. Further, the impact of CEO
actions can be thought of in terms of the *operational* effectiveness of the organization as well as the organization's *bottom-line* performance. Thus, there are three
generic classes of CEO performance: leadership effectiveness, operational impact,
and bottom-line impact.

### (a) Bottom-Line Impact

Although it is difficult to test in the short term, except in extreme cases of brilliant
decisions or egregious errors, an underlying assumption of almost all CEO evaluation and pay-for-performance plans is that the CEO has a direct and significant
impact on corporate performance. Accordingly, the CEO is held accountable for
the company's overall financial health relative to industry peers. Exhibit 5.2 shows
the types of the bottom-line metrics used to evaluate the effectiveness of a CEO
in the telecommunications sector. While it is critical to keep the CEO focused on
corporate financial success, these bottom-line measures have severe deficiencies
as sole indicators of a CEO's performance. As the person at the top "pulling all

---

**Exhibit 5.2**    Bottom-Line Impact Dimensions Used in Evaluation of a
Telecommunications CEO

---

- Net Operating Revenues
- Operating Cash Flow
- Net Income
- Earnings per Share
- Capital Expenditures
- Share Price

The compensation and personnel committee measures the company's
actual performance, then compares this performance against the CEO's
projections in his/her annual plan.

---

*Source: Board Alert* (April 1999).

the levers," CEOs recognize that their ability to affect the organization's bottom line is not exactly direct and not always overwhelming.

Exhibit 5.3 provides an example of why this is the case in the area of customer relationship management (CRM). In this example, the CEO has engaged in direct action to improve customer relations, directly intervening with key customers and sponsoring organizational programs to build CRM capabilities. The impact of these actions on the strength of the customer relationship (in this case measured by customer satisfaction) can be quite strong, diminished or enhanced by only a handful of extraneous factors. However, the impact of the CEO's actions on the bottom line (in this case defined as growth in earnings from existing customers) is mediated by a bewildering array of external factors. As the desired impact moves further away from the CEO's direct action, the more actual results are influenced by things outside his or her control.

## (b) Operational Impact

"Operational impact" refers to the CEO's effect on the company's operational and organizational effectiveness. This addresses the question of: What changes or improvements has the CEO made in the organization's ability to function and perform? Operational impact measures include indicators of organizational functioning (e.g., retention rates, employee satisfaction scores), operational effectiveness (e.g., quality ratings of products, time to market), and strategic implementation (e.g., number of acquisitions, total headcount reduction). When surveyed, *Fortune* 1000 directors point to company morale, organizational flexibility, company image, research and development, and customer satisfaction as the most important dimensions of

**Exhibit 5.3** The Impact of CEO's Actions on Company Operations and the Bottom Line

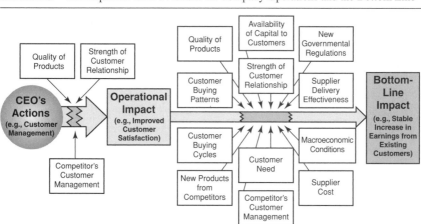

© Mercer Delta Consulting LLC, 2003.

operational impact for evaluating CEO performance.[7] These types of operational measures are important to include in a CEO evaluation process. They are less influenced by market volatility than traditional outcome measure such as stock price and therefore are often more indicative of what the CEO actually does. Additionally, because they reflect organizational capability to perform, they are good predictors of a company's long-term potential to create value.[8]

## (c) Leadership Effectiveness

This class of performance refers to those things totally under the CEO's control—his or her behaviors. As such, this category is quite different from the previous two—the emphasis here is on the CEO's actions and personal impact, not on organizational outcomes. Essentially, this speaks to the question of how the CEO is behaving in terms of whether the CEO is carrying out specific responsibilities (e.g., identifying a successor, meeting with key customers, meeting with the investment community, developing a long-term strategy, etc.) and on the quality of those actions (e.g., improving relationships with external stakeholders, energizing the organization, developing innovative and compelling strategies, etc.). Exhibit 5.4 identifies three key leadership effectiveness dimensions used to evaluate the CEO of a major consumer products company.

## 5.5   SELECTING OBJECTIVES AND SPECIFYING MEASURES

The three categories just identified simply describe the waterfront of CEO performance in generic terms. The specific dimensions and objectives used in a particular evaluation process will vary for each company. Nonetheless, leading companies follow some general principles in selecting CEO performance objectives:[9]

- *Go beyond bottom-line performance:* As discussed, financial measures of corporate performance, while critical, capture only one aspect (and often a tenuous one, at that) of CEO performance. To perform a more holistic evaluation of the CEO and to compensate for some of the limitations of bottom-line measures, it is important to include objectives that relate to leadership behavior as well as the CEO's impact on the organization's operational effectiveness.
- *Focus on a manageable number of objectives:* One risk with attempting to define a mix of objectives that captures multiple aspects of CEO performance is

[7]*Fortune 1000 Director's Survey* (Greenwich, Conn: Directors Publications Inc., 1992), p. 57.
[8]*Corporate Boards: CEO Selection, Evaluation and Succession,* Report Number 1103-95-RR (New York, New York: The Conference Board, 1995).
[9]Korn Ferry International, *Evaluating the Chief Executive Officer* (New York, New York, 1998).

**Exhibit 5.4**   Leadership Dimensions at a Major Consumer Products Company

---

**Strategic Leadership:** Leads the development of appropriate strategies for the enterprise and in achieving support and commitment for the strategies from management and the board.

**Enterprise Guardianship:** Sets the "tone at the top" in such matters as enterprise reputation, ethics, legal compliance, customer relations, and ensuring results.

**Board Relationships:** Works collaboratively with board members and committees; communicates information in a timely manner to ensure full and informed consent about matters of enterprise governance.

---

that the list of performance dimensions may grow so large as to be unworkable. It is important to get the number of dimensions right: too few and the process is likely to be dominated by short-term financial objectives; too many and the CEO and his or her management team risk losing focus. Of course, there is no magic number; this has to be determined for each company individually. Best practice companies typically have between 5 and 10.[10]

- *Include separate objectives for chairman and CEO performance (where appropriate):* In most American companies, the CEO also serves as the chairman of the board. It is important that performance in both roles is evaluated. The chairman may be assessed as part of a formal board evaluation process; if not, dimensions of chairman effectiveness can be added to the CEO's evaluation process.

- *Define measures for each objective:* It is critical that each objective has clearly stated measures that will be used to track performance against that objective. This is simple enough for all bottom-line and most operational impact objectives. These dimensions lend themselves to hard, quantitative measurement. There are robust methods for reliably and validly measuring the "soft stuff" as well. For instance, leadership behaviors can be measured through behavioral rating methods that ask board members to indicate the frequency with which the CEO engages in desired behaviors and to what perceived effect.

- *Specify performance levels for each rating measure:* Having clearly identified measures for each objective greatly facilitates the sharing of performance expectations with the CEO. For any given measure, multiple levels of performance can be "scaled." For instance, 0 to 10 percent earnings growth is poor, 11 to 21 percent is acceptable, and 22 percent and above is outstanding. Although this scaling is rarely done, these levels can help the board and CEO develop a shared understanding of the performance standards.

---

[10]J. A. Conger, E. E. Lawler III, and D. L. Finegold, *Corporate Boards: New Strategies for Adding Value at the Top* (San Francisco: Jossey-Bass, 2001).

## 5.6    LEADING AND PARTICIPATING IN THE PROCESS

CEO evaluation is a complex and, in the case of compensation decisions, highly regulated and scrutinized process. By virtue of company bylaws and other regulations, oversight of the evaluation process is almost always the responsibility of the board committee charged with determining compensation—typically the compensation committee but possibly also the governance or executive committee. In any case, to preserve the integrity of the process, it is critical that the key committee that oversees the evaluation is led and managed by outside directors. In fact, CalPERS offers this as one of their Core Principles and Guidelines:

> The independent directors establish performance criteria and compensation incentives for the CEO and regularly review the CEO's performance against those criteria. The independent directors have access to advisers on these subjects, who are independent of management.[11]

Although leadership of the process is in the hands of the CEO and key outside directors, many others can participate in the process—greatly increasing the amount of information and quality of decision making. One increasingly popular practice in CEO evaluation is multisource feedback. In this process the CEO is evaluated on a range of leadership effectiveness behaviors by multiple stakeholders—the board, the executive team, customers, and others. If done well, a multisource assessment can provide the CEO with a clear picture of which actions and behaviors are facilitating and which are impeding his or her effectiveness. Exhibit 5.5 illustrates how Dow Chemical structured a multisource feedback process for the CEO.[12]

There are two criteria to consider in inviting additional voices to provide feedback on the CEO's performance:

1.    Does the individual or group have a valuable point of view on the CEO's performance? For example, the CEO's management team is likely to have much more exposure to his or her leadership behavior than the outside members of the board.

2.    Are there collateral benefits to involving the person or group in the CEO evaluation process? One potential upside of including customer input in the evaluation, for example, is a stronger relationship with the customer and the increased sense of ownership in the success of the company. Similarly, when

---

[11]Corporate Governance Core Principles and Guidelines, California Public Employees' Retirement System (CalPERS), Sacramento, CA, 1998.
[12]"Corporate Boards: CEO Selection Evaluation and Succession," Report Number 1103-95 (New York: The Conference Board, 1995).

**Exhibit 5.5**   Multisource CEO Feedback

---

**Purpose:** Improve CEO's performance as a "people" manager, not influence compensation
**Led by:** Director of global compensation/benefits
**Who is involved:** 10–12 direct reports or people who have regular contact with the CEO
**Areas covered in assessment:** Leadership, teamwork, communication, integrity, development and coaching, interpersonal skills, and diversity

---

the CEO's direct reports are involved, it can help to foster an environment of constructive feedback and diminish a yes-man mentality.

The decision to include additional people in the CEO evaluation should not be taken lightly. It increases the complexity of the process and introduces a set of political and interpersonal dynamics that have to be managed. In the end, for the feedback to have the appropriate impact, both the board and the CEO have to be comfortable with the source.

## 5.7   IMPLEMENTING A CEO EVALUATION PROCESS

Effective CEO evaluation requires much more than clear expectations and clarity on performance dimensions and objectives. Successful implementation requires a detailed process map that identifies the various steps and ties the process to the company's existing calendar of business planning and compensation review.[13] Three broad steps define the beginning, middle, and end of the process.

### (a) Steps in the Process

#### (i) Defining the CEO's Objectives and Evaluation Criteria    Before the start of the fiscal year, the executive team works with the board to review and refine the strategic plan and establish key long- and short-term business objectives for the coming year. Using the strategy as a starting point, the CEO formulates an initial set of personal performance targets for the coming year, specifying how progress against each target will be measured. If the previous year's evaluation highlighted critical areas for development, the CEO can add these to the full set of objectives for the coming year.

The CEO then shares the targets with external members of the board, normally the compensation or board governance committee. After reviewing the targets

---

[13]Korn Ferry International, *Evaluating the Chief Executive Officer* (New York, New York, 1998).

and amending them, if needed, the final set is presented to the board for discussion and final approval. Once finalized, the targets can be cascaded down through the organization in a goal-setting process that aligns the objectives of each leadership level.

***(ii) Midyear Performance Check-in***     Six months into the year, the board and CEO should take time to review the targets and progress against them. Although many boards skip this midyear review or do it informally, it can provide great value for two reasons.

1.   It helps boards monitor progress against the objectives—to see how the CEO is meeting or exceeding targets and to identify areas that require closer attention.
2.   It provides an opportunity to amend the targets in light of new circumstances, such as rapidly changing business conditions. This capability is crucial in industries with rapidly changing market dynamics.

***(iii) Year-End Assessment and Feedback***     The final step in the evaluation process occurs at the end of the fiscal year when the CEO's performance is measured against the previously established objectives. As with the creation of the targets, this process should begin with the CEO who supplies a self-evaluation and has an opportunity to address areas where targets were not met. The self-assessment is shared with all external directors, along with a guide for how to conduct their own assessment of the CEO's performance.

These evaluations are collected and given to the compensation committee, who uses the results to determine the portion of the CEO's pay that is linked to performance. Before providing feedback to the CEO, the recommendations and the results of the evaluation process should be first discussed in the board, without the CEO or other inside directors present. Once the results are discussed and fully understood, the final step is for the CEO to receive the feedback.

It is important to ensure candid and timely reporting of the feedback to the CEO. The ability to deliver impactful feedback is so critical that it demands careful selection of the feedback provider (or, as is often preferable, two providers). This skill should be a selection criterion for any position that has CEO evaluation and feedback as a job requirement (e.g., chair of governance committee). For example, General Motors specifically charges the (nonexecutive) chairman with that task or a designated lead director when the chair and CEO positions are combined. One scenario for delivering the results of the evaluation has two board members doing the initial private feedback to the CEO. Following that event, the outside directors can convene for a group discussion of the evaluation with the CEO present.

This entire process is repeated yearly. Ideally, the committee responsible for corporate governance also will periodically review the evaluation process itself and seek ways to improve it.

## (b) Ongoing Performance Discussions

In addition to the three major evaluation events, the CEO should also plan for regular discussions about his or her performance with selected board members. The objective of these discussions is for the CEO to get real-time feedback on his or her leadership style and impact, including the effectiveness of interactions with the board. These discussions need not be formally scheduled, but should be viewed as part of the CEO's ongoing dialog with the board.

The choice of which directors to engage in discussions of CEO performance is up to the CEO. Directors who have been CEOs themselves as well as those who bring an outsider's perspective are often best suited to provide unique and valuable guidance. In addition, though, the CEO should plan to meet at least occasionally with the chair of the committee responsible for the CEO evaluation (e.g., the compensation committee), to keep them informed of strategic decisions that may have a bearing on their evaluation.

## (c) Barriers to Effective Implementation

Successfully carrying out an evaluation at this level of the organization is a difficult undertaking. Understanding and working to minimize potential hurdles at the outset increases the likelihood of a successful and sustainable process. Some of the most common pitfalls to avoid are listed next.

- *Uncertainty concerning roles and responsibilities:* As with any detailed, multi-stakeholder process, there is likely to be some confusion over roles and responsibilities at first. Much of this confusion can be alleviated through attention to principles of effective process design—a clear charter, descriptions of roles and accountabilities, time lines, and milestones. The director leading the process also should contract with the various members of the board to clarify expectations for how they should participate in the various aspects of the process (e.g., as "judge" vs. "coach," providing input to decisions vs. making decisions, etc.).

- *Lack of time and energy:* One of the major constraints that all boards face is how to find the time needed to monitor short-term financial performance, shape long-term strategy, and fulfill the many other duties of the board—all within the limited amount of time the board spends together. Given these constraints, an elaborate CEO evaluation process requiring significant input from the board is likely to meet with resistance. Yet a well-designed CEO evaluation can bring structure and efficiency to many of the board's oversight responsibilities, actually saving the board time in the long run. A well-designed process, with clear roles and adequate administrative support to manage the paper trail, also can reduce the amount of effort required of each individual board member in the process.

- *Disagreement over criteria for assessment:* In the early stages of designing a CEO evaluation, a debate over the appropriate criteria for assessing performance actually is quite healthy, indicating that the relevant stakeholders are thinking carefully about the process. Before the process can be enacted, however, the CEO and the board must agree that the dimensions of performance and objectives used are the right ones. The ultimate standard by which disagreements should be resolved is an appeal to the strategy and business needs of the organization—ultimately all criteria for CEO evaluation should have a direct line of sight back to the needs of the business.

- *Lack of direct information about nonquantitative performance:* Financial and key operational metrics are readily available in most organizations. However, measures of "softer" aspects of performance, such as leadership effectiveness, often have to be designed specifically for the purpose of the evaluation. These measures can be quite effective and informative if based on a well-understood model of leadership effectiveness and developed with appropriate concern for psychometric validity by a professional trained in attitude and behavioral assessment.

Ultimately, the CEO's own behavior and attitude toward the evaluation is the greatest single determinant of the effectiveness of the process. Performance reviews are most valuable when they are characterized by a complete and candid discussion of the CEO's strengths and areas for improvement. Of course, the CEO and the board share responsibility for setting the right tone. However, because the CEO is a major figure throughout the process as well as the "beneficiary" of the feedback, the bulk of the responsibility rests with him or her. Defensiveness, detachment, or antagonism can change an otherwise helpful evaluation into a yearly unpleasantry. Board members often report that the difference between a good evaluation process in which everyone wants to participate and an evaluation process that becomes mere window dressing is the CEO's attitude toward the process and reactions to the feedback. At the same time, an ad hoc evaluation process sprung on the CEO can send the wrong signals about the nature of the board/CEO relationship. The board therefore needs to make a similar investment to ensure that the process is well thought out and part of the normal course of business.

## 5.8   SUMMARY

The promise of an effective CEO evaluation process is great: heightened performance accountability, stronger link between performance and rewards, support for CEO development, and better board/CEO relations. Realizing these benefits, however, requires a well-designed process. A set of questions derived from the principles and practices emerging from the research described in this chapter follows. These questions can be used as criteria for judging the effectiveness of a current or planned CEO evaluation process. These criteria are divided into three categories—procedural elements, roles and responsibilities, and content and measures.

## (a) Procedural Elements

- Is there an explicit description of the CEO evaluation process, with articulated goals, roles, and responsibilities?
- Is there an explicit process calendar with detailed deadlines and milestones?
- Is the process calendar aligned with the corporate calendar (i.e., do CEO evaluation events fit with preexisting governance and management schedules)?
- Does the process include a midyear check-in on CEO performance?
- Does the process include a focus on CEO development and opportunities for developmental feedback?
- Is the process consistent with the company's values and culture?
- Does the process have quality assurance mechanisms designed in, allowing the process to be revised as needed?

## (b) Roles and Responsibilities

- Does the process have a clear owner?
- Is the process sufficiently controlled (led and managed) by outside directors to preserve the integrity of the evaluation?
- Is there a clearly identified administrative support role (or external consultant) for the collecting and compiling of performance data and ratings?
- Is the CEO considered a partner at each stage of the process, with ample opportunity for input?
- Are the people with the most valid information about the CEO's actions and leadership impact given the opportunity to provide feedback?
- Has the feedback deliverer been identified? Does this person have the skills required to deliver CEO performance feedback effectively?

## (c) Content and Measurement

- Have performance standards and criteria for evaluating the CEO been identified and made explicit?
- Does the mix of performance criteria sample effectively from all relevant aspects of CEO performance?
- Do performance criteria encompass both CEO and chairman roles?
- Is there a clear link between the performance criteria that comprise the evaluation and the company's strategic objectives and business requirements?

- Can a business rationale be articulated for each performance criteria?
- Is there a valid, feasible measure identified for each relevant performance criteria?
- Are statistically sound methods used to gather and interpret performance data?

This chapter has defined performance dimensions and measures for the CEO, looked at various means of gathering feedback, and mapped out both the steps to implementing the process and the barriers to effective implementations. These steps will facilitate the development of an effective CEO evaluation process that is an important part of the top leader's success—and survival.

# Chapter 6

# Executive Pay and the Shareholder Perspective

**K. Kelly Crean**

Institutional shareholders and other governance organizations always have played an integral role in the implementation of a company's executive compensation programs. However, their interaction with companies often occurred during a short period of time just prior to the annual meeting of shareholders. Most often this interaction was limited to reaction to a proposed executive compensation plan or a request for additional shares under an existing compensation program. Until recently, it was unusual for the human resources (HR) department to play an active role in the communication with shareholders. Typically, interaction with a company was limited to the investor relations area or with the corporate secretary. The role of the HR department was very limited except in the few isolated cases where compensation issues were highlighted in specific shareholder proposals or intensified shareholder activism.

In all but a few isolated cases, most stock plans and compensation programs that were submitted to shareholders were approved routinely and overwhelmingly. Despite the growing spotlight on executive pay, the opposition to executive stock plans averaged less than 15 percent in the mid-1990s. Executive bonus plans received even less opposition due to the potential tax savings resulting from shareholder approval of a bonus plan under Section 162(m) of the Internal Revenue Code. "Discretionary broker voting" procedures also increased the percentage of favorable votes as broker votes virtually always were voted with management. (Under New York Stock Exchange [NYSE] rules, a broker could, if instructions were not received from a beneficial owner, vote the shares on its own for routine proposals, including certain stock and compensation plans.) To avoid negative scrutiny from investors, a number of companies completely bypassed the shareholder approval process for large reserves of shares by adopting plans for individuals below the management levels without shareholder approval. However, the landscape for compensation issues has undergone a significant change beginning in early 2000. And with the growing number of corporate scandals and the intensified spotlight on executive pay issues, this high level of shareholder acceptance quickly evolved into a greater level of shareholder angst.

## 6.1 OVERVIEW OF KEY TRENDS

Shareholder activism has become an increasingly important concern for many companies and their boards of directors. The importance of adopting strong corporate governance practices within a sound compensation philosophy and strategy has never been more important. Volatile market conditions, the significant decline in shareholder value, increasing equity dilution levels, continued public scrutiny over perceived aggressive compensation levels, and several emerging trends have resulted in unprecedented levels of shareholder interest and activity in the executive pay arena.

The most dramatic indicator of shareholder activism has been the increasing percentage of votes cast against compensation programs. No longer can management count on an 80 percent approval level for its compensation proposals. And with the growing spotlight on governance concerns and pay abuses, boards of directors and compensation committees are becoming increasingly more uncomfortable with an opposition level in excess of 25 to 30 percent. According to data from the Investor Responsibility Research Center (the IRRC), the average vote against executive stock plans has risen from about 3.5 in 1988 to above 20 percent by 1999. While the number of plans that actually are voted down by shareholders remains relatively small (less than 12 per year over the past five years according to IRRC data), the number of companies receiving opposition above 30 and 40 percent has grown significantly. Where the dilution level for companies routinely exceeded 20 percent, the level of "no" votes averaged almost 30 percent, even with a more active communication effort by the company. With the new stock exchange listing requirements, including the elimination of discretionary broker voting on equity compensation matters and the requirement that companies obtain shareholder approval of all equity compensation plans, these percentages are likely to continue to increase (see Chapter 4). As a result, maintaining the status quo or emulating the compensation programs of peer companies may no longer be a viable alternative.

In response to this growing opposition, companies are becoming more proactive in incorporating the "shareholder perspective" into their planning process and compensation philosophy. A dialogue with shareholders is being established before the proxy materials are finalized. Human Resources departments are being asked to provide more detailed information in proxy statements and to highlight the pay-for-performance relationship and shareholder protection provisions within all compensation plans. Human resource departments are now working closer with the investor relations function in communicating with shareholders and conducting road shows with investors to discuss compensation philosophy and specific compensation issues. This chapter provides an overview of the key aspects to include in developing a shareholder-friendly compensation program and also identifies the potential pitfalls to avoid.

## 6.2   UNDERSTANDING THE KEY STAKEHOLDERS

Investors in a company are not a homogeneous group, as the views of mutual funds differ from those of public pension funds, which differ from those of financial institutions (i.e., banks) and individual investors. Depending on the specific ownership composition of a company, the impact of the various ownership groups could vary significantly. Therefore, it is important for companies to gain a detailed understanding of their primary stakeholders. This would include identifying the key shareholder groups and developing a profile of each significant investor (i.e., the key "red flags" and expectations of the investor, the factors influencing the investor, and the potential voting tendencies [frequency as well as active vs. passive voting] and ownership patterns [long-term vs. short-term focus] of the investor). When analyzing institutional investors, companies should seek insight into the investing/portfolio manager issues as well as the proxy voting/governance policy issues. An illustrative breakdown is provided in Exhibit 6.1.

**Exhibit 6.1**   Illustrative Ownership Analysis

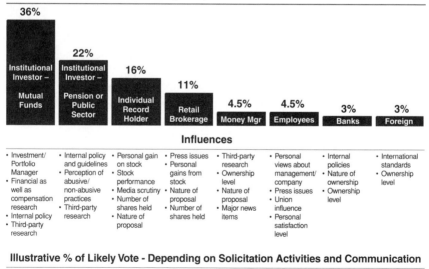

| | | | | | | | |
|---|---|---|---|---|---|---|---|
| **36%** | | | | | | | |
| | **22%** | | | | | | |
| | | **16%** | | | | | |
| | | | **11%** | | | | |
| | | | | **4.5%** | **4.5%** | **3%** | **3%** |
| Institutional Investor – Mutual Funds | Institutional Investor – Pension or Public Sector | Individual Record Holder | Retail Brokerage | Money Mgr | Employees | Banks | Foreign |

**Influences**

| | | | | | | | |
|---|---|---|---|---|---|---|---|
| • Investment/ Portfolio Manager <br> • Financial as well as compensation research <br> • Internal policy <br> • Third-party research | • Internal policy and guidelines <br> • Perception of abusive/ non-abusive practices <br> • Third-party research | • Personal gain on stock <br> • Stock performance <br> • Media scrutiny <br> • Number of shares held <br> • Nature of proposal | • Press issues <br> • Personal gains from stock <br> • Nature of proposal <br> • Number of shares held | • Third-party research <br> • Ownership level <br> • Nature of proposal <br> • Major news items | • Personal views about management/ company <br> • Press issues <br> • Union influence <br> • Personal satisfaction level | • Internal policies <br> • Nature of ownership <br> • Ownership level | • International standards <br> • Ownership level |

**Illustrative % of Likely Vote - Depending on Solicitation Activities and Communication**

| | | | | | | | |
|---|---|---|---|---|---|---|---|
| 90–100% | 80–85% | 35–40% | 30–70% | 60–65% | 40–60% | 80–95% | 35–40% |

Most companies can look to their investor relations and/or corporate finance department for guidance on the company's shareholder composition. Concurrently, many companies utilize their external proxy solicitation firm to provide information on specific shareholder concerns, issues, and voting patterns. With the growing interest in compensation issues and equity programs, many companies are becoming more proactive in obtaining additional information by direct contact with investors.

## 6.3   OVERVIEW OF KEY STAKEHOLDERS

While the actual shareholder composition will vary from company to company, the key stakeholders can generally be divided into common groups, based on their voting patterns and policy issues. Specifically, the most common groupings may include:

- Individual investors
- Employee owners
- Institutional shareholders
- External influencers

### (a) Individual Investors

Whether through brokerage accounts or as a record holder, individual investors may hold a significant number of company shares, but typically they represent the smallest actual voting percentage. Overall, they tend to vote with management but may be significantly influenced by negative issues in the general media and business press. Stock price performance also may have a major impact as their personal financial experience will weigh heavily on their voting decisions. Additionally, their decision on whether to vote will increase if they have a significant ownership position or if they are upset with the company or management. Typically, less than one-third of these shares can be expected to be voted by the actual holder in a normal proxy solicitation (i.e., only contact is made through the annual mailing of the proxy statement). This percentage will increase significantly with a more aggressive solicitation (personal contact, additional mailings, etc.). However, companies that historically exercised discretionary broker voting procedures often benefited from lower voting percentages and the high probability that brokers would support management.

Based on information from various proxy solicitors, up to two-thirds of the votes cast by this group were in support of management on typical issues, with a higher percentage if individuals have been satisfied with the stock price performance. Companies that have historically relied on discretionary broker votes for previous proposals may be required to provide more active communication efforts with individual investors in order to offset the potential negative impact from the loss of discretionary broker voting procedures.

## (b) Employee Owners

Employee owners also may play an important part in the process. Unlike other individual shareholders, employees have a greater personal stake in the company and the overall plan objectives. Their voting patterns will depend heavily on their personal views and satisfaction with management, the company, and their own compensation level. Voting tendencies are influenced if employees are affected directly by the proposed compensation issue. Overall, this group is more likely to vote than other individual investors, but their support of management could vary greatly. Additionally, if the shares were issued in connection with a company-sponsored employee ownership plan (i.e., an ESOP or 401(k) plan), the plan provisions could dictate the voting procedures for shares that were not voted by employees (i.e., unvoted shares will be voted in the same percentage as the actual votes cast by employees). Therefore, the employee's vote could impact other non-voted shares. Employee voting patterns also may be influenced significantly by the presence of labor unions, which have become more actively involved in executive compensation issues.

## (c) Institutional Shareholders

Institutional investor voting patterns will differ, depending on the type of investor and the internal voting policies. While a significant number of institutional investors subscribe to third-party organizations to obtain research and potential voting recommendations, their views and opinions may also reflect the research and the views of the internal policy individual or committee. Most pension funds and public sector funds rely on internal policies, corporate governance practices, and external research. Mutual funds may have voting patterns similar to the public sector, but often they include information and insight from portfolio managers or investment advisors. Money managers and financial institutions historically have spent less time focusing on individual matters such as compensation and more time on the financial prospects and performance of the company. The investment strategy and ownership levels of many institutional investors also may play a role in voting patterns and the overall likelihood of voting, as long-term investors or institutional investors with a significant ownership position tend to take a more active role in executive compensation decisions.

## (d) External Influencers

In addition to the internal policies and individual views, a number of external organizations influence the voting process. Clearly the business press and general media play an important role in shaping public opinion on executive compensation. Many major business publications, including the *Wall Street Journal, Fortune, Forbes*, and *Business Week*, conduct annual surveys on executive compensation. In recent years executive pay issues have moved from the business pages to the front pages. The increased number of business-oriented news shows and television channels also has contributed to the growing spotlight on pay issues. Chief executive officer (CEO) pay levels and gains from stock transactions often are reported by news services within minutes of Securities and Exchange Commission (SEC) filings and even before public announcements are made or communication documents are published.

Labor unions continue to exert influence over employee groups, especially for companies with strained labor relations or a heavily unionized population. Other firms, such as Institutional Shareholder Services (ISS), Glass, Lewis, & Co. (GL&C), the Corporate Library, and the IRRC provide research and data on executive compensation programs. ISS and GL&C also offer voting recommendations on company proposals as well as shareholder proposals within the proxy statement. A number of institutional investors and investor groups, including the California Public Employees' Retirement System (CalPERS), the State of Wisconsin Investment Board (SWIB), and the Council of Institutional Investors, also take a stance on compensation issues by actively publicizing questionable compensation practices, publishing their specific voting practices, and leading a proactive campaign against certain companies. Other firms, such as the Corporate Library and Governance Metrics International, as well as ISS, GL&C, and CalPERS, provide corporate governance or other ratings systems that incorporate aspects of executive pay into the analysis process.

## 6.4  UNDERSTANDING SHAREHOLDER POLICIES

As investor scrutiny over executive compensation plans continues to grow, the need to obtain shareholder insight has become increasingly important. The elimination of discretionary voting procedures and the requirement to have all stock plans approved by shareholders has placed an even greater level of oversight in the hands of shareholders. With the increasing level of attention to design elements as well as pay levels, companies are seeking shareholder input earlier in the design process. Although the federal securities laws limit a company's ability to solicit input directly from, or provide detailed information to, institutional investors, companies can be proactive about their general policies and provisions prior to the filing of solicitation materials.

Companies now have easier access to detailed public information on the governance policies and proxy voting practices of many institutional shareholders. Recent SEC changes now require mutual funds and many institutional investors to disclose their policies via the Internet, company web site, or written inquiry. Others funds and investors voluntarily improved their disclosure information in an effort to increase their control over perceived abusive compensation practices. Many of these policy statements contain broad terms and provisions but may include a summary of key hot buttons and potential red flags.

Additionally, many companies find it important to identify the key decision makers of their institutional investors and build a solid rapport well in advance of the annual meeting. General discussions can be held throughout the year, whereby companies can monitor broad trends and policies on an ongoing basis. With the abundance of annual meetings occurring during a relatively short time frame, and with most companies allowing for only a few weeks between the filing of their proxy materials and the annual shareholders' meeting, many institutional investors may be unable to commit significant one-on-one attention during the proxy season. Therefore, it is beneficial for companies to develop an ongoing relationship with their institutional investors throughout the year.

Finally, a company could obtain additional research and information from various third-party research and/or advisory groups. Some companies, like ISS, offer consulting advice or online modeling tools to gauge potential reaction to a company-sponsored plan proposal. Other firms which do not offer an online modeling tool or consulting services may provide historical analyses or an overview of their policies and concerns. A company's proxy solicitor also can provide insights as to the key concerns of a majority of shareholders and can help weigh the impact of various design features. Additional research should be obtained on competitor practices to address key questions from investors.

Regardless of their stated policies and practices, most institutional investors continue to analyze companies on a case-by-case basis. Although institutional investors are becoming more vocal on executive compensation plans, they have, for the most part, moved from an active "opposition" role at the time of the proxy statement to a more interactive "negotiating" role at various stages of the approval process. Many continue to express the importance of open dialogue with management and interaction beyond the traditional proxy-only disclosure approach. The overall goal of most institutional investors is not to micromanage a company's compensation programs, but to ensure that compensation plans align management interests with those of shareholders and avoid excessive dilution and structural red flag design elements. Many institutions note that it is extremely difficult and challenging to meet these objectives if their only interaction with management occurs only in response to a negative vote, or within days prior to the annual meeting, well after the proxy statement and plan documents have been finalized.

## 6.5   RED FLAGS AND EMERGING COMPENSATION CONCERNS

With the significant changes in the landscape for executive compensation, virtually all institutional shareholders are reviewing and/or refining their voting practices and guidelines. Investor groups are modifying their guidelines (or incorporating new requirements) in response to several recent compensation concerns. The renewed interested in restricted stock programs creates significant challenges for investors trying to analyze different plan designs. Since stock plans are the predominant compensation issue presented to shareholders, the primary concern for most companies is investor reaction to equity compensation plans. Although the importance of key plan attributes and design issues varies among investors, there are a number of common policies and potential red flags (see Exhibit 6.2). These issues are discussed next.

**Exhibit 6.2**   Key Compensation Issues

Historical Plan Usage
- Dilution level
- Annual burn rate
- Historical repricing practices
- Megagrants/participation rates
- Performance-based grants

Proposed Plan Provisions
- Share request
- Repricing provisions
- Evergreen provisions
- Discounted options
- Reload options
- Vesting period
- Unlimited nonperformance stock grants

Company Policies
- Ownership guidelines
- Holding period for stock
- Annual share commitment
- Use of nonapproved plans
- Option expensing

Other Company Issues
- Independent administering committee
- Other compensation plans/practices
- Stock buyback programs
- Dividend policy
- Other governance issues

## (a) Dilution Level

Dilution level remains the primary concern for a number of institutional investors. The dilution formula varies by institution; however, typical dilution guidelines for most established or mature companies range from 10 to 15 percent of common shares outstanding (CSO), with higher levels for high-tech companies or traditional all-employee option plan industries. Many of these guidelines serve as a rule of thumb rather than an absolute maximum. Companies that exceed these limitations may not necessarily receive an automatic "no" vote, as most of the institutional investors will use a case-by-case approach. However, companies that exceed the guidelines of institutions will need to provide a detailed rationale and acceptable justification for the higher dilution level and/or any potential share request.

## (b) Annual Grant Rate or "Burn Rate"

Annual grant rates (or "burn rates") are becoming more important and soon may become equal to, or perhaps more important than, actual historical dilution levels. Many institutional investors are beginning to place a greater emphasis on annual stock usage and develop policies surrounding maximum annual limitations for various awards. In fact, some institutions structure their voting policy on burn rate rather than aggregate dilution level. Additionally, others may overlook historical dilution levels if the company commits to an acceptable annual share usage limitation going forward (e.g., no more than 1.5 percent of CSO on a net basis). In response to burn rate concerns, a number of companies have incorporated a stated share limitation in the proxy statement and plan proposals. A few companies have even incorporated performance-based modifiers in their expected grant rate that would increase or decrease annual share usage, based on company performance.

Typically, grant expectations fall between 1 and 3 percent of CSO, depending on a company's industry group, comparator data, and the level of plan participation. However, to address the growing use of restricted stock, some institutions are expecting to see a bifurcated approach, with one limit for options and a significantly lower limit for the use of restricted stock and other stock awards. For example, one institutional investor allows a maximum annual grant of 2 percent of CSO in the form of service-based options. The maximum annual limit for service-based restricted stock is 0.67 percent of CSO (one-third of the option total, reflecting a three-to-one ratio for options vs. restricted stock). For companies that provide multiple award types, the sum of options plus restricted stock (converted to a three-to-one ratio or multiplied by three) cannot exceed 2 percent of CSO. Although not stated, it appears that a higher level of grants could be supported if awards were performance-based as opposed to service-based.

### (c) Repricing

Option repricing is the one common plan design feature that continues to take precedence over dilution levels and annual grant practices for many institutional investors. Some institutions are opposed to the concept of repricing, but most opposition is for plans that provide for option repricing without shareholder approval. In fact, some institutions actually may favor a repricing program (if structured properly) that would significantly reduce dilution levels. The NYSE listing standards have eliminated a company's ability to reprice stock options unless the plan expressly permits this type of transaction. However, the existence of such an express provision for discretionary option repricing may cause some institutional investors to vote against a proposed equity plan. Additionally, programs which promote cash replacement alternatives in lieu of underwater options (which may not require shareholder approval) may also result in shareholder scrutiny. The revised Nasdaq standards do not currently require companies to include the express ability to reprice, but they do strongly suggest that companies consider seeking shareholder approval prior to repricing. Nasdaq's stance could change based on potential shareholder response.

### (d) Evergreen Provisions

Evergreen provisions (plan features that automatically increase the number of shares available for grant on an annual basis—i.e., 2 percent of CSO is added per year) are also a strong negative plan provision. A number of institutional investors, including Vanguard and CalPERS, actually vote against a plan that includes an evergreen provision. Most evergreen provisions would result in a significant number of shares reserved under the plan (2 percent per year over 10 years is a 20 percent dilution) and would result in unacceptable dilution levels. However, a growing concern is that an evergreen provision eliminates shareholder input in future compensation decisions (i.e., shareholders could not vote on the plan for 10 years). In fact, GL&C notes that shareholder input is a key factor in its vote process, as it prefers to see shareholders having input on a regular basis (e.g., at least every four years). Therefore, companies that disclose an annual share usage level also would need to provide an aggregate share level for expected grants.

### (e) Discounted Stock Options

Many institutional investors also view the potential ability to grant discounted stock options as a significant red flag. For some, the ability to grant a discounted stock option would result in an automatic no vote. Others would require a minimum acceptable price (i.e., 85 percent of the stock price on the date of grant) or be more willing to allow discounted stock options if the plan limits such grants to a small portion of the available shares. If a company intends to consider discounted stock options, institutions would prefer to have these limited to options only under special circumstances (i.e., a merger or new hire). It is interesting that many would find a discounted stock option of more concern than the grant of restricted stock (which is substantively a short-term option with a zero strike price).

## (f) Reload Options

Reload options also have been identified as potential red flags for a number of companies. A reload feature would provide for the automatic grant of additional options following certain option exercises. The most common (and typically more acceptable) reload grant occurs when an option is exercised in a stock-for-stock exchange exercise (the individual surrenders shares of stock to pay the exercise price and tax liability) whereby the optionee receives a new option only for the shares they actually surrendered. In limited cases, another type of reload option (the full-share reload) is structured to provide the individual with a new option grant to cover the full number of options exercised, regardless of the method of exercise. Most of the objections to reload options have derived from the full-share reloads, which many institutional investors consider to be an abusive way for companies to enrich management. However, the swapped share reload also has been criticized as being, in essence, either an interest-free loan for executives or a mechanism to capitalize unfairly on future stock price appreciation.

For a significant number of institutional investors, reload grants are, at worst, only a minor negative issue, and the inclusion of reload provisions would not result in an automatic vote against a proposed equity plan. Additionally, some of the potential concern could be eliminated if reloads were only issued in a stock-swap transaction and/or if companies limit how reloads can be used (no more than two reloads per grant; inability to reload a reload grant, holding or vesting period for reloads, etc.).

## (g) Plain-Vanilla Stock Options

A number of institutional investors have expressed concern over the lack of a true "performance requirement" in stock options. Much of this concern has been raised against the large stock option gains resulting from general market conditions rather than company performance. Additional concern has been expressed on the overuse of plain-vanilla stock options, in that the sheer number of options being granted to individuals would ensure a generous payout, even with a small to modest stock price improvement, and could result in exorbitant payments in a bull market. Along with the perceived erosion to the pay-for-performance aspect of stock options, many observers also express concern that stock options actually encourage management actions that are misaligned with long-term shareholder interests, including the manipulation of financial data, the short-term holding and the dumping of shares, the need to provide overly dilutive annual grant levels, and the pressure to reprice upon a stock price decline. As a result, one of the most common shareholder proposals during the 2003 proxy season was to require companies to implement performance-based option programs or, at a minimum, to require that all options for executives be performance-based. A small number of companies even received shareholder proposals demanding the elimination of stock options entirely. Although most institutional investors prefer to see performance-based grants for senior executives, there were mixed views on the percentage of options that should be performance-based.

### (h) Ownership Guidelines—"Post-Exercise" Holding Period

Executive ownership of stock always has been a prime focus for many institutional investors. Following a number of recent corporate scandals, there has been an emergence of a new type of ownership feature—the mandatory holding period. A number of institutional investors have begun pressing companies to adopt mandatory holding periods for all or a portion of the stock compensation received by an executive. While the duration of the holding period (ranging from one year to until some period after the executive leaves the company) and the share level (all or a portion of the net or gross shares) varies, an increasing number of institutional investors have incorporated these expectations into their voting policies. Overall, institutional investors are focused on two issues: the actual ownership level of executives (to ensure "skin in the game") and/or the focus on long-term shareholder interests (to avoid immediate or short-term flipping of shares).

Virtually all institutional investors would encourage executive ownership of stock but vary on their preferred approach. Many currently expect either a stated minimum ownership level or a minimum holding period for stock provided through company-sponsored stock plans. However, a growing number of institutional investors are placing greater importance on the mandatory holding period, as they note that an adequate holding period would eliminate the need for ownership guidelines. Others note that strong ownership requirements (or actual ownership position) would eliminate the need for holding periods. The inclusion of both components would foster a strong investor perception of the company's ownership culture.

### (i) Megagrants of Options

A number of institutional investors also have expressed concern over the growing use of megagrants to executive officers (particularly at the CEO level). While it is unclear what would constitute a megagrant, institutional concern regarding the size of grants to senior executives continues to grow.

## (j) Percentage of Grants to the Named Executive Officers

Some institutional investors look at the total number of shares issued to the top five executive officers, as a percentage of all option grants during a specific period. Aggregate grant levels to the top five in excess of 10 to 15 percent of the annual grant may raise concerns, unless the company's annual burn rate is well below typical standards. CalPERS recently adopted a requirement for companies with broad-based stock programs, stipulating that no more than 5 percent of the aggregate grants may be issued to the top five executives.

## (k) Discretionary Grants to Directors

An increasing number of institutional investors have expressed concern over discretionary equity grants to directors. This concern includes both the type of grant that could be issued as well as the level of grants to be issued. Institutional investors are becoming more vocal in their concern that discretionary programs could jeopardize the independence of the director if compensation levels become too excessive.

## (l) Independent Administering Committee

The independence of the members of the board compensation committee has garnered increased attention. Key concerns from institutional investors include a stricter definition of independence, a greater time commitment to compensation decisions, and greater interaction with independent consultants. Investors are also looking at the background and qualifications of the committee members and demanding more disclosure on potential conflict-of-interest relationships. Some governance experts are even demanding term limits and rotations of the chairman position in order to foster independence.

## (m) Dividend Policy

There has been some modest inclusion of dividend policy in the analysis of institutional investors as there is some negative sentiment that companies deliberately avoided paying dividends due to significant option grant levels. (Options do not pay dividends and the value of the grant could decline if companies focus too much on dividends rather than stock price appreciation.) This concern may be one minor reason for the growing support for restricted stock, as these grants typically would include provisions for dividends. And with the recent favorable tax provisions for dividend payments, the pressure for companies to increase their dividend payments (which are not reflected in traditional stock option gains) continues to grow.

## (n) Policy on Expensing Stock Options

Although most institutional investors believe that stock options should be expensed, many indicate that this policy would have a moderate impact on their voting decision (e.g., might be the tie-breaking issue). A significant number of institutions would view voluntary expensing of options as a positive factor, noting that the voluntary expensing will help foster more transparent disclosure and restore trust in the management team. But for most institutions, stock option expensing is not a major element that would cause a stock plan to receive a "no" vote. Many stock analysts also believe that option expensing is a decision that would have a greater impact on the investment decision of their organization (i.e., whether to invest in a stock) than with the actual voting or governance policies. Additionally, companies that elect to replace stock options with other long-term incentive measures may receive close scrutiny if they did not elect to adopt Financial Accounting Standards (FAS) 123 accounting.

## (o) Use of Non–Shareholder-Approved Plans

Based on the recent actions of the NYSE and the Nasdaq, concerns about the use of non–shareholder-approved plans have diminished for most institutional investors. Although there may be some limited concern over companies that continue to use the shares under these plans, it will be only a modest point. The elimination of these plans (or the lack of a history of nonapproved plans) could, however, be a modest positive for companies that need institutional support for a share reserve that exceeds normal guidelines. Conversely, companies implementing a plan or additional share reserve just prior to the adoption of the new listing standard will receive considerable scrutiny. In addition, recent examples of companies replacing option programs with cash-based appreciation plans (e.g., cash-based stock appreciation rights) may also garner negative reaction if they result in windfall profits or encourage artificial price appreciation. Overall, this scrutiny may have a greater impact on the election of directors than on an equity plan proposal.

## (p) Governance Ratings Systems and Scoring

Over the past few months, many organizations have developed "governance" ratings systems to assess the governance profiles of various companies. Key examples include the ISS Corporate Governance Quotient (CGQ) score, the Governance Metrics International (GMI) analysis, the Corporate Library Board Effectiveness Rating, and CalPERS' governance and compensation ratings systems. Typically these ratings may have less importance on the voting decision of institutional investors than their internal research; however, these ratings systems could have a significant impact on the investing decisions of certain investors (whether to buy a certain stock or dispose of shares of a company with a low rating). However, many have said a higher governance score could be an important tiebreaker if all other factors do not result in clear voting preference.

## (q) Other Potential Factors

In addition to the factors just discussed, many institutional investors also may use several company-specific factors when reviewing an equity incentive plan. These factors may include the level of cash compensation being provided, severance or change-in-control provisions, company performance, peer group information, disclosure information, and other interaction with shareholders.

## 6.6   REACTION TO OTHER COMPENSATION ELEMENTS

Historically, equity compensation has received the highest level of scrutiny from institutional investors for four primary reasons:

1.  Equity compensation comprised the greatest portion of executive pay and therefore results in the highest compensation amounts.
2.  Unlike many elements of compensation, shareholder approval was required for many executive stock programs. For some companies, the implementation of an executive stock plan without shareholder approval was not a viable alternative. And the recent NYSE and Nasdaq listing requirements discussed above will require shareholder approval.
3.  More detailed information on plan provisions and stock usage is available than on other company programs.
4.  The growing number of shares being issued under stock plans significantly impacts the ownership position of many institutions.

   With the recent number of corporate scandals and the growing spotlight on executive and management pay, other elements of compensation are beginning to face a heightened level of scrutiny. As companies begin to place a greater emphasis on cash compensation, base salaries and annual bonus payments are being included in many investor analyses. Base salaries that exceed those of industry peers are being heavily scrutinized; for some organizations, a salary in excess of $1 million is of significant concern. Bonus programs, both the annual plan and intermediate cash plans, are being closely monitored and tracked against company performance. Many investors have expressed a growing level of concern over the perceived misalignment of management compensation with the increase in shareholder value, as large bonuses continue to be paid despite declining stock prices and low to modest dividend programs. An additional concern centers on the impact that higher salaries and bonus payments have on other benefit programs (i.e., severance arrangements and retirement plan benefits are often calculated using an individual's current annualized cash compensation).

Benefit programs and executive perquisites also have generated a great deal of negative scrutiny recently in light of several well-publicized corporate scandals. Executive retirement programs (e.g., Supplemental Executive Retirement Plans, or SERPs), deferred compensation programs, and severance arrangements have been the subject of significant debate as a result of the large payments offered to ousted executives. Investors continue to express concern over lavish perquisites being offered within the executive ranks at a time when stock prices were declining, massive layoff programs were being conducted, and the portfolio value of many investors (not to mention the retirement plans of many rank-and-file employees) were being significantly eroded. Criticism has been focused on both the cost and the appropriateness of the benefits as well as the lack of public disclosure over the company's use of executive-only perquisites.

Recent legislation and SEC actions have addressed some of these programs (i.e., the Sarbanes-Oxley Act of 2002 prohibited the issuance of company loans to executives and impacted the use of "split-dollar" insurance benefits). Other issues have been addressed in shareholder proposals (see the next discussion) or intensified campaigns by the institutional investor (a targeted campaign by institutions against specific companies).

## 6.7  SHAREHOLDER PROPOSALS

Perhaps the most revealing trend in increased shareholder activism has been the number of proposals deriving from individual investors that specifically address compensation issues. Of the initial 762 shareholder proposals tracked by the IRRC in 2003, almost half addressed executive compensation. The number for 2003 exceeded the entire number of proposals tracked in the previous three years combined. Even more telling is the level of support these proposals received, despite being opposed by management. Although most of these proposals are nonbinding (i.e., management does not have to adopt the proposed action), they appear to be impacting several major companies.

Companies are not required to include all shareholder proposals in their proxy statements. Proposals that are too vague or that attempt to address the company's routine business matters can be excluded from the proxy with the approval of the SEC. Additionally, a number of companies look to avoid inclusion by working with the proponents of these proposals in advance of the proxy filing. Institutions often submit a shareholder proposal either to get the company's attention or to start a dialogue with the company on key issues. In a number of cases, companies do not have to change their internal policies, but simply need to increase the disclosure of their current practices. Or, in some cases, the company has to "commit" to certain practices that have been unwritten historical company practices (i.e., minimum vesting period for stock options or the commitment not to reprice options without shareholder approval). If the company's efforts are successful, it can exclude the proposal from the proxy statement and avoid any potential adverse reaction resulting from the proposal.

The most successful compensation-related shareholder proposals for 2003 are related to severance packages to executives, especially payments provided to ousted executive officers. Specifically, these shareholder proposals require management to seek shareholder approval of severance packages in excess of some multiple (typically 2.99 times) of the executive's annual income (or to limit payments above a target amount). The 2.99 limitation is a direct correlation to Section 280(G) of the Internal Revenue Code, which provides unfavorable tax treatment for payments in excess of 2.99 times an executive's current compensation level. This proposal surfaced as a result of the disclosure of general severance packages provided to several ousted executives in connection with a number of recent company failures. Investors express concern that the excessive value of the severance benefits provided to these "failed" executives underscored the misalignment between management pay and shareholder interests as well as with sustained company performance. Investors also criticize the board of directors (and the compensation committee) and question whether the directors themselves are misaligned with their role as protectors of shareholder interests.

During 2003 these proposals received support from a majority of shareholders at 9 of the first 12 companies that announced the results. Two additional proposals received a majority of support in 2002. In response to this support, more than half of the companies where these proposals received a majority vote adopted specific severance-related programs that potentially would require shareholder approval of certain severance payments. At least three other Standard & Poor's 500 companies avoided the inclusion of a similar proposal in their proxy by adopting a special severance policy requiring shareholder approval.

The expensing of stock options was also a significant issue for shareholders in 2003, as more than one-third of the compensation-related shareholder proposals for the year sought to require companies to begin expensing stock options. Early results indicated that more than a dozen proposals received majority support from shareholders. Although this issue may become a moot point if, as expected, the Financial Accounting Standards Board (FASB) requires companies to expense stock options, in the short term the 2003 proxy season does provide an indication of the current view of many institutional investors.

Other common issues addressed in shareholder proposals include the requirement that option grants be performance-based; the potential elimination of certain equity plans, including options and restricted stock; and the growing pay disparity between the CEO and the average employee. It appeared that many institutional investors and advisory groups agreed with management on many of these other issues, as the proposals received modest to minimal support, at best.

In addition to the items just discussed, other examples of special or unique shareholder proposals would require companies to:

- Exclude pension income from bonus plan calculations
- Link bonus plans to social/worker relation issues
- Conduct more detailed reviews of executive compensation
- Link pay to worker turnover
- Link pay to dividend policy

## 6.8  COMMUNICATING WITH INVESTORS: AVOIDING PITFALLS

Whether a company is submitting a compensation plan for shareholder approval, or reacting to a specific shareholder-initiated proposal and/or heightened investor concerns, the communication process should not be overlooked. An effective strategy of clear and detailed disclosure, coupled with ongoing dialogue with investors, will help companies avoid any potential roadblocks and unnecessary confrontations during the communication process. Exhibit 6.3 presents a checklist of items that will help companies avoid many of these potential pitfalls.

### (a) Know Your Shareholders

An understanding of the company's shareholders and their key hot buttons is critical in the communication process. With the increased focus on corporate governance and executive compensation, it has become increasingly important to identify these hot buttons in the design process instead of during the communication process. Important questions to ask include:

- Who are our shareholders/stakeholders?
- What are their key issues and concerns?

---

**Exhibit 6.3**   Potential Pitfalls to Avoid

---

- Not knowing the key stakeholders/shareholders
- Disorganized communication effort
- Limited or infrequent interaction with shareholders
- Reactive, not proactive, dialogue
- Proxy disclosure
- "Keeping up with the Joneses"
- Overdependence on the status quo
- Confrontational dialogue
- Last-minute planning

---

- When should they be contacted?
- Who is, and how do I contact, the key decision maker?
- Why would shareholders vote in opposition to management?
- How have shareholders voted on our previous proposals?

## (b) Coordinated Effort

With the increased external spotlight on executive pay, compensation issues are no longer limited solely to the human resource department. Investor relations individuals are dealing with increasingly complex compensation questions. Corporate finance is being asked questions regarding the link between pay and performance and key performance goals. Corporate accounting is being asked about the impact of stock option expensing. Corporate treasury is responding to questions about executive ownership levels and stock transactions. Internal and external legal counsel have been faced with significant changes in key legal and stock exchange requirements. As a result, the design process should incorporate input from throughout the organization. In many cases, the integration among internal stakeholders is just as challenging as working with external investors.

## (c) Frequent and Ongoing Interaction with Shareholders

Companies that receive high marks for their corporate governance policies often incorporate frequent and ongoing investor dialogue into their communication strategy. As noted previously, federal securities laws limit a company's ability to communicate specific information or conduct limited solicitation efforts. But communication channels can and should remain open and active throughout the year. Investor discussions can be used to begin tilling the soil on key compensation issues. Feedback on emerging trends or broad policy changes can be received throughout the year. Communication efforts should not be limited to the two months surrounding the annual meeting.

## (d) Be Proactive Rather than Reactive

Companies should strive to be proactive in working with their investors. Although many investors have developed standard policies for addressing compensation issues, these policies are simply guidelines. By being proactive, companies can avoid the uncertainty caused by adverse reaction from shareholders. More important, a company can minimize any potential misperception about key compensation issues. Since many institutional investors often obtain research from outside sources, additional contact may be needed to clarify inaccurate or misinterpreted information or to address compensation concerns. Additionally, many investors react favorably to proactive communications from management, and their final vote is impacted most often by the information obtained through additional dialogue.

## (e) Effective Proxy Disclosure

Perhaps the most common oversight in the communication process is the use of a boilerplate proxy statement. Historically, the proxy statement focused on the typical SEC requirements and incorporated a limited amount of disclosure. Proxy preparation often was left to the legal department, with much of the attention focused on pay numbers rather than philosophy. With the larger spotlight on pay programs and growing investor angst over compensation issues, many companies are including more detailed information in their proxy statements. Companies are also being more forthcoming with information and highlighting the shareholder-friendly provisions of compensation programs. Where possible, companies should accentuate positive features and strong governance provisions. Key financial data and information highlighting the pay-for-performance relationship should be incorporated into stock plan proposals and compensation discussions. Companies that use the proxy as a detailed presentation to shareholders instead of just a necessary legal filing have seen a significant improvement in their communication efforts. As one institutional investor commented, investors have more "trust" in companies that offer detailed and forthright disclosure. And this trust often is demonstrated in the shareholder response to key compensation issues.

## (f) Incorporate Company-Specific Issues into Compensation Discussions

Another common pitfall to avoid is to base decisions about future equity strategy solely on competitive data (i.e., keeping up with the Joneses). With the significant changes to the landscape of compensation programs (highlighted in Chapter 8), it has become even more apparent that compensation is not a one-size-fits-all issue. Since most investors will react on a case-by-case basis, companies should tailor their equity principles and communications to the facts and circumstances unique to their organization.

## (g) Avoid Maintaining the Status Quo Just for the Sake of Simplicity

The significant changes to the compensation landscape, coupled with the uncertainty surrounding stock option expensing, have caused a number of companies to adopt a short-term focus to maintain the status quo. However, historical experience is no longer an effective predictor of the future. The increased level of shareholder activism and the push for tighter corporate governance controls are impacting all companies, even those noted for strong governance principles and excellent performance.

## (h) Foster Dialogue Rather Than Confrontation

Another common misperception among companies is that meeting with institutional investors or shareholder groups will lead to confrontation as opposed to dialogue. Although there are some instances in which confrontation is unavoidable, most institutional investors would welcome additional interaction with management. If institutional investors are willing to invest in a company and maintain an ownership position, it is in their best interests to work with the management team. Often they are looking for a strong rationale to continue to support the management team. The effort to dialogue with the voting side of institutional investors should mirror that used with the investment group. This dialogue always should be viewed as a golden opportunity to strengthen relations with the investment community rather than as a necessary evil of doing business.

## (i) Begin the Planning Process as Early as Possible

Timing is also an important factor in the communication process with investors. The increased need for input from individuals outside the Human Resource department should be factored in the planning process. Communications with the board and the compensation committee also are resulting in the need for additional planning efforts. The increasingly complex financial, legal, and disclosure requirements have increased the need for input from external accounting and legal resources. And all of this effort is being demanded from the HR department that continues to feel the impact of limited resources and staff constraints.

The potential need for more focused communication efforts (and potential one-on-one interaction) with institutional investors also has increased the level of detail and time commitment the HR department must dedicate to the communication process. Consequently, many companies are filing SEC materials (i.e., the proxy statement and annual report) earlier to allow for more time to interact with shareholders prior to the annual shareholders' meeting.

## 6.9 CONCLUSION

As discussed, the need for effective communications with shareholders has never been more important. Knowing and understanding the population of shareholders, their key compensation concerns and requirements, and their voting practices remains the key challenge for many companies. Although many institutional investors continually are developing their voting practices and adapting their public policy statements (as a result of recent SEC requirements), most continue to use a case-by-case approach in analyzing companies. All shareholder groups have a number of common requirements and expectations. And a number of compensation provisions would help maintain shareholder confidence in management and the board of directors.

Disclosure documents (i.e., the proxy statement) should address these issues in a clear and direct manner. Given the volume of analyses that must be completed during proxy season, a company must make sure analysts can gain a quick understanding of the proposal and the shareholder-friendly features. Confusing disclosure language, or the lack of information, may result in misconceptions and/or potential mistrust that could trigger an automatic against vote recommendation.

Ultimately, companies that foster a strong corporate governance environment will incorporate as many shareholder-friendly features into their compensation programs as possible. These provisions play an important role in building trust with the institutional investors and often persuade them to be supportive of management, even if management's proposal falls outside the investors' standard guidelines.

# Chapter 7

# Option Valuation: Accounting and Executive Incentive Design

Susan Eichen

## 7.1 BACKGROUND

### (a) Introduction

Who ever imagined a day when concepts such as fair value option expense, Black-Scholes, and modified grant date would appear regularly in the business press? Over the past two years, these concepts have become familiar, as U.S. and global standard setters examine the accounting treatment of equity-based compensation.

The accounting rules governing equity-based compensation are changing. Few would argue that accounting should drive pay policies—we would be surprised to find a proxy statement with a compensation committee report stating that the primary objective of its company's pay policies is to minimize accounting costs. But few would doubt that stock options' "free" nature, as accounted for under Accounting Principles Board Opinion No. 25 (APB 25), was a key driver of their exponential growth over the past 10 to 15 years. So the accounting rule changes are likely to play a significant role in shaping future compensation policies. As of this writing, the specific provisions of the new accounting rules have not yet been finalized. But we have a good indication of the standard setters' preferences, in the U.S. and globally.

This chapter reviews the status of the current debate regarding accounting for equity-based compensation, presents a primer on the binomial and Black-Scholes option pricing models, introduces simulation or Monte Carlo modeling techniques, highlights some of the issues regarding valuation of employee stock options for various purposes, and presents some implications of the changing accounting rules for executive incentive plan design.

## (b) Who Are the Key Players?

The Financial Accounting Standards Board (FASB) is responsible for the establishment of generally accepted accounting principles (GAAP), to which financial reporting by U.S. corporations must conform. The FASB, organized in 1973, is an independent organization headquartered in Norwalk, Connecticut, comprised of seven board members who serve five-year terms.

Publicly held companies in the United States also must follow accounting rules established by the Securities and Exchange Commission (SEC). The SEC and the FASB generally work together to ensure consistency in accounting rules. In general, the SEC defers to the FASB on rule making.

The International Accounting Standards Board (IASB) consists of representatives from the accounting rule makers in eight countries. The IASB was formed by the International Accounting Standards Committee (IASC), which represents accounting organizations throughout the world. Companies are not required to comply with standards established by the IASB unless the standard setters for the country in which they are listed have agreed to adopt them.

Companies listed in European Union (EU) countries generally must comply with IASB standards by January 1, 2005, while nonpublic companies in the EU have longer to comply.

The FASB and the IASB have been working together to achieve "convergence" in global accounting standards. This means that they are attempting to devise standards that are consistent in terms of overall principles, although not necessarily identical in terms of specific rules.

## (c) Accounting Rules for Stock Compensation Are Changing

Both the FASB and the IASB have undertaken projects to revamp the accounting rules governing equity-based compensation. The IASB's exposure draft on this issue was published in November 2002. Following a period of public comment and redeliberation, the IASB plans to issue a final standard in the first quarter of 2004. The FASB's project follows close behind, with an exposure draft expected in the first quarter of 2004 and a final standard planned for issuance in the third quarter of 2004.

As of this writing, it appears that the effective date for most companies for the IASB's proposed standard will be January 1, 2005, and for the FASB's proposal, fiscal years beginning after December 15, 2004 (for companies reporting on a calendar year, the effective date for the FASB's standard would be January 1, 2005, consistent with the IASB). The new standard will apply prospectively for any awards granted after the effective date, as well as any awards granted before, but that remain unvested at, the effective date. (For the IASB, the latter provision will apply only for awards granted after November 2002 that remain unvested at January 1, 2005.)

The final standards are likely to resemble in many ways the current "preferred" method of accounting for equity-based compensation, as set forth in Statement of Financial Accounting Standards No. 123 (FAS 123)—particularly in terms of general principles. It can be expected that, for example, companies will have to recognize the fair value cost of equity-based compensation in their financial statements; fair value generally will be determined at the grant date; the cost will be spread over the service period (generally the vesting period); and total cost will generally be trued up at the vesting date based on the number of awards that actually vest. It is also expected, however, that the new standards will correct some of the shortcomings in the FAS 123 approach.

Concurrent with the equity-based compensation project, the FASB is moving toward standards that are broader than the traditional "rules-based" U.S. GAAP. This movement toward "principles-based" accounting standards is part of the convergence effort with the IASB, since U.S. accounting standards traditionally have been far more detailed than non-U.S. standards. One of the criticisms of U.S. standards is that they allow companies to record transactions based on their form, not necessarily their substance. A transaction that meets the "letter of the law" may be recorded in a way that is inconsistent with its actual substance. The SEC has endorsed this principles-based approach.

In accounting for equity-based compensation, a principles-based approach would, among other things, require companies to become more conversant with option valuation methods other than the Black-Scholes option pricing model, which are discussed in this chapter.

While the winds of change continue to bring the likelihood of mandatory expensing, as of this writing companies in the U.S. still have the choice of recognizing compensation cost for stock-based awards under APB 25, which has been the standard since 1972, or under FAS 123. Companies that continue to use APB 25 principles in their financial statements are required to disclose in the footnotes to those statements the pro forma impact on their earnings of FAS 123 principles.

During the years following the issuance of FAS 123 in 1995, nearly all companies continued to follow APB 25, recognizing stock compensation costs using the intrinsic value method in their financial statements, while disclosing the FAS 123 fair value cost in their footnotes. The absence of any expense for the conventional employee stock option under APB 25 helped fuel the tremendous growth in option grants. But since July 2002, in response to shareholder concerns, hundreds of companies have opted to use FAS 123 recognition principles in their financial statements. For a detailed description of APB 25 and FAS 123, see Chapter 18 of *Paying for Performance*.[1]

---

[1]Peter T. Chingos, ed., and consultants from Mercer Human Resource Consulting, Inc., *Paying for Performance: A Guide to Compensation Management*, 2nd ed. (Hoboken, NJ: John Wiley & Sons, 2002).

## 7.2   WHY VALUE STOCK OPTIONS?

This chapter addresses the use of option valuation models to satisfy current and proposed accounting requirements and the implications of changing accounting rules for incentive plan design. However, option pricing models have other uses in connection with compensation. Some of the more common ones include using the models to:

- Determine competitive value of long-term incentive grants
- Show expected present value of current year's grants in the proxy statement
- Communicate value of option grants to employees
- Value outstanding options as part of a new hire or termination package
- Value options in accordance with certain tax law provisions

Because different sets of rules and guidelines govern the assumptions used when estimating option values for these various purposes, different option values may result for the same option grant. For example, for purposes of determining competitive long-term incentive values, the full option term frequently is used. In contrast, for FAS 123 purposes, the option's "expected life" (estimated exercise date) is used, and to value outstanding grants, the remaining term is used.

These differences can be quite confusing to the layperson. People must understand the purpose of an option value calculation in order to evaluate the results of the calculation properly.

## 7.3   OPTION VALUATION BASICS

This section presents a primer on how to value a stock option, focusing on financial models used to value publicly traded options. Section 7.4 discusses valuation issues specific to employee stock options.

### (a) How Much Is an Option Worth?

The old rule of thumb that options are worth about 33 percent of the value of the underlying stock is based on a particular set of assumptions, some of which often are invalid in today's environment: an option with a 10-year term, dividend yield of 3 percent, volatility of about 25 percent, and a 10-year risk-free interest rate of about 7 percent will have a Black-Scholes value of 33 percent. It is tempting to avoid the many pitfalls of option pricing models and revert to the comfort of that one-third figure. Although this approach certainly simplifies the whole process, it bears no resemblance to the economic value of a stock option except, in some cases, by coincidence.

## (b) Random Stock Price Movement

Most economic option pricing models assume that stock prices move randomly over time. The mathematical models underlying this randomness assumption generally view the stock's past history as irrelevant for predicting the future.

Most common valuation models produce a distribution of stock prices; the methods differ, however, in the extent to which they allow the price path leading to the distribution to be analyzed.

For most employee option holders, this very basic concept of randomness can immediately make all option pricing models suspect. Most employees perceive that the future performance of their company's stock depends largely on its historical trend (up or down). For example, if the stock price has increased significantly, they may assume that future appreciation will be less rapid. Of course, actions of the company's management influence stock price movement, but most of the movement in a typical stock is influenced by random market and industry factors. The random movement of stock prices takes the form of a lognormal distribution. The shape of the curve is determined by the volatility, or variability (explained below) of the stock, as shown in Exhibit 7.1.

## (c) Six Basic Variables

Most common option pricing models incorporate six basic variables. Assuming all other inputs remain constant, these variables, and their impact on an option's value, are summarized in Exhibit 7.2:

1.  *Stock price:* A higher stock price produces a higher option value, since it increases the potential dollar gain for a given rate of stock price appreciation.
2   *Exercise price:* A higher exercise price produces a lower option value, since the gain on the option will be lower.
3.  *Option term:* A longer term produces a higher option value, since there is greater opportunity for the stock to trade above the exercise price.

**Exhibit 7.1**   Lognormal Distribution of Stock Prices

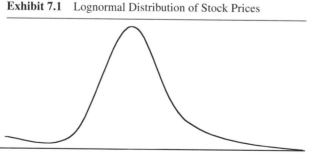

**Exhibit 7.2**   Option Model Variables

| Increase in . . . | Impact on Value of Option |
|---|---|
| Stock Price | ↑ |
| Exercise Price | ↓ |
| Option Term | ↑ |
| Risk-free Interest Rate | ↑ |
| Stock Volatility | ↑ |
| Dividend Yield | ↓ |

4.  *Risk-free interest rate:* A higher rate produces a higher option value, since it increases the value of delaying the purchase of stock while still gaining from price appreciation (i.e., the present value of the exercise price is lower at higher interest rates).

5.  *Stock volatility:* Higher volatility produces a higher option value, since there is greater opportunity for the stock to trade significantly above the exercise price. Volatility is one of the most important concepts in option valuation—and one of the most challenging to get right. For option valuation purposes, volatility is defined as the standard deviation of the rate of return on the stock, and is based on the assumption that stock prices move randomly over time. For publicly traded options, volatility typically is based on the percentage change in the stock price from day to day over a period of time. It is not the same as a stock's beta, which is the stock's volatility relative to the overall market. Instead, it is the "ups and downs" of a stock price.

    The greater the volatility of the stock, the more valuable the option to the option holder. For example, take two stocks that, on average, maintain their price over time. Suppose Stock A does so by remaining at the same price forever, say, $10, while Stock B remains at $10 on average by trading at $5 one day and $15 the next. Stock A has a volatility of 0, while Stock B's volatility is greater than 0. The holder of an option with an exercise price of $10 would never benefit or lose from Stock A, but could clearly benefit from Stock B on its "up" days, while never losing.

6.  *Dividend yield:* Higher dividend yield produces lower option value, since it decreases the potential for price appreciation.

## (d) Binomial Model

Although it may seem daunting at first, a binomial option pricing model is actually a good introduction to the economics of option valuation. Unlike Black-Scholes, the basic concepts underlying binomial models can be illustrated graphically.

Binomial option pricing models use probability theory to estimate the value of a stock option. The term "binomial" refers to a situation where there are always two potential outcomes, each with an associated probability, such as flipping a coin. As with most option pricing models, binomial models assume that stock prices move randomly over time.

Exhibit 7.3 shows a highly simplified illustration.

The probability of the price going up or down, as well as the magnitude of the upstep and downstep, is derived from the stock's volatility.

The expected value of the stock after one period can be calculated as equal to the weighted average of the two potential outcomes:

$$(60\% \times \$10 \times 150\%) + (40\% \times \$10 \times 50\%) = \$11$$

This approach, carried out for two periods, is shown in the lattice or tree diagram in Exhibit 7.3.

If the same process is carried out for multiple periods, for example, 52 weeks, a more complex and useful version of the lattice diagram can be developed. The result at the last set of values is a probability distribution for the stock price at the end of the 52 weeks.

A stock option can be introduced into this theory of stock price movement by comparing its exercise price to the expected stock price at each of the final points in the lattice. The expectation is that where the option is projected to be in the

**Exhibit 7.3**   Binomial Model of Stock Price Movement

*Assumptions*
- Initial stock price                                                        $10
- Probability of the price going up                                  60%
- Probability of the price going down                            40%
- Magnitude of an upstep (amount the price
  increases the 60% of the time that it goes up)        150%
- Magnitude of a downstep (amount the price
  decreases the 40% of the time that it goes down)     50%

```
                                                    $22.50
                                                    (0.36)
                        $15.00
                        (0.60)
$10.00                                              $7.50
                                                    (0.48)
                        $ 5.00
                        (0.40)
                                                    $2.50
                                                    (0.16)
```

money, it would be exercised. In the simplified case shown in Exhibit 7.4, the exercise price equals $10, and the option would be exercised only if the stock price were $22.50, for a gain of $12.50. The probability of this gain is 36 percent. The resulting expected value, $4.50 (36% × $12.50), is then valued back to today using a risk-free rate—let's say 6 percent. Assuming our model represents one year, the resulting present value is $4.25. Thus, $4.25 is the value of the option using this highly simplified binomial option pricing model.

## (e) Black-Scholes Option Pricing Model

The Black-Scholes option pricing model was developed by Fischer Black and Myron Scholes in 1973 (and further developed by Robert Merton) to calculate the economic value of publicly traded call options. During the past 10 to 15 years, the model has been widely used to value employee stock options, even though they differ from publicly traded options in a number of ways, which are discussed in Section 7.4 (a).

The Black-Scholes model is a special case of the binomial model. It was developed assuming the underlying stock pays no dividends. For that reason, the highest value one could obtain from the option would be to wait until the end of its term to exercise it. Exhibit 7.4 shows that the greatest opportunity for gain from the option occurs at the end of its term, where the probability of the option being in the money is greatest. As discussed in Section 7.3 (f), the binomial model has the advantage of accommodating the impact of dividends on the timing of exercise and therefore on the option's value. In practice, the original Black-Scholes model frequently is adjusted to roughly accommodate dividends by reducing the stock price used in the formula by the present value of the expected dividend stream.

Exhibit 7.5 gives the Black-Scholes formula.

A simplified concept of the formula is that the value of the option is essentially a function of the spread between the stock price ($S$) and the exercise price ($X$). The first term of the equation, $S[N(d_1)]$, represents the discounted expected value of the stock price at the end of the term times the probability that the ter-

**Exhibit 7.4**  Binomial Option Pricing Model Illustration

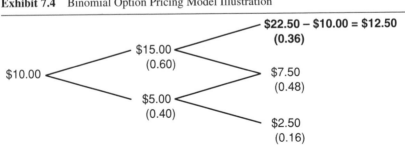

**Exhibit 7.5**  Black-Scholes Formula

$$C = S[N(d_1)] - Xe^{-Rt}[N(d_2)]$$

where

$$d_1 = \frac{\ln(S/X) + [R + (V/2)]t}{(Vt)^{1/2}}$$

$$d_2 = d_1 - (Vt)^{1/2}$$

$C$ = Call (option) value

$S$ = Current stock price

$N(d_1)$ and $N(d_2)$ = areas under a standard normal distribution

$X$ = Exercise price of option

$e$ = Exponential constant (equal to 2.71828)

$R$ = Risk-free rate

$t$ = Time until option expires

$V$ = Variance of the rate of return on the stock (volatility)

minal price will exceed the exercise price. The second term, $Xe^{-Rt}[N(d_2)]$, represents the present value of the exercise price times the probability that the terminal price will exceed the exercise price.

The derivation of the formula is based on the concept of a riskless hedge. An investor can create a risk-free investment position by simultaneously buying shares of a stock and selling options on this stock. Gains on the stock would exactly offset losses on the option, and vice versa. This riskless position must earn a rate of return equal to the risk-free rate: otherwise, an arbitrage opportunity would exist, and people trying to take advantage of this opportunity would drive the price of the option to the equilibrium level specified by the Black-Scholes model.

## (f) Comparison of Black-Scholes and Binomial Option Pricing Model

Both Black-Scholes and binomial models use the same variables. Both produce a stock price distribution. But with the Black-Scholes model, the path to that distribution cannot be analyzed—it is a "closed form" solution. With the binomial model, each node can be a decision point about whether to exercise. The model can incorporate factors such as changes in volatility and interest rates, changes in the underlying stock price itself, and dividends.

If a stock pays no dividends, and the option is granted at the money, the Black-Scholes and binomial models will generate equal values, if the same set of assumptions are used for each, since both will assume that the optimum exercise date is just before the option expires.

However, if the stock pays a dividend—particularly if it pays a high dividend—the Black-Scholes model will tend to undervalue the option. This occurs because the future dividend stream obtained from early exercise of an option on a high–dividend-paying stock is expected to provide greater value than the potential appreciation in the stock price over the remaining option term. A binomial model can capture the value realized from early exercise, while the Black-Scholes model cannot. A binomial model can be programmed to reflect payment of dividends on the underlying stock at the appropriate time, or node in the decision tree.

Examples of the differences between the binomial and Black-Scholes values are shown in Exhibit 7.6.

Binomial models also tend to give higher values than the Black-Scholes model for options that are significantly in the money.

Unlike the Black-Scholes model, binomial models also can be programmed to reflect changes in other assumptions, including volatility and interest rates. Performance contingencies can be incorporated into binomial models as well. For example, an option that vests only if the stock price appreciates 50 percent from the initial grant date could be valued by excluding all possible probability paths where the stock price is lower than the vesting trigger.

Both Black-Scholes and binomial models are permissible under FAS 123 and proxy disclosure rules. The FASB has expressed a preference for a binomial-type model, rather than Black-Scholes, for reasons discussed in Section 7.4(b).

## (g) Monte Carlo Simulations

As the name implies, this approach to option valuation consists of running thousands of iterations of possible stock price movement over the life of the option.

**Exhibit 7.6** Comparison of Black-Scholes and Binomial Option Pricing Model Values for Selected Stock Options Based on Varying Dividend Yields

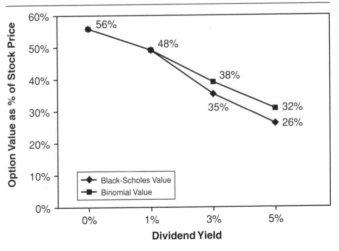

The Monte Carlo method can be thought of as the next stage of the binomial approach. It uses the same variables and assumes random stock price movement. Unlike binomial models, however, which allow just two paths from each node, Monte Carlo simulations allow for a large number of possible paths.

For at-the-money options with service vesting, simulation models generally will produce results that are equivalent to Black-Scholes or binomial models. Since simulation models are computer-intensive, they may not be the ideal choice for valuing conventional options. However, they are well suited to valuing options with certain performance contingencies such as target or trigger stock price hurdles that must be met for options to vest. This feature of simulation models may be important as companies move toward performance-based equity (see Section 7.6(b) and Chapter 8). In addition, the results of the simulation model can be used to produce an array of likelihood estimates of options' potential cost, rather than just the single value estimate produced by Black-Scholes.

## 7.4   VALUING EMPLOYEE STOCK OPTIONS

### (a) Why Do People Hate Using the Black-Scholes Model to Value Employee Stock Options?

Few people dispute that Fischer Black, Myron Scholes, and Robert Merton deserved the Nobel Prize for their contribution to valuation of publicly traded options. But when it comes to valuing employee stock options, even Myron Scholes has noted the shortcomings of the eponymous model.

Why do people hate using the Black-Scholes model to value employee stock options? There are six reasons, some of which also apply to other valuation models.

1. The basic Black-Scholes model cannot effectively recognize the differences between publicly traded options, which it was developed to value, and employee stock options. Publicly traded call options differ from employee stock options in several significant ways:
   - *Longer times to expiration:* Call options generally expire within 1 year, while employee stock options typically have 10-year terms. This fact makes estimating future interest rates, volatility, and dividend yield for employee stock options more difficult than for call options.
   - *Delayed exercisability:* Employee stock options typically include vesting provisions that restrict the holder's ability to exercise. The "forfeiture risk" discount applied to the fair value of an option for accounting purposes helps account for the possibility that the employee will be dismissed before his or her options vest, but it does not factor in the value of lost opportunities to exercise during the vesting period. (The original Black-Scholes

model assumes the stock pays no dividends. Therefore, there is no reason to exercise until the end of the term. Also, unless the option is issued well in the money and dividends are very high, the decision not to exercise during a three-year vesting period for an option with a five-year term, for example, also would be rational.)

- *Nontransferability:* Unlike call options, employee stock options generally cannot be bought or sold in an open market transaction. Therefore, in order to realize value from an employee stock option, the employee must exercise the option and sell the stock. This is the basis for the FAS 123 "expected life" concept. (Some employee options include a transferability feature for estate planning purposes, and some companies, from time to time, offer to repurchase or exchange employees' underwater stock options, but these differ from an arm's-length transaction with a third party.).

  A nontransferability "haircut" sometimes is applied to employee stock options to account for their lack of liquidity. This haircut might range from about 20 to 40 percent applied to the option value, based on conventional discounts used when a nontradable security is valued relative to a publicly traded one.

2. It is a "black box" or "black hole." The typical layperson finds the Black-Scholes model inscrutable. The impact of changes in the variables is less than transparent and, as discussed below, is sometimes counterintuitive.

3. An at-the-money option is worth more under all option pricing models when the grant-date stock price is higher than when it is lower, if all other assumptions are the same. Take a company that awarded an employee 1,000 options with an exercise price of $25 when the stock price was $25. Assume that the stock price subsequently doubles to $50, and the company grants 1,000 new options to the employee with an exercise price of $50. The employee's perception is that the new options are less valuable than the old ones were when they were granted, because the employee perceives that it is less likely for the stock to appreciate above $50 than it was when it was trading at $25. However, assuming all other inputs are the same (term, interest rate, volatility, etc.), option pricing models would say the new options are worth twice as much as the old ones were when they were granted. Since most option pricing models assume that stock prices move randomly, the likelihood of the company's stock price doubling again from $50 to $100 may be the same as the likelihood that the stock price would double when it was trading at $25.

4. Option recipients are "penalized" with smaller option grants when their stock price increases. An increase in the stock price means a company will award fewer options if the company is targeting a specific dollar value to determine stock option grant sizes. As described, an at-the-money option at a higher price is worth more than a comparable one at a lower price. So, in the previous ex-

ample, if the company wanted to convey the same dollar value opportunity at both grant dates, the award at $50 would consist of only 500 options instead of 1,000. This situation can be remedied by setting option grant guidelines at least partially based on competitive annual run rates and managing aggregate share usage on the basis of overall dilution levels.

5. Black-Scholes significantly overvalues options on technology stocks and others that are highly volatile and pay no dividend. Few investors would be willing to spend $7 to purchase an option on a stock that's trading at $10. However, most option pricing models will value a 10-year option on a non–dividend-paying stock with high volatility at about 70 percent (or more) of the underlying stock price. A quick fix is to cap volatility at, say, 50 percent—but the resulting value still is not likely to look reasonable.

6. What does an economic pricing model like Black-Scholes have to do with the real value of the option to the employee, which is realized when it is exercised? This is an apples-to-oranges comparison. Option pricing models are based on a set of statistical assumptions that determine the value of an option in a transaction between a willing buyer and seller. Certain underlying assumptions—such as the use of riskless interest rates and absence of taxes—are just some of the features of option pricing models that differentiate them from an employee's perception of an option's value. Any equivalence between an option's Black-Scholes value and the value realized at exercise is most likely due to coincidence. In addition, accounting standards do not consider an option's value to the employee. Instead, the standards are aimed at obtaining an objective "fair value" of a stock option.

Despite these shortcomings, Black-Scholes has been the most commonly used model for estimating the value of employee stock options. Often it is used to value employee stock options, because its inputs are easily verifiable and it is easy to calculate. Furthermore, it is widely regarded as a reasonable estimate of the economic value of a publicly traded option—which, despite its differences, is more closely related to an employee stock option than are other types of securities or derivatives.

## (b) Selecting Assumptions for Accounting Valuation

The Black-Scholes and the simplest forms of binomial and simulation models assume that interest rates, stock price volatility, and dividend yield are constant throughout the life of the option. The assumptions used in the model should be one's best guess of what those variables will be during that time. Since it is difficult, if not impossible, to predict the future movement of these variables, it is common practice to use current figures or recent history to estimate interest rates, volatility, and dividends as discussed in the following list.

- *Stock price:* Employee stock options are valued most frequently as of the date of grant. Therefore, the stock price at the date of the option grant typically is used. In certain cases, stock prices as of other measurement dates may be appropriate. For example, if an option is repriced, the current stock price would be used to calculate the accounting cost under FAS 123.
- *Exercise price:* Typically, this is a given value, fixed at the grant date.
- *Option term:* The full contractual term commonly is used in valuing stock options for competitive purposes. Doing this facilitates comparisons of the value of opportunities granted by different companies. For example, a company that awards options with a 5-year term is providing less of an opportunity for employees to realize value than a company that grants options with a 10-year term.

For FAS 123 purposes, an estimated exercise date is used to value employee stock options instead of the full option term. The purpose of this assumption is to recognize the fact that employee stock options generally cannot be transferred, so, as discussed above, in order to realize any value prior to expiration, the employee must exercise them early. The shortest expected life permissible under FAS 123 is generally equal to the full vesting period of the option. For example, an option that vests 100 percent four years after grant date can have an expected life of no less than four years.

The new accounting standards may provide for an alternative to the single-date "expected life" assumption typically used with the Black-Scholes model, thus opening the door to a more accurate valuation of employee stock options. The path outlined in binomial models can incorporate assumptions about employee exercise and forfeiture behavior, and be used to determine the most likely exercise patterns. Employee demographics, such as age, length of service, stockholdings, and salary, as well as historical exercise and forfeiture patterns can be analyzed to refine the precision of estimating the timing of exercise. For example, a model could be adjusted to reflect the fact that a company's employees historically have tended to exercise options two years after they vest, or when the stock price is double the exercise price, or two years before expiration, and so on. Incorporation of these factors can help the models account for employees' risk aversion and wealth concentration in the company stock, which are key determinants in the timing of exercise. And characteristics of the company's stock, including its volatility and dividend policy, also can be used to depict a more accurate picture of likely employee exercise timing. Employees at companies with highly volatile stock tend to exercise earlier than employees at companies with lower volatility. At each node, these models can evaluate whether the option will be forfeited, exercised, or held until the next node. This may produce a value very different than using a single expected exercise date and one grounded in a more realistic assumption about employee exercise patterns.

- *Risk-free interest rate:* Generally, this is assumed to be the yield on U.S. Treasury securities with the same maturity date as the option, measured as of the same date as the stock price (i.e., date of grant, current date, or other). FAS 123 requires the use of the rate on zero-coupon Treasury securities (strips).
- *Stock volatility:* Stock volatility is represented by the standard deviation (variance squared) of the rate of return on the stock. This input is the most complex (and controversial) one in option pricing formulas. It can be estimated using many different approaches. The estimated volatility is supposed to represent one's best guess regarding the future movement of the stock price over the life of the option.

  The classic method for calculating volatility for publicly traded call options is to use the standard deviation of the log of the daily change in the company's stock price over a historical 6- to 12-month period—typically the period immediately preceding the measurement date of the option.

  The 6- to 12-month period is considered appropriate for publicly traded options, which have relatively short terms. For employee stock options, a longer base period often is used to estimate volatility; for example, weekly or month-end closing prices over 3 to 5 years.

  FAS 123 provides specific guidance on how to estimate volatility, including the use of historical volatility over the most recent period that is generally commensurate with the expected option life. In general (though not for all companies), longer historical periods yield lower volatility figures, since the market has become more volatile in recent years and because, over time, volatility on an individual stock tends to revert toward the average volatility of a broader group of stocks.

  FAS 123 permits companies to calculate volatility based on changes in closing prices, average prices, or high prices. For example, volatility can be calculated based on changes in month-end closing prices, or on changes in average monthly prices from one month to another, or on changes in the highest stock price from one month to another. The latter approach tends to yield lower volatility figures than the other two.

  In addition to historical volatility, implied volatility sometimes is used as an estimate. This figure is derived from the quoted market value of a publicly traded option. For a publicly traded option, we know the value the market places on it, as well as the value of all of the inputs required to calculate an option value except volatility. Therefore, we can use these figures in the Black-Scholes equation to solve for the volatility "implied" by the market's valuation.
- *Dividend yield:* As described, the basic Black-Scholes formula does not include a provision for dividends, while binomial models can include dividends. The simple shortcut method for adjusting the Black-Scholes formula for dividends was described earlier: Deduct the present value of the estimated

future dividend stream from the current stock price prior to performing the calculations. Future dividends can be estimated based on historical dividend yields on the underlying stock or on a company's stated dividend policy.

In some cases, a discount is applied to the Black-Scholes value of unvested options to account for the risk that the employee will forfeit the option prior to vesting. As discussed in Section 7.6(b), FAS 123 and the new standard require companies to true up the cost of their options based on the actual number that ultimately vest.

## 7.5   VARYING THE ASSUMPTIONS

### (a) Sensitivity of the Black-Scholes Model to Changes in Assumptions

Changes in the underlying assumptions used in option pricing models have different effects on the option value because of the interrelationships of the variables. Exhibit 7.7 illustrates the impact of a 10 percent increase in each assumption while all other assumptions are held constant.

From a practical standpoint, given an at-the-money option, the only variables that a company can vary for accounting purposes are volatility and, to a lesser extent, expected life (and, therefore, the associated interest rate). As shown in the example in Exhibit 7.7, a 10 percent increase in volatility results in an 8 percent increase in the Black-Scholes value, assuming all other assumptions remain constant. The following sections explore in more detail the sensitivity of option values to changes in volatility.

### (b) Sensitivity Analysis Using Alternative Volatility Assumptions

It is not yet clear how much flexibility the FASB and the IASB will permit companies to use in estimating inputs to option pricing models, such as volatility. As described, FAS 123 currently provides a great deal of leeway.

Exhibit 7.8 shows the impact on the Black-Scholes value of an at-the-money option at different levels of volatility, assuming different expected lives.

An option with a 3 percent dividend yield is worth about 15 percent of the underlying stock price, assuming an expected life of 5 years and relatively low volatility of 20 percent. At a more average volatility level of 35 percent, the Black-Scholes value rises to about 25 percent. And if volatility increases to 50 percent, the option's value jumps to about 35 percent of the underlying stock price. Using an expected life of 10 years, the Black-Scholes value is about 25, 35, and 45 percent of the underlying stock price, given volatility of 20, 35, and 50 percent, respectively.

**Exhibit 7.7**  Illustration of the Impact of Changes in Assumptions on ABC Co.'s FAS 123 Black-Scholes Value

|  | Black-Scholes Value as % of Stock Price | Increase in Option Value due to 10% Change in Assumption |
|---|---|---|
| *Base Case[1]* | 27.6% | – |
| *10% Increase in ...* |  |  |
| Stock Price[2] | 31.2% | +13% |
| Exercise Price[2] | 24.3% | −12% |
| Option Term | 28.9% | + 5% |
| Risk-free Rate | 28.1% | + 2% |
| Volatility | 29.9% | +8% |
| Dividend Yield | 27.3% | − 1% |

[1]Base case assumptions are: stock price and exercise price $20; term 5 years; risk-free rate 2.5%; volatility 30%; dividend yield 1.0%

[2]Note that, if the exercise price is equal to the stock price, the Black-Scholes value as a percentage of the stock price will be the same, regardless of the stock price, assuming all other assumptions hold constant. In other words, the Black-Scholes value remains at 27.6% of the stock price regardless of whether the option is granted at $16 or $24 or any other value, as long as it is granted at the money and all other assumptions remain unchanged. The percentage changes only if the stock price is more than the exercise price or vice versa.

Exhibits 7.7 and 7.8 illustrate the sensitivity of the Black-Scholes model to changes in volatility and expected life assumptions. Exhibits 7.9 and 7.10 show how FAS 123 permits a company to select a wide range of volatility figures, which can have a significant impact on the accounting cost of its options.

Exhibit 7.9 shows historical volatility for the stock of a large financial services company calculated based on monthly and weekly prices—defined as high, low, or closing—over a period of five years. The results range from a low of 26.1 percent (monthly high price volatility) to a high of 40.7 percent (weekly closing price volatility). Given the same expected life assumption, this company inadvertently could use a volatility estimate that is 56 percent higher than an alternative that would be acceptable under FAS 123.

Although the illustration shows data for a large financial services company, the implications are applicable to companies of any size, across industries: The volatility of a stock can vary significantly depending on the method used to calculate it—and, although not illustrated here, depending on the time period selected.

Exhibit 7.10 shows the sensitivity of the company's Black-Scholes option value to the alternative volatility estimates in Exhibit 7.9.

Using the highest volatility assumption, the company's Black-Scholes value would be 35.7 percent of the underlying stock price, which is much higher than

**Exhibit 7.8**   Sensitivity of Black-Scholes Model to Changes in Assumptions

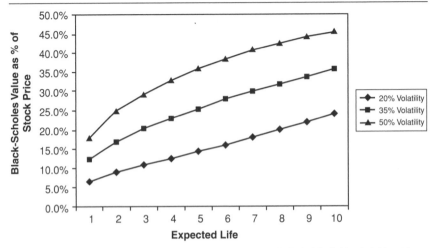

Figures shown are for "at the money option." Other assumptions include 3% dividend yield and interest rate that increases with expected life.

the Black-Scholes value of 24.6 percent that results from the lowest volatility assumption.

The aggregate cost savings could be quite significant. Assume, for example, that the company has granted 1 million options with an exercise price of $20. Using the highest volatility assumption, the total cost of the options would be about $7

**Exhibit 7.9**   Alternative Volatility Estimates

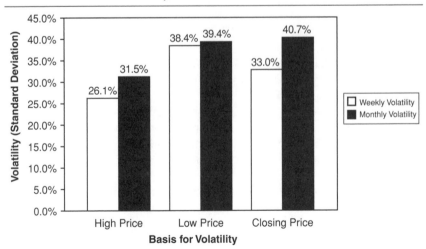

**Exhibit 7.10**   Sensitivity to Black-Scholes to Alternative Volatility Estimates

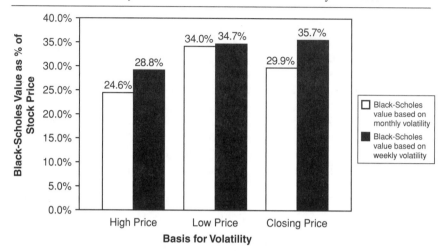

(Other assumptions include expected life of 5 years, dividend yield of 1.0%, and risk-free rate of 2.5%)

million (35.7% × $20 × 1 million). The lowest volatility assumption would re-
duce that cost by 31 percent, to about $5 million (24.6% × $20 × 1 million).

Many companies have missed the opportunity to legitimately reduce their FAS
123 costs (even if only for footnote disclosure purposes) simply by estimating alternative volatility figures.

## 7.6  INCENTIVE PLAN IMPLICATIONS

The pending accounting rules will provide both management and boards with
greater opportunities to link pay programs more closely with business strategy.
This increased flexibility will be accompanied by more challenges. As discussed
in Chapter 8, management and compensation committee members will have to
understand, among other things: how to translate a company's business plan into
performance measures that can be linked to long-term incentives; how to interpret
the risks and potential rewards of competitors' executive incentive programs; potential dilution costs to shareholders from alternative incentive plan approaches;
and, of course, potential accounting costs.

This section discusses some of the incentives that companies are likely to
adopt—assuming the final rules are consistent with current expectations.

### (a) Why Is Everyone Talking about Restricted Stock?

As discussed in other chapters of this book, restricted stock has begun to surface
as the vehicle of choice among many companies seeking alternatives to stock

options. Chapter 8 discusses the incentive value of restricted stock. Restricted stock also presents the opportunity for companies to save on accounting costs while delivering an incentive to employees that is potentially more valuable than options.

Let us look at an example to illustrate the accounting impact of restricted stock. Take a company with a current stock price of $15. Assume the option's fair value, for accounting purposes, is $5. In the past, the company might award an employee, say, 10,000 options, for a total accounting cost of $50,000. A restricted stock grant with an equivalent accounting cost would require 3,333 shares (3 to 1 options to restricted shares). However, let us assume that most of the company's prior option grants are underwater, and therefore employees do not value new grants highly. In addition, its stock plan is running out of shares. Therefore, from an employee's perspective, a restricted stock grant of equivalent value might require only 2,000 shares (5 to 1 options to restricted shares). The accounting cost would be reduced from $50,000 to $30,000; the company would use 8,000 fewer shares than if it granted options and 1,333 fewer shares than if it granted restricted stock with an accounting cost equivalent to the original option grant—and the employees would place greater value on the restricted stock grant. (Employees' perception of the relative value of options and restricted stock could differ, of course, if their prior option grants were significantly in the money.)

### (b) How Are Performance Contingencies Handled under the Accounting Rules?

The treatment of performance contingencies in valuing employee stock options is one of the most important determinants of future developments in equity-based compensation.

FAS 123 specifies that compensation cost "shall be based on the number of instruments that eventually vest." This general rule applies to both service-based and performance-based vesting conditions. The final FASB and IASB standards will include a similar provision, as both bodies have tentatively agreed to this approach.

It is this true-up provision that makes a plan such as Microsoft's well-publicized performance contingent awards for executives attractive from an accounting perspective. The Microsoft plan provides that the number of shares participants will receive after a three-year performance period (and subsequent two-year vesting period) will depend on the company's performance regarding the number and satisfaction of its customers. Under FAS 123, the cost of any shares that are earned under the plan is fixed at the initial grant date, with no requirement to recognize any future stock price fluctuations. The final cost true-up will factor in only those shares actually earned, multiplied by the initial value per share. If the customer growth and satisfaction goals are missed completely, the company will issue no shares under the plan—and will recognize no cost under FAS 123, reversing any previously recorded expense for the plan.

FAS 123 includes an exception to this true-up provision, which applies to awards whose vesting or exercisability is conditioned on meeting "a target stock price or specified amount of intrinsic value." The cost of these awards *cannot* be reversed if the awards are forfeited due to failure to meet that condition.

This exception refers to contingencies based on the issuing company's own (absolute) stock price performance, such as:

- 1,000 stock options will vest if ABC Co.'s stock price increases from $25 to $50 by the third anniversary of the date of grant
- 1,000 restricted shares will vest if ABC Co.'s stock price increases by at least 50 percent by the third anniversary of the date of grant

It also applies to awards with relative market performance goals. Referring to the example above, a common type of plan currently under consideration by many companies consists of 1,000 stock options with a fixed exercise price of $25 that will vest if ABC Co.'s total shareholder return (TSR; stock price appreciation plus dividends) equals the growth in the S&P Insurance Index at the end of three years. If ABC Co.'s TSR exceeds that of the S&P Insurance Index, more options will vest. If ABC Co.'s TSR is less than that of the S&P Insurance Index, no options will vest.

This relative TSR plan provides that the options could vest even if the stock price declines below $25 and they are underwater at the end of three years. (A similar performance condition could be applied to a restricted stock or stock unit award.)

FAS 123 does not provide a clear rationale for this exception to the treatment of awards with performance conditions. Footnote 10 states that "The existence of a target stock price that must be achieved to make an option exercisable generally affects the value of the option. Option-pricing models have been adapted to value many of those path-dependent options" (a reference to the flexibility of binomial and simulation models discussed in Section 7.3). The suggestion is that a market-based performance contingency affects the *value* of the award, rather than the *number* of awards that may be earned. Since FAS 123 requires the value of each award to be fixed at the grant date, allowing the cost to be trued up only for the number of awards actually issued, the FASB took the position that a market-based performance contingency would exclude the plan from the true-up provision.

In its deliberations on the new standard, the FASB appears to have expressed a preference for treating *all* equity-based awards in the same "fixed at grant date, nonreversible" approach as awards with market-based contingencies. In effect, the FASB would prefer that this approach become the rule rather than the exception: All awards would be valued at the grant date with no subsequent adjustments for any future events. However, the FASB has concluded that other types of performance contingent awards, such as those based on EPS or ROE, cannot reasonably be valued at the grant date since there is no objective way to evaluate the probability of meeting those "internal" goals. Therefore, the FASB decided that, under the new standard, the expense for all awards with service or performance-based vesting (except market-based goals) should be trued up at the vesting date based on the actual number of shares (or options) issued. This is consistent with the FAS 123 approach.

Relative market performance measures are attractive to both companies and shareholders. Such measures respond to the criticism that the typical stock option provides value to executives in a bull market, even if the company is underperforming—the often-heard rising-tide-lifts-all-boats issue.

Plans often are designed with a relative TSR contingency to exclude from the determination of incentive payouts those random, external factors that company management cannot influence. Companies in the same industry are subject to common factors that influence the movements of their stock prices. Relative performance comparisons that use an industry index help filter out these common influences. As a result, relative performance measures generally provide a better gauge of management's contributions to shareholder value than do absolute measures and therefore provide a better incentive than options with traditional service-based vesting (see Chapter 9).

The exclusion of relative performance plans from the true-up provision may discourage many companies from adopting them, since the full accounting cost would have to be recognized even if none of the awards vests.

## (c) Are Options with Indexed Exercise Prices the "Ideal" Plan?

In the debates about the best way to structure executive pay plans, options with indexed exercise prices are mentioned often. In fact, many companies have seen shareholder proposals that would require executive options to carry exercise prices indexed to the S&P 500 or some other market index.

Chapter 8 discusses the pros and cons of indexed options. The most straightforward approach to indexing an option's exercise price is to provide that it will change in parallel with a market index. If the index increases 10 percent, so would the exercise price. So, for the option to have value, the stock price must increase faster than the index. Proponents of indexed options see them as the perfect linkage between executives and shareholders: Executives do not benefit from stock price gains unless shareholders realize a return in excess of alternative investments.

Under FAS 123, options with an indexed exercise price are valued similarly to conventional options with fixed exercise prices, with a few wrinkles. The FAS 123 approach uses the cross volatility between the stock and the index, instead of the stock's own volatility. And the dividend yield on the index is used instead of the risk-free interest rate. (In addition, although not specified in FAS 123, simulation models are well suited to valuing options with indexed exercise prices.)

The resulting accounting cost under FAS 123 is usually lower than that of a conventional option. Therefore, a company will have to deliver more indexed options than conventional options to provide equivalent value. But the accounting cost may not be as low as the perceived value to the executive. As an example, assume a conventional option has a FAS 123 cost of $5 per share. Using the FAS 123 methodology, the value of an option on the same stock with an indexed exercise price is, for example, $2.50 per share. The equivalent accounting cost would require the company to grant twice as many options—which may be a challenge for many companies that are running out of shares under their stock plans. To further complicate the equation, assume that executives perceive that their company will have a very difficult time beating the index because the risk profile of their stock differs significantly from the companies that comprise the index. Therefore, they will expect three times as many indexed options as conventional options. This fact increases both the accounting cost and the potential dilution from stock plans.

### (d) What about Broad-Based Stock Purchase Plans?

Broad-based stock purchase plans, such as those that qualify under Internal Revenue Code Section 423, fall under the FAS 123 classification as stock options and must be expensed (in contrast to their "noncompensatory" treatment under APB 25).

There are significant public policy issues associated with expensing broad-based plans—both in the United States and abroad. The FASB and, in particular, the IASB, have been under pressure to carve out an exclusion from the new standard for broad-based plans such as Section 423 plans and their equivalent tax-qualified stock plans in other countries. However, it does not appear likely that the standard setters will find any solid accounting concepts that would allow them to exclude broad-based plans while maintaining the integrity of the new standard.

FAS 123 does include a very narrow exception that permits a stock purchase plan to be treated as noncompensatory. The plan must have a purchase price of at least 95 percent of the stock price at the end of the purchase period, and employees must have no more than 31 days to enroll after the price is fixed. In practice, few, if any, companies have a plan that meets these requirements. Some companies are considering adding a one- or two-year holding requirement that might allow them to maintain a purchase discount of 15 percent, while applying a discount to the accounting value of the plan to recognize the postvesting restriction. Doing this could reduce the effective discount for accounting purposes to the FAS 123 5 percent threshold. However, it is unlikely that this 5 percent "safe harbor" will be maintained under the new standard, which is more likely to include a noncompensatory exclusion only for those plans that provide an employee discount no greater than that available to all shareholders (such as through a dividend reinvestment plan).

Most 423 plans include a look-back feature, which allows employees to purchase shares at a discount from the stock price at the beginning or end of the purchase period, whichever is lower. FASB Technical Bulletin (FTB) 97-1 presents very detailed guidance on how to value nine types of look-back plans. (In fact,

FTB 97-1 may be cited as a perfect example of the rules-based approach that FASB is cutting back.)

Under FTB 97-1, look-back plans can cost companies two or more times the discount actually realized by employees, yielding a highly unsatisfactory cost/benefit relationship. Seemingly modest plan design features—such as whether employees are permitted to change their withholding elections during the year—can have a significant impact on plan costs. In fact, FTB 97-1 requires that when an employee changes payroll withholding elections during the year, it must be accounted for as a modification under FAS, with the incremental value, if any, accrued as an additional compensation expense. Although doing this might not add any significant accounting cost, the administrative requirements may be overwhelming.

Companies considering the impact of fair value expensing on their broad-based stock plans must invest time in modeling alternative plan designs that might be more cost effective. But any design changes that make the plan less costly also will make it less attractive to participants. As companies review the components and costs of all of their stock programs, some are finding it tempting simply to eliminate broad-based plans that they do not consider necessary for competitive purposes and that may not produce a benefit commensurate with their accounting costs.

# Chapter 8

# Changing Role of Equity Compensation

Diane L. Doubleday

A confluence of factors is dramatically changing the role of equity in compensation programs. These factors include the impact of the sustained economic downturn on equity markets, the focus on corporate governance following the recent corporate accounting scandals, the likelihood that the accounting rules for equity compensation will change, high dilution levels, and the rise in shareholder activism. Companies are reducing the emphasis on equity, using a wider variety of equity vehicles rather than relying almost solely on options, and incorporating financial performance measures into their equity programs to strengthen the link between pay and performance. Although the primary focus is executive compensation programs, these changes also will materially alter the use of equity in broader-based programs, including global equity plans.

## 8.1 OVERVIEW OF TRENDS IN EQUITY COMPENSATION

Over the past decade, the emphasis on the long-term incentive component of senior executive pay increased dramatically. According to the Mercer 350, a database of 350 public companies with revenues of $1 billion or more, for chief executive officers (CEOs), long-term incentives grew from 49 percent of pay mix in 1994 to 71 percent in 2001. In 2002, the long-term incentive component dropped to 68 percent; many believe that year will mark the first year of a trend to create more balance among pay elements. Stock options continue to be the most popular long-term incentive opportunities in large public companies—96.5 percent report using them in 2002. But here, too, there is a growing trend toward using other vehicles.

Along with these changes, total CEO pay dropped in 2002, when stock option grant values declined and fewer CEOs received grants. These changes—shift in emphasis, increased prevalence of different equity vehicles, and declining long-term incentive values—are not just a phenomenon at the CEO level. These tactics are cascading down through the executive level and deep into the lower levels of employees as companies respond to the changing environment and the demands of multiple stakeholders.

## 8.2  FACTORS INFLUENCING CHANGE

### (a) Spotlight on Corporate Governance

The dramatic collapse of Enron Corporation in late 2001 spawned the movement to strengthen corporate governance. The reform movement gained momentum when additional corporate accounting scandals followed in early 2002. Congress responded by enacting the Sarbanes-Oxley Act of 2002, which regulates the relationship between corporate auditors and the audit committees of public companies boards and establishes the Public Company Accounting Oversight Board.

The New York Stock Exchange (NYSE) and the Nasdaq proposed changes to their listing requirements that addressed weaknesses not only in the audit arena but also in the compensation committee function. The changes, although not identical, focused on board membership, such as tightening the definition of independence and requiring that only independent directors sit on the audit and compensation committees. The changes also addressed key board tasks, such as executive sessions to be led by an independent "lead" director, the charter of compensation committees, and CEO evaluation. The proposals had an immediate effect on boards of public companies. Many companies moved to comply with the proposals as a kind of "best practice" rather than waiting for the proposals to become effective. Final requirements were issued late in 2003. (See Chapters 4 and 5 for a more detailed discussion of these topics.)

### (b) Accounting Treatment of Equity Compensation

Stock options became widely cited as a contributing cause for the corporate accounting failures. Observers theorized that executives had so much opportunity to benefit from short-term market fluctuations that their decisions had become biased and their ethics compromised. Options had been abused or, at best, overused because they carried no earnings charge and therefore were perceived to have no cost.

In response to shareholder concerns, companies began announcing that they would record the cost of options as a charge to earnings using Statement of Financial Accounting Standards No. 123 (FAS 123). Members of Congress began calling for mandatory expensing. Meanwhile, the International Accounting Standards Board (IASB) had taken a position that options should be expensed. These developments increased the pressure on the Financial Accounting Standards Board

(FASB), which announced in early 2003 that fair value accounting, including the expensing of stock options, should become mandatory for all public companies. (See Chapter 7.)

The biggest consequence of fair value accounting is that it creates a level playing field for equity vehicles. Under Accounting Principles Board Opinion No. 25 (APB 25), plain vanilla options carried no earnings charge; all other equity vehicles—restricted stock, indexed options, performance shares—carried a charge, and in some cases, the charge was variable or marked to market. Because unpredictable costs are anathema to chief financial officers, those vehicles that incurred a variable expense were rarely used.

## (c) Dilution Levels

Shareholder dilution is another factor that is changing the role of equity compensation. Outstanding options and reserves for future grants—which represent future dilution of earnings per share—are at unsustainable levels in many organizations. For example, in large companies, *median* overhang levels grew to 15 percent in 2001, but dropped to 14.7 percent in 2002, reflecting a market pullback in options. Some industries fared worse. For example, in the Mercer 350, the technology sector's median 2002 overhang was 23.7 percent.

Companies that have used options broadly in their organizations are particularly vulnerable to high dilution levels. And if a company's stock price has suffered a sustained decline, underwater options may make it difficult to reduce dilution levels. If the market is rising or earnings per share are growing, shareholders may tolerate higher dilution. In a tough economic market, shareholders take a dim view of their ownership stake being further weakened by dilution from substantial equity compensation levels.

The root causes of high dilution levels are past grant practices and poor stock price performance. Shareholders, particularly institutions, are pressuring companies to more tightly manage how much equity they are granting ("burn rates"). In large general industry companies in the Mercer 350, the median annual burn rate was 1.9 percent of shares outstanding in 2002. In contrast, the technology sector median burn rate for 2002 was 3 percent. Along with a more general concern about the magnitude of executive compensation and particularly the use of equity, grant levels are starting to decline.

## (d) Investor Influence

Shareholders are quickly gaining a greater voice and wielding more power. The number of shareholder proposals addressing issues related to executive compensation—including topics such as option expensing and severance—has increased dramatically, and the number of successful shareholder proposals also has grown. (See Chapter 6 for a discussion of institutional investor issues.)

Large institutional shareholders, in particular, are influencing the design of equity programs by supporting requests for approval of new shares only if certain conditions are met, such as burn rate limits, performance-based awards, extended vesting, and holding and ownership requirements.

Shareholder concerns have been reinforced by the media, which have covered extensively the corporate failures and executive compensation excesses. Severance packages, excessive stock option compensation, executive benefits, and the failure to link pay to performance are among the most common topics.

A change in the rules on voting uninstructed shares strengthened institutional shareholders and their influence over the design of equity programs. The NYSE eliminated discretionary voting of "street name" shares on equity compensation plans. Previously, when brokers did not receive instructions from owners of record, they voted the shares with management on routine matters. Under the new NYSE standard, these uninstructed shares cannot be voted. The Nasdaq also does not permit broker voting of uninstructed shares.

The NYSE and the Nasdaq implemented new listing standards in 2003 requiring shareholder approval of most equity plans as well as material amendments to plans. In the case of the NYSE, this includes approval of any repricing of underwater options unless the plan specifies that shareholder approval is not required.

## 8.3 NEW ROLE OF EQUITY

Equity compensation will continue to be the largest component of executive pay in publicly traded companies. However, the design and the delivery of equity compensation are undergoing dramatic changes in response to the factors just described. The need to manage burn rates and lower dilution already has begun to reduce grant levels. Companies are reconsidering the mix of cash and equity in their programs and the mix between short- and long-term incentives. They are considering a broader range of equity vehicles with new design features to support a long-term business view, executive share ownership, and, most important, a much stronger linkage of pay to performance. And finally, although the spotlight has been on executives, these changes in how equity is used will filter through organizations. In particular, we expect broad-based stock programs to be revamped to better manage dilution, burn rate, and accounting expense.

In making decisions about future equity strategy, compensation committees will find competitive data to be of limited use. Rather, committees should adopt guiding principles tailored to the facts and circumstances of each organization to inform their decision making. The balance of this section focuses on the broad principles that committees should take into consideration as they restructure the equity component.

## (a) Align Pay Mix with Business Strategy and Compensation Philosophy

Compensation committees should revisit the current pay mix of the senior management team. Pay mix addresses the relative emphasis on specific elements, including cash vs. equity, fixed vs. variable, and short- vs. long-term incentives. Delving deeper into pay mix raises questions about the emphasis on specific vehicles, such as options vs. performance shares, and how to measure performance, including relative vs. absolute and entity vs. division vs. individual.

The pay mix should be aligned with the organization's compensation philosophy and should clearly support the business strategy. One key concern should be to achieve the correct balance between short- and long-term business focus. Many observers have bemoaned the market's obsession with short-term performance. Even though option plans are ostensibly a long-term vehicle, frequently they have been designed or administered to reward short-term gains. The correct balance between short- and long-term results will depend on factors such as type of industry, company maturity, business strategy, and company financial condition. A desperate turnaround situation may require a short-term focus while a biotechnology company with a long product development cycle may emphasize a longer-term view.

Early indications are that most companies' rebalancing efforts are focused on reducing the emphasis on stock options and adding new equity vehicles or on increasing the annual incentive opportunity. (See Exhibit 8.1.) Nonetheless, compensation committees should revisit executive base salaries, how they are established, and the appropriate weight they should have in the total compensation package.

## (b) Strengthen the Link between Performance and Compensation

In a mandatory fair value accounting environment, many equity vehicles will be no more expensive (and perhaps even less expensive) than the plain-vanilla options

**Exhibit 8.1**   Rebalancing the Equity Program

|                                                                        | Percent of Respondents |
| ---------------------------------------------------------------------- | :--------------------: |
| Reduced number of options to be granted                                | 63%                    |
| Reduced number of option recipients                                    | 46%                    |
| Added long-term cash-based incentive plan                              | 9%                     |
| Reduced number of options and substituted cash for at least some lost value | 8%                |

*Source:* Mercer 2003 Future of Equity Survey.

that have been widely used. As it will be possible under fair value accounting to have performance-contingent vehicles without adverse accounting consequences, shareholders are likely to demand that at least some portion of executives' equity compensation be linked directly to company performance. Companies should take advantage of this leveling of the playing field and consider shifting at least some of their long-term incentive program value to performance-contingent equity.

Performance goals can strengthen the long-term focus of equity plans by moving away from absolute, short-term measures, such as earnings per share. Instead, longer-term measures, such as return on invested capital or return on equity, can be incorporated. Goals may be absolute or relative. Absolute goals are fixed, such as "5 percent annual revenue growth." A relative goal is measured against a benchmark, such as "annual revenue growth equal to the median annual revenue growth of a specified peer group of companies." A popular relative measure is the total shareholder return (TSR; stock price appreciation plus dividends) of a peer group or industry sector. (For accounting issues raised by using relative TSR, see Chapter 7.) Goals may be linked to internal quantifiable initiatives, such as product development, or to external measures, such as market share. A range of performance can be used with the magnitude of the equity award calibrated to the performance level achieved.

Committees should fully understand that adding performance requirements to equity awards is complex and puts significant pressure on the performance measurement capabilities of both the management team and the board. Many organizations have trouble establishing effective and accurate goals for their annual incentive programs; the challenges substantially increase when the performance horizon extends beyond the next year. Relative performance measures are a sound alternative in many cases but also raise problems with implementation. For instance, industry consolidation combined with the uniqueness of some organizations can severely limit the number of peer company candidates. (See Chapter 9.) Poor goal setting may undermine shareholder confidence. Yet even the most disciplined goal-setting process may require skilled communication: Executives may receive equity awards based on achieving goals in years when the share price is depressed. (See Chapter 13.)

## (c) Use a Portfolio Approach

Given the challenges of establishing the "right" performance metrics, we expect companies to move cautiously into the performance-contingent arena by using a portfolio approach: A portion of the equity program will continue to rely on absolute share price improvement, and a portion will depend on relative or absolute financial or operational performance. The portfolio approach relies on using more than one equity vehicle, including restricted stock, performance shares, stock appreciation rights and options, perhaps with new design features, such as options with indexed exercise prices. Each vehicle has strengths and weaknesses relative to issues such as cost, dilutive impact, line of sight, retention, alignment with shareholders, and complexity.

Indexed stock options respond to a common objection to options that a rising market tends to boost share prices of all companies, regardless of underlying performance. Certainly, in the late 1990s, this phenomenon enabled many employees to exercise options and reap substantial gains in companies that later collapsed and even disappeared. The fair value accounting rules enable companies to index the exercise price of options without adverse accounting treatment. Using this strategy, the exercise price would rise or fall relative to an external index of industry peers or even a broad market index, such as the Standard & Poor's 500. The option holder would benefit from the option only if the company's stock price outperformed the index.

Indexing is likely to be debated more than used. Implementation raises a number of challenges, including selecting an appropriate index, administering the exercise price changes, and explaining exercise price increases and decreases to option holders and to shareholders. It can be particularly challenging for shareholders to understand how an indexed option can have value when a company's share price, and investor value, drops. Almost no stock plan documents include indexing provisions, so implementation would have to include submitting a plan amendment to shareholders. Finally, an indexed option may not satisfy the requirements for deductibility under Section 162(m) of the Internal Revenue Code.

Restricted stock has long been used by large companies and selectively used by others to help manage the risk inherent in options, to support retention, and to replace benefits (usually equity) that a new hire left behind at the prior employer. Historically, restricted stock has been service-vested; after a specified period, the stock vests if the holder remains employed by the company. Restricted stock accomplishes two objectives: It supports retention, and it rewards for share price improvement. However, restricted stock generally was criticized as a "gift" because it lacked a performance link (even share price decline was rewarded) and reinforced notions of entitlement in the workplace. Its complexity—tax and withholding issues—and the fact that it carried an earnings charge operated to limit its widespread use. Restricted stock was virtually never used with vesting contingent on achieving performance goals because this type of restricted stock incurred a variable charge to earnings.

Restricted stock is making a resurgence. In light of the perceived abuse of stock options, the first move that many companies made was to add or increase their use of restricted stock, usually with service-based vesting. However, with the onset of fair value expensing, performance-contingent restricted shares are likely to gain in popularity. These shares would become vested only on attainment of certain performance goals within a specified period of time. And under fair value accounting, the expense is determined by the value at grant, not marked to market over time. This form of restricted stock responds to the "gift" criticism by eliminating the entitlement component and focusing on goal achievement. In either form, restricted stock is gaining popularity because it uses fewer shares than stock options to deliver comparable value, but it also provides less upside opportunity to employees. (See Exhibit 8.2.)

Performance share or unit plans, which have been in use for decades, are likely to increase in popularity. Under these plans, participants are awarded shares or units for performance over a multiyear cycle, typically three years. Goals typically are based on financial or operational performance, and the number of shares or units awarded is calibrated to the performance level achieved. These plans received variable accounting treatment under APB 25; usually this was managed by paying the units in cash rather than in shares and establishing maximum payout levels. In a fair value accounting environment, the accounting for the awards paid in shares is comparable to restricted stock. Thus these plans are likely to increase in popularity. Of course, as discussed, the ability to set performance goals may be a barrier to implementation in some companies.

Stock appreciation rights (SARs) entitle the holder to cash or shares equivalent to the appreciation on a fixed number of shares and historically were issued in tandem with stock options. Exercise of a SAR canceled one option. By drawing down enough in-the-money SARs, the participant could generate the cash necessary to exercise the remaining options. SARs have been used only sparingly in the last decade because of their adverse accounting treatment under APB 25 (variable charge to earnings) and the advent of cashless exercise programs. With fair value accounting, SARs that are payable in stock are treated favorably and may become more common because they minimize share dilution. SARs payable in cash will continue to have marked to market accounting and are not likely to become widely used. Many stock plans no longer contain provisions regarding SARs, which means companies would have to submit a plan amendment to shareholders before using SARs.

**Exhibit 8.2**    Adoption of New or Rarely Used Equity Vehicles in 2003

|  | Percent of Respondents |
| --- | --- |
| Service-based restricted stock | 63% |
| Performance-contingent restricted stock | 14% |
| Performance share/unit plan | 14% |
| Stock appreciation rights payable in cash | 4% |
| Performance-contingent options | 3% |
| Options price-indexed to external benchmark | 3% |
| Stock appreciation rights payable in stock | 1% |
| Other | 17% |

*Source:* Mercer 2003 Future of Equity Survey.

The new role of equity enables companies to offer executives choice. If a company moves to a portfolio of equity vehicles such as options, restricted stock, and performance shares, the company could offer the executive the choice (above a specified minimum level) to receive incremental equity in the vehicle that best meets personal financial needs and risk profile. This kind of flexibility could be very attractive and result in the delivery of greater perceived value.

## (d) Balance Cost and Value

Compensation committees will have to take into account the earnings impact of any proposed equity strategy. For many companies, the earnings impact of fair value accounting will be significant. However, while the cost of equity awards can be substantial, it may align poorly with the perceived value to executives. Balancing cost and perceived value includes assessing the probability that the goals will not be achieved and the reward never earned. Thus an important part of the compensation committee's work is to find vehicles that provide the strongest incentive or perceived value to the executive while minimizing the company's earnings impact.

## (e) Manage Overhang and Burn Rates

Shareholders have revolted against high overhang (outstanding options as a percentage of options outstanding) and continuing high burn rates (annual awards issued as a percentage of shares outstanding). Overhang levels tend to be high because of underwater options, historically high burn rates, and long option terms, often 10 years, which means that even in-the-money options remain outstanding. Some repricing strategies have been used to bring overhang down, but for most organizations it will simply take time for the backlog of outstanding options to diminish through attrition, exercise, and the issuance of fewer new options.

Institutional shareholders have been particularly active in conditioning approval of share replenishment requests on managing dilution, particularly by demanding that burn rates drop. Companies should consider these types of actions:

- Limiting eligibility to those employees where equity awards are most valued and most needed for attraction, retention, and motivation
- Reducing awards recognizing that past grant levels can no longer be sustained
- Shortening the term of options, which both reduces their cost and minimizes their long-term impact on overhang
- Using a larger portion of whole-value equity, such as performance shares or restricted stock, rather than options

- Repricing underwater options in an appropriately designed program that is consistent with shareholders' views

## (f) Design Plans that Reflect Compensation Strategy

The terms and conditions of equity vehicles often receive little attention or, once established, are not revisited to ensure that they continue to support the company's compensation strategy. This revisiting includes ensuring design features are appropriately aligned with the needs of different employee groups. For example, one strategy used during the late 1990s to attract new employees in a tight labor market was shortened vesting schedules. However, the company perhaps should have focused on retaining the management team, which might require longer vesting schedules for executives.

Vesting terms continue to be a key feature for discussion. Vesting raises attraction and retention issues and, in a fair value accounting environment, defines the period over which cost usually is recognized. Vesting also reinforces a long-term view of performance, an objective that many companies are trying to instill in their compensation programs. Other key features that should be addressed include posttermination rights, such as how long an employee can exercise an option. The operation of special rules for retirement, death, and disability will have to be reconsidered for each new equity vehicle. And, finally, the treatment of awards in the event of involuntary termination, particularly in connection with a transaction, should be evaluated carefully. Severance arrangements, including the acceleration of equity awards, receive particular scrutiny from shareholders, employees, and the media.

Recent events are giving rise to new design features. One of the most popular with boards of directors is holding periods. In a number of corporate scandals, executives exercised options and sold shares prior to the corporation's collapse. Observers believe that the ability to exercise and sell immediately—even in a healthy organization—reinforces a short-term focus that is not in the best interests of shareholders. In response to these concerns, companies have begun instituting holding period requirements, where executives are required to hold the shares acquired on exercise of options or vesting of restricted shares or grant of performance shares, net of the exercise price and any taxes. The length of the holding period varies; in some organizations it is a specified time, such as one year, but in others it is until termination of employment and even beyond. This holding period concept is being extended to members of the board of directors.

The holding period requirement is in addition to any ownership requirements that the company may have in place. Ownership requirements have been increasing in prevalence over the last decade, but are receiving new attention. Ownership requirements typically are expressed as a multiple of salary or a fixed number of shares and are intended to align executives more closely with the interests of shareholders. Volatility in share prices has led a growing number of companies to define ownership guidelines based on a fixed number of shares.

## 8.4 IMPACT OF CHANGE ON THE BROADER EMPLOYEE POPULATION

Broad-based employee stock plans raise human resource, compensation philosophy, and employee communication challenges for compensation committees. These are in addition to the accounting cost, dilution impact, and burn rate concerns that are the focus of executive compensation design.

High dilution levels and pressure to manage burn rates and future accounting expense are forcing companies to consider reducing eligibility, cutting back grant levels, and even eliminating broad-based programs. For many companies—particularly high-growth companies and technology industry members—reducing the use of options is completely antithetical to long-standing principles about how to best motivate and reward employees. These organizations are likely to continue broad use of plain-vanilla options, but not at the levels common in the late 1990s.

The future of discounted employee stock purchase plans (ESPP) is unclear. These plans enable employees to purchase employer stock at a discount through after-tax payroll deductions. If structured appropriately (and most are), employees are not taxed until sale of the shares, even though the purchase is at a discount. ESPPs generally have been viewed favorably by shareholders, because they represent a relatively small use of shares. They also have been a popular alternative to broad-based options because the tax rules require broad eligibility. ESPPs have provided an opportunity for virtually all employees to purchase shares at a discount and thus have reduced the pressure on some companies to grant stock options more broadly.

Under the fair value accounting rules as proposed, ESPPs would no longer receive favorable accounting treatment. Under APB 25, these plans—if structured appropriately—did not incur a charge to earnings. That is not the case under FAS 123, which makes most ESPPs quite expensive. (See Chapter 7.) Many commentators have urged the FASB to revisit the ESPP treatment. If ESPPs incur a charge to earnings (and the charge could be substantial under fair value accounting), then companies likely will eliminate these plans or substantially alter the design to make them less expensive. Design changes would include shortening the purchase period, capping the maximum number of shares that can be purchased in a period, limiting the contributions, eliminating opportunities to change contribution rates, and reducing the discount.

## 8.5 CHALLENGES FOR DECISION MAKERS

Designing an appropriate equity compensation program is becoming more complex than ever before. The first question that must be asked, how much equity should be distributed, is much more challenging to answer than in the past. Boards will need to assess the organization's existing equity situation, particularly overhang and historical burn rates, and how well equity aligns with the organization's business and human resource strategies. Looking at the competitive environment provides context for this decision, but the data lag market practice. While this has always been true, it is particularly a problem in a fluid environment and may not mirror the circumstances of a particular company.

The most common criticism of fair value accounting is the flaws in the valuation methodology. Companies, of course, try to minimize the cost using the flexibility that the accounting rules permit. If that lower value then is used to compare relative competitiveness of compensation, companies could be induced to increase the size of equity awards under the guise of maintaining competitive market pay levels.

The second issue is the difference between the cost of equity and its perceived value. As discussed, employees' perceptions about the value of an equity award may be much lower than the award's accounting cost. These considerations may drive employers to use different vehicles or to shift a portion of equity compensation to cash compensation, at least for some employees.

The challenges do not end with the cost/value analysis; other considerations affect the choice of vehicle, including tax treatment, retention value, and disclosure issues. Perhaps the most important consideration is performance. Shareholders are demanding that boards strengthen the link between pay and performance. With fair value accounting, it will be feasible to link at least some portion of the equity program to true company performance. Establishing appropriate performance measures is difficult. The issues include identifying which measures drive long-term shareholder value and are within the control of the management team. A second-level issue is whether the measures should be relative, absolute, or a combination. The third issue is time frame. For some organizations, the time horizon in which they can project performance reasonably is very short.

The final challenge is the calibration of pay to performance. This has long been an issue in annual incentive plans, but the magnitude of long-term incentive compensation and the longer time horizon puts more pressure on the calibration.

Most boards have relatively limited experience coping with these challenges. This, like many board tasks, will now require a greater investment of time and resources.

## 8.6 CONCLUSION

The executive compensation environment is changing dramatically. The first indications showed up in the proxies reflecting 2002 decisions. Boards that have relied heavily on market data have to take a more skeptical approach now, since looking in the rearview mirror is less helpful than it used to be. Equity continues to be the largest portion of the compensation program for most executives and will continue to be monitored closely by shareholders, employees, retirees, and the press. In this environment, boards will focus on balancing pay elements, managing costs, and strengthening the link of pay to performance. And more than ever, boards will ensure that their decisions and the rationale for those decisions are communicated more expansively in the proxy and elsewhere.

# Chapter 9

# Relative Performance Evaluation and the Selection of Peers

Haig R. Nalbantian and Wei Zheng

## 9.1 INTRODUCTION: CURRENT DIFFICULTIES WITH PAY FOR PERFORMANCE[1]

One of the basic tenets of the American model of executive compensation is the alignment of the long-term interests of management with shareholders. This alignment is effectively achieved, or so the theory goes, by awarding some portion of the company to executives in the form of stock or stock options. This approach was pursued vigorously in the 1990s. Companies in the United States and in many of the western industrial countries dramatically increased their reliance on stock-based rewards, particularly stock options.

Unfortunately, this story has not had a happy ending. The highly publicized accounting scandals of Enron and WorldCom drove home the sad reality that financial information can be distorted to influence investor perceptions about a company and that executives with large stakes in their company's stock may have incentives to try to drive up stock price in unsustainable ways. But the scandals are really the exceptions that make the headlines. More to the point, in the aftermath of the recession and the stock market "correction," many companies found

[1]This chapter draws on material from a previous article by the authors, "Worth the Risk?: When and How to Use Stock in Executive Incentives," *WorldatWork* 10, No. 3 (2001). The authors are grateful for research assistance provided by Lingzi Liang and Susan Merino of Mercer Human Resource Consulting and for the cooperation of Steve Sabow and Colin Hinkson of our Executive Compensation Research unit, who provided us with relevant data from the Mercer 350 database on compensation of top executives in the United States. We have benefited from insights concerning methodology and policy implications offered by our colleagues Bruce Wang and Susan Eichen, respectively, by our former colleague Yale Tauber, and from collaboration on projects with colleagues in both our Strategy and Metrics practice and Mercer's Executive Compensation practice.

their incentive compensation programs in disarray. The stock options of many executives were driven deeply underwater, while the wealth accumulated during the 1990s in various stock programs quickly and substantially eroded. Ironically, these incentives weakened precisely when they were most needed to help drive a revival of company fortunes and to protect against cherry-picking of top talent.

These experiences point to some inherent problems and instability in pay-for-performance programs. They make plain something that serious practitioners of incentive compensation have long known: Pay for performance is easy to support in principle, but it is much harder to achieve in practice. You cannot simply link rewards to some business outcome, such as stock price, and set the program on automatic pilot, because "performance" often is difficult to define and even more difficult to measure. All too often, companies fail to determine whose performance they mean to pay for: the individual, the group, the business unit, the organization as a whole? To understand this point, just think of the many executives who not long ago were extolled as strategic or operational wizards, who suddenly find their company's stock price in the hole and little or no value left in their stock awards. For them, "pay for performance" had more to do with the performance of the Federal Reserve than with the quality of their own decisions. Whose performance were their companies truly paying for?

In response to these upheavals, compensation committees, shareholder groups, and public policy makers have been looking for ways to restore investor confidence in pay practices for company executives. Some are simply throwing down the gauntlet and blocking pay packages proposed for top executives. Others are trying to find ways to rationalize pay systems and rescue the pay-for-performance concept. In this vein, much attention is being given to the potential to use relative performance evaluation (RPE) as the basis of incentive compensation—that is, to link payouts directly to how well a company performs in comparison to some designated peer group, either a specified set of comparator companies or the market as a whole (or both).

Although few companies incorporate relative performance criteria in their stock option plans in the United States, the number of companies using some form of peer group comparison in their executive incentive programs is quite substantial and has risen in recent years. Data from Mercer Human Resource Consulting's annual survey of top executive compensation in 350 U.S.-based industrial and service companies with revenues over $1 billion show that 40 percent of the 135 companies that awarded long-term incentives in 2002 used peer group comparisons to determine payouts. Of the 347 companies with short-term incentives, about 15 percent incorporated peer comparisons in their payout formulas.[2]

In the United Kingdom the use of relative performance is even more established, due in part to the demands of institutional investor groups that have strongly supported the concept. Reliance on relative performance has become more the

---

[2]These data are compiled by Mercer's Executive Compensation Research Unit.

rule than the exception among leading UK firms. A Mercer survey of the FTSE 100 companies shows that 65 percent of those that have long-term incentive programs now measure performance relative to comparator companies. Interestingly, UK companies appear to be shifting away from comparisons against the broad market index—FTSE 100 performance—and relying more heavily now on industry peers. Tailored peer groups now are seen as a more reliable basis for measuring performance than the FTSE 100 index. RPE is becoming increasingly sophisticated in its application.[3]

RPE is intuitively appealing in that it conforms to ingrained notions of the value of competition, of "winning." As we shall see, it also has a strong basis in the economics and finance literature, where research has highlighted its efficiency both in delivering performance incentives and in effectively managing the risks associated with *externally driven* volatility in performance.

In this chapter we review the economic rationale for RPE and the conditions under which it is likely to prove effective for delivering performance incentives to the top leadership of organizations. We outline a well-tested and practical proprietary statistical tool—what we call Performance Sensitivity Analysis[SM] (PSA)—to determine if and how to use RPE in incentive compensation programs, including stock-based rewards. We focus in particular on the issue of peer group selection, offering a more objective method that addresses some of the difficulties companies face in determining their peer groups. Finally, we draw on our actual work with clients to illustrate several alternative performance measures that embody the RPE principle and consider how they might be used in incentive design. In the process we speak to the challenges of getting RPE right, recognizing that while RPE has many properties that commend its use for compensation purposes, it is not a panacea for the current problems of incentive design.

## 9.2 ECONOMIC RATIONALE FOR RELATIVE PERFORMANCE EVALUATION

### (a) Limitations of the Pay-for-Performance Concept

At first glance, the decimation of stock incentives experienced by many companies in the past few years actually might be construed as a healthy manifestation of "pay for performance." After all, the primary mandate of executives is to create shareholder value. What better way to encourage this result than by directly linking their fortunes to those of shareholders through actual or potential stock ownership? And since shareholders have seen the value of their investments tumble, why shouldn't the rewards to executives fall as well?

[3]These data are drawn from a survey of FTSE 100 companies' annual reports and accounts (as of June 2003) conducted by Mercer UK's Executive Compensation Research Unit.

While intuitively compelling, this argument, in fact, flies in the face of some of the most basic economic tenets about risk and rewards. It fails to acknowledge that two transactions are involved in incentive compensation: (1) pricing and allocating labor to motivate productive behavior, and (2) pricing and allocating the risks associated with volatility in performance, what we call performance risk. Failure to manage the second transaction effectively can seriously undermine the first and drive up the costs of providing performance incentives.

An important distinction must be made. While stock price is, perhaps, the ultimate measure of *company* performance, it is a very imperfect measure of *executive* performance. It does not distinguish between effort and luck, between the results of hard work and business acumen and the effects of the many random market and industry factors that influence stock price performance and over which executives have little or no control. This creates two problems. First, these random market and industry fluctuations are imparted to rewards. These risks thereby are transferred from capital markets that are made to handle them to individuals who bear the burden often at higher personal cost. Risk-averse executives will discount the value of their grants because of these risks, making stock and stock options potentially expensive forms of compensation.[4] Second, the true productive efforts of executives may be masked by the many external factors driving stock price, thereby weakening the incentives associated with stock-based rewards.

These problems could be resolved if there were some way to disentangle the influences of broad market and industry factors (i.e., the "systematic" components of performance) from those reflecting managerial actions (the "unsystematic" or firm-specific parts of performance), and reduce their influence on rewards. This is where relative performance evaluation comes into play.

Consider this example. All hotel chains and resorts were affected by shockwaves that followed the attacks of 9/11. As both business and personal travel plummeted, demand for accommodations and vacation facilities dried up as well. But the financial repercussions were not identical for all companies in the industry. Management clearly made a difference. Indeed, the difference between an individual company's performance and the average performance of comparable companies in the industry—if the sample of companies is large enough—is highly informative about the quality and effectiveness of management decisions. Some of these were decisions about market positioning and operations that were made before the event occurred. These decisions made some companies less vulnerable to random shocks. Others were made during and subsequent to the attack as responses to customer concerns and market pressures. They involved decisions about pricing, level of service, provision of security, staffing, and capital investments. Clearly they mattered.

---

[4]For estimates of the costs associated with executive discounting of stock options, see Brian J. Hall and Kevin J. Murphy, "Stock Options for Undiversified Executives," NBER Working Paper, No. W8502 (November 2000).

But in most instances, if one looked only at absolute measures of performance—the company's own performance alone—the broader macroeffects would obscure the effects of management actions completely. Without the added information conveyed by the performance of others, we could not detect superior executive performance. And, therefore, rewards for superior management could well be indistinguishable from those associated with average or even poor management. That is hardly a recipe for effective incentives, hardly the basis for true pay for performance. Relative performance can help mitigate this problem. Properly used, it can help companies filter out from compensation the purely external risks associated with performance, allocating them to those who can bear them at lowest cost—usually shareholders. And in the process, it can help tighten the link between executive rewards and that part of performance that they most influence through their actions. RPE is implemented by directly incorporating measures of other firms' performance or market performance into a company's reward formulas so that payoffs to executives depend not only on how their company performs but how other companies perform as well.

## (b) Evidence on the Efficacy of Relative Performance Evaluation

Although the theoretical case for RPE is strong, there is very little evidence as to its efficacy in actual practice, at least with respect to executive compensation. Some interesting studies have been conducted at the individual level, looking at how RPE functions in perhaps the purest form of contests, professional sports. Studies of performance on the PGA golf tour and the NASCAR circuit show that the major theoretical predictions about relative performance evaluation do materialize in practice.[5] Specifically, the researchers found that average performance rises directly with the size of the spread in payoffs between winners and losers. Even with all the intrinsic motivation that might be assumed to exist among professional athletes, the data reveal that the higher the financial returns associated with winning the contest—of securing a higher *relative* position—the higher the performance of those competing. Similar results have emerged in laboratory experiments on the effects of relative performance and so-called competitive compensation systems.[6]

We know of no rigorous studies of the impact on performance of the use of RPE in executive compensation. The simple question to address is whether all else being equal, companies that rely on relative performance assessments in determining executive compensation outperform those that link pay to absolute mea-

[5]R. Ehrenberg and M. Bognanno, "The Incentive Effects of Tournaments Revisited: Evidence from the European PGA Tour," *Industrial and Labor Relations Review* 43, Special Issue (February 1990), 74S–88S; B. Becker, and M. Huselid, "The Incentive Effects of Tournament Compensation Systems," *Administrative Science Quarterly* 37 (1992): 336–350.
[6]C. Bull, A. Schotter, and K. Weigelt, "Tournaments and Piece Rates: An Experimental Study," *Journal of Political Economy* 95 (1987): 1–33; H. Nalbantian and A. Schotter, "Productivity Under Group Incentives: An Experimental Study," *American Economic Review* 87, No. 3 (1997): 314–341.

sures, as theory would predict. In the late 1990s we conducted a simple test of this proposition. Using data from the Mercer annual top executive compensation surveys, we examined performance patterns among companies that differed in the degree to which they used relative performance in determining executive pay.

We divided companies into two classes: those for which year-to-year variation in their chief executive officer's (CEO's) pay tracked more closely with changes in stock price we called "absolutists"; those for which CEO pay tracked more closely with stock price movements relative to the Standard & Poor's (S&P) 500 we called "relativists." We considered only companies whose CEO remained unchanged over the period 1993 to 1997. Total pay was defined to include base salary, annual bonus, long-term incentives payouts, value of restricted stock grants as well as paper gains on options and restricted stock granted during the period. Of the 119 companies that survived our data requirements, 52 were found to be relativists. Comparison of total shareholder returns (TSR) between the two groups is shown in Exhibit 9.1.

**Exhibit 9.1**   "Relativists" Hold a Performance Edge over "Absolutists"

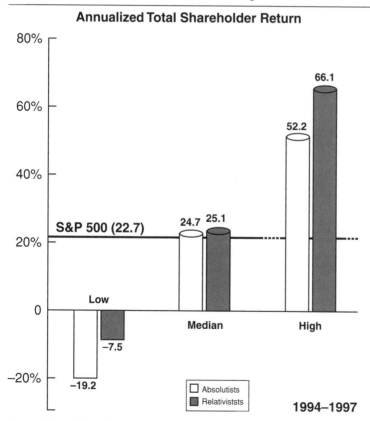

*Source:* Mercer Human Resource Consulting.

While median performance was indistinguishable, the two groups clearly separated at the extremes of high and low performance. It is interesting that among the higher performers, relativists delivered higher returns; and their losses were less among the lower performers as well.

These are at best rough comparisons of performance that do not account for multiple factors beyond RPE that might explain performance differences. Still, the findings add to the weight of evidence that RPE can improve the effectiveness of rewards.

## 9.3   MEASURING AND UNDERSTANDING PERFORMANCE RISK

### (a) Sources of Risk

When should RPE be used? The answer to this question depends not only on the level of risk associated with performance but on its sources. In the discussion that follows, we focus on stock price. But the basic observations are equally pertinent to many performance measures, particularly financial ones.

Variations in stock price arise from three distinct sources:

1.  Fluctuations driven by movements in the overall stock market
2.  Those reflecting changes in the performance of the specific industry or sector(s) in which a company operates
3.  Those specific to the company, reflecting investor perceptions of the value of the company independent of the larger macro considerations

Volatility arising from the first two sources is called "systematic risk."[7] Volatility coming from the last source is called "unsystematic risk." The breakdown of risk among these sources provides important information concerning the likely effectiveness of incentives tied to absolute vs. relative performance measures.

From the standpoint of executives, systematic risks represent the uncontrollable external elements inherent in all performance. Executives make decisions about such things as capital structure, size, and the degree to which their operations are diversified across different industries or sectors. These unquestionably affect a company's susceptibility to both market and industry risk, which varies across companies. But executives have little or no influence on the factors that *drive* market and industry dynamics, such as economic growth, interest rates, fiscal policies, trade balances, or regulatory and technological change. Tying their

---

[7]This risk classification more directly reflects the executive's point of view. But, adopting an investor's perspective, conventional finance theory considers only that part of stock price variation driven by the market as "systematic risk" and the remaining part as "unsystematic risk."

incentive compensation to these factors turns their rewards into a form of lottery where chance dominates actions in determining outcomes.

Unsystematic risk, in contrast, captures most directly how investors perceive and value the individual company, how they assess the strategy and operational performance of the company and its management. It is independent of broader market and industry dynamics. Executives have the most direct control over this element of performance risk through their strategic choices, management practices, and communications with investors. Incentives, therefore, will be strongest when they are pegged to the unsystematic component of performance risk.

The distinctions among the different sources of risk are important for compensation purposes because executives and investors are not identically positioned to deal with them. Let us consider each in turn. The risks originating from general market movements cannot be diversified away *within* the market. Therefore, their costs cannot be avoided. Indeed, this is a part of risk that drives the cost of equity capital. The higher the relative market risk to which a company is exposed, the higher the return investors will expect if they are to keep investing at current stock prices. Neither investors nor executives are in an advantageous position to bear these risks. Both parties will demand compensation to bear them.

The same is not true, however, for the industry-specific and firm-specific components of risk. Investors can reduce or eliminate these risks through diversification. Using equity markets, they can invest their assets in different industry sectors and companies, precisely balancing their portfolio to suit their investment objectives and risk tolerances. Executives cannot diversify similarly their human capital investment across industries and individual companies. For all intents and purposes, they are stuck with a single company. If a significant portion of compensation is stock-based rewards, their exposure to these risks is magnified. Their human capital and net wealth are tied up in company stock or options and therefore fluctuate with the ups and downs of the market, industries, and the unique fortunes of their own companies.

This situation imposes an inescapable cost on executives. Since investors are better positioned to bear these risks, all parties could gain if shareholders insured executives against their consequences. This is certainly true for industry risk. But when it comes to firm-specific risk, there is a complication. Executive actions also create firm-specific volatility in company TSR. If executives were fully insured against firm-specific volatility, they would have little financial incentive to work to maximize value or avert those risks that undermine value. This is the classic insurance problem of moral hazard,[8] and it makes full insurance untenable. Unless there are other measures to readily gauge the effectiveness of executive actions,

---

[8]"Moral hazard" is the observed phenomenon whereby insuring against a particular contingency increases the likelihood that it will actually occur. It is the reason for deductibles in insurance policies. For those insured to maintain adequate diligence, they must assume some of the costs associated with the insurance loss.

**Alignment of Incentives Doesn't Mean Symmetry in Rewards**

The lack of symmetry in the position of executives and investors regarding the different forms of risk suggests that to achieve real alignment of the interests of these stakeholders, in fact, may require *asymmetry* in their rewards. Depending on the risk profile of a company, insisting that executives and shareholders always be in the same boat may be incompatible with essential criteria for efficiency either in the provision of incentives or in the allocation of risk. Failure to take account of these differences can lead to higher compensation costs, higher executive turnover, and/or perhaps, a skewing of strategic decisions as executives allow their own tolerance of risk to influence decisions rather than an unbiased evaluation of potential shareholder returns. Therefore, it is important for companies to measure and understand their risk profiles and use the information in incentive design.

some portion of firm-specific risk needs to remain with executives by way of their compensation. Hence there is little chance for organizations to allocate performance risk efficiently and, at the same time, deliver optimal performance incentives. Some trade-off of efficiency is inevitable. The trade-off is lessened to the extent one can separate the systematic from the unsystematic components of performance. That is a key property of relative performance evaluation.

## (b) Statistical Methodology for Decomposing Risk into Its Three Sources

The preceding discussion shows the importance of understanding the risk characteristics of the performance measures that are used in incentive compensation programs. An objective risk profile of a company's performance can be developed using PSA, which identifies and measures the relative impact on a company's TSR of indices of both industry and general market performance.[9] Specifically, for a given time period (usually three to five years), it statistically decomposes the overall volatility of TSR into three parts:

1.  *General market volatility*, as measured by an index of stock market performance (e.g., S&P 500, Morgan Stanley Capital International World Equity)
2.  *Industry volatility*, as measured by an index of peer group performance
3.  *Company-specific volatility*—that part not statistically explained by industry and market movements

[9]PSA also can be applied to other performance measures so long as there are a sufficient number of observations of their values both for the company and for a relevant peer group.

Three steps are required to decompose TSR volatility into its component parts.

1.  Identify an appropriate peer group to represent the industry or segment of the company of interest.

2.  Create an index representing the performance of these peer companies. Of course, such an index itself will be influenced by market performance. Therefore, to truly isolate industry drivers of performance, we need to remove or statistically filter out (via regression analysis) the market effects on the index. The result is what we call a filtered peer group performance index. For reasons to be discussed, the performance of each peer company is weighed in the index by the degree of comovement in its stock price with that of the subject company.

3.  Estimate statistically, once two independent performance indices—general market and industry performance indices—are at hand, how changes in those indices drive TSR volatility. The part of TSR volatility that is not explained by changes in these indices—the residual—then can be classified as the firm-specific component.

## (c) Outputs of PSA Analysis: A Case Illustration

The results of such an analysis for a high-tech company are shown in Exhibit 9.2.
    The figure shows the risk profile of 15 select high-tech peers for our client—HiTech—in the period from November 1999 to May 2003. Risk is measured as the

**Exhibit 9.2**    Risk Profile of High-Technology Companies Varies Substantially

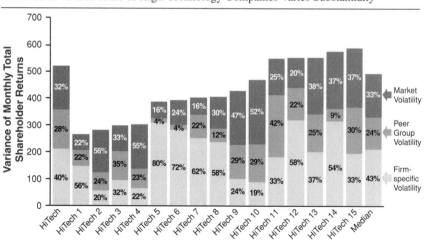

Mercer Human Resource Consulting, © 2003.

variance of monthly TSR and is represented on the vertical axis. Market performance is represented by changes in the S&P 500 index. Industry performance is captured by changes in a customized index of peer group TSR. This peer group was selected based on the empirical patterns of comovement among stock prices, a method we will explain shortly.

Aside from differences in overall volatility, the breakdown of risk varies considerably across companies. Some companies, such as HiTechs 2, 3, 4, 10, and 11, are extremely susceptible to fluctuations in market and industry performance, whereas others, such as HiTechs 5 and 6, are not. Some companies, such as HiTechs 10 and 11, share high levels of systematic risk, but the breakdown of that risk between market and industry influences differs significantly. For HiTech 10, over 50 percent of volatility is explained by changes in market performance. For HiTech 11, industry performance dominates. Market sensitivity is about half that of HiTech 10.

The observed differences in the risk characteristics of the technology companies are important because they bear directly on the potential impact and cost of transferring risk from investors to executives via stock-based rewards. As noted, risk imposes costs to the extent that it cannot be diversified. In this respect, industry risk is the great divide between investors and executives, since the latter are limited in their ability to reduce the costs of industry risk through diversification or, unlike firm-specific risk, to reduce the influence of industry risk through their actions. Industry risk will impose a differential cost on executives that ultimately will have to be compensated—often in the form of larger stock grants. Therefore, firms with high levels of industry risk—such as HiTech 11—are the strongest candidates to benefit from some form of relative performance evaluation. Companies with high levels of market risk also might benefit from RPE strictly for incentive reasons. Although it might have little bearing on the costs of risk, RPE would reinforce the contingent relationship between actions and rewards.

### (d) How to Use PSA to Determine if an RPE-Based System Is Warranted

The preceding discussion illustrates the practical value of PSA as a guide to deal with the risks embedded in any performance measures used in incentive design. By measuring the sources of risk, PSA provides an objective basis to determine whether an RPE-based system is worth considering. Exhibit 9.3 outlines the decision rules companies can use in determining whether to introduce RPE-based incentives. Based on the PSA results, companies can be grouped into two categories:

1. Those whose TSR volatility is dominated by systematic risk independent of its peers (the vertical axis)
2. Those whose TSR displays high levels of systematic risk in comparison to that of peers, but not in absolute terms (the horizontal axis)

**Exhibit 9.3**   When Is RPE Most Likely to Work?

| | |
|---|---|
| Relative performance evaluation is preferable. | Relative performance evaluation is preferable. |
| Standard absolute performance evaluation is preferable. | Other considerations are critical in determining the use of relative performance evaluation. |

*(y-axis label: Systematic Risk on an Absolute Basis)*

**Systematic Risk on a Relative Basis**

*Source:* Mercer Human Resource Consulting.

Our client HiTech, for example, would fall into the upper right-hand box, even though its risk profile is about the median of its peers. Most (60 percent) of its TSR volatility is associated with changes in industry and general market performance combined. Further, its susceptibility to systematic risk is higher than its peers, albeit modestly. The high levels of systematic risk—in particular, variations driven by industry performance—raise a red flag about the likely effectiveness of standard stock-based awards. An RPE system where rewards are tied to how the firm performs relative to its peer group or general market performance could well be more effective. The same can be said for HiTechs 2, 4, 9, 10, and 11, which have high systematic risk both in absolute and in relative terms.

For those peers with high levels of firm-specific variation, such as HiTech 5 and 6, more conventional stock-based rewards should work quite well. Because the effects of systematic market and industry volatility are limited, their executives would have a clearer line of sight between their actions and rewards. The advantage of using RPE would be slim, if any.

Occasionally there may be situations where a company's TSR does not show high levels of systematic risk in absolute terms, but is nonetheless more susceptible than the TSRs of its peers. In these situations, one must consider other factors such as run rate, overhang, competition for talent, and the like in determining whether to use RPE.

## 9.4   KEY QUESTIONS FOR IMPLEMENTING RELATIVE PERFORMANCE EVALUATION

Once a company decides to introduce RPE into its incentive program, it must determine how to measure relative performance and then what formula to use to link this measure to rewards. Assessing relative performance is a more complex exercise than it might appear. Several key questions need to be addressed:

- Against whom should performance be compared—to the industry alone? to the general market, or both?
- If industry comparisons are relevant, which firms should be included, those that operate in any segment in which the company operates significantly or simply its dominant line of business?
- Beyond line of business, what other criteria (e.g., size, financial structure, workforce profile, etc.) should be used in defining the peer group?
- On what basis should performance relative to peers be measured—by some form of ranking against industry peers, or against some weighted average of industry performance?
- If the latter approach is taken, should a customized index be developed, or is a standard published industry index sufficient?
- If a customized index is required, how should it be constructed? For example, how should one weigh the performance of companies that comprise the peer group—equally? by market capitalization? by some other means?

Developing an empirical understanding of the risk characteristics of a company in comparison to its peers—as is possible through a PSA analysis—helps answer many of these questions.

## 9.5  CONSTRUCTING THE PEER GROUP

### (a) What Is a Peer Group?

The first and perhaps most important challenge in implementing RPE is determining who the comparator group should be. In some instances, where systematic variations in performance are driven predominantly by market movements, simple comparisons against a market index may be sufficient. But if industry factors dominate, then developing an appropriate set of peer companies is critical.

Needless to say, this is not always a simple exercise. Large conglomerate organizations with multiple business lines increasingly are hard-pressed to specify who belongs in their peer group. Should the peer group be dominated by companies in that line of business in which it has the largest revenues, or should some composite group covering other business segments also be used? Should the group be comprised primarily of other conglomerate companies of similar size and scope of operations? These are challenging questions.

Also, certain sectors have undergone substantial consolidation in recent years, such that only a few companies remain against which to be compared. The oil industry offers a classic example of this problem. Selecting a peer group among the few remaining global oil companies would strain the statistical validity of measures of the industry impact. The small number of companies also would mean that the assessment of relative performance would be highly susceptible to chance events or even minor perturbations among a single one of these peer companies. This susceptibility would introduce another form of randomness or risk to incentive compensation, creating just the sort of problems that relative performance is supposed to remedy. The effectiveness and stability of the incentive program would be compromised again. Our solution, pointed to in our discussion of PSA, is to follow the market, tapping into the mass of information captured in stock price movements to determine how investors actually group companies in making their investment decisions. Observed empirical regularities open a window on how perceptions of "industry" dynamics are evolving.

But this discussion begs a larger question: What constitutes a "peer group" anyway? In our view, there are at least three types of peer groups relevant to reward decisions:[10]

### (i) Product/Service Market Peers

These are the companies against which the company competes for customers. They are rivals in the traditional sense of the word. They have a direct impact on the company's growth and profitability and directly affect such measures of customer value as customer satisfaction, customer retention, and, most significantly, market share.

### (ii) Labor Market Peers

These are the employers against which the company competes for labor. They may not be in the same industry sector, but they employ similar types of people. They need similar skills, competencies, and types of experience or may be similarly positioned in terms of their employment brand.

### (iii) Capital Market Peers

These are the companies against which the company most competes for capital. Although in some sense every company is such a competitor, considerations of risk significantly narrow the relevant group of capital market rivals. Since investors weigh potential returns against the risks they entail, collectively they will group the company with others that have a similar risk profile or costs of capital. Competitive markets will force stock price adjustments to equilibrate returns on a risk-adjusted basis.

All three types of peer groups are relevant, depending on the issue of concern. If the focus is on overall pay levels, labor market peers may be the most relevant,

---

[10]Certainly other types of peer groups can be used as well. For instance, some companies like to compare themselves directly to recognized high-performance companies. Others might select strictly by size. We focus on the most generic categories of comparison because we believe these distinctions often are lost in designing incentive compensation programs, to the detriment of shareholders and executives alike.

since competitiveness of pay is essential to attracting and retaining the requisite talent. If short-term incentives are at issue, more traditional product/service market rivals may be most pertinent, since sustained growth or advantage in revenue and/or profitability are typically antecedents of market value. But if long-term incentives are the concern, in particular stock-based programs, nothing is more relevant than capital market dynamics. Sharing value should be tied to creating value. Creating value means generating returns that exceed the cost of capital. The latter, ultimately, is a reflection of the risk characteristics of a company, and investors will make comparisons based on an assessment of the relevant risks. To sustain or grow value, it would seem, therefore, that incentives must be aligned with investor perspectives. This fact suggests that capital market peers should dominate peer group determination when long-term incentives are at stake.[11]

## (b) Statistical Methodology for Constructing a Peer Group

PSA provides an objective method to screen companies for inclusion in the comparator group based on the empirical pattern of comovements in stock price or TSR. This approach draws on the fact that stock prices of companies exposed to common external risks tend to move more in concert over time than those with less common risk exposures. The observed stock price changes result from the investment decisions of millions of investors based on their expectations about how different factors will affect the company's future performance. For example, changes in interest rate policies likely will change investor expectations about the attractiveness of equity as an investment alternative. The ensuing investment decisions will have an influence on the stock prices of all companies in the market. The extent to which any company's stock price reacts depends on its susceptibility to market risk.

Similarly, developments specific to an industry or sector will affect investor expectations about the future performance of the industry. The latter will result in portfolio reallocations that increase investments in companies that make up the industry if developments create positive expectations or take money out of such companies if the consensus is more negative. This portfolio effect will cause stock prices of some companies to move more in concert than those that are less affected by the common "industry" factor. Therefore, after accounting for the effects of broader market movements, the remaining observed comovement among company stock prices or TSR—what we call the "partial" or industry correlation—reflects investors' judgments about comparability of those specific companies. Those whose stock prices move more closely together can be regarded as stronger industry peers than those whose stock price movements are more independent.

[11]We recognize the difficulties and costs of using multiple peer groups and do not mean to suggest that companies ought to adopt that approach. We simply wish to emphasize the importance of weighing the different considerations identified and making choices based on the most compelling business need.

Unlike the first two factors that tend to move stock prices of the relevant companies in concert, firm-specific factors tend to move their stock prices independently. Within the same industry, different companies generate different investor expectations. Most differences are due to differences in operating performance and assessments of future earnings prospects.

The PSA-based approach empirically estimates and isolates the comovements of company stock prices that are caused by industry-related factors. The identification of potential peer companies for a specific company involves four steps. (See Exhibit 9.4.)

1.   Identify a pool of firms from which potential peers can be selected. Most often the subject company will have a list of competitors based on either product or labor market rivalry or what securities analysts are tracking. This list is usually a good starting point. As an independent validation, additional candidate firms also can be screened based on two- to four-digit Standard Industry Classification (SIC) codes or some other standardized industry groups in which the subject company operates. The screening is based on all the industry segments in which the company operates. We typically invoke additional criteria, such as revenue or market capitalization, to ensure that the selected peer group is credible to executives and shareholders. Obviously, the time period covered for the analysis of stock price movements must be selected to strike a balance between capturing the most current market dynamics and

**Exhibit 9.4**   Building a Peer Group: A PSA-Based Process

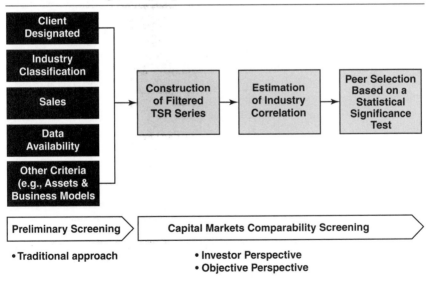

© Mercer Human Resource Consulting, 2003.

ensuring statistical robustness (stability) of estimated results. Typically we rely on three to five years of stock price performance, tracked monthly.[12]

2.  Construct a "filtered" time series of TSR for the subject company and each candidate firm within the pool to account for the effects of stock price of the broader market movements. Most often we use either the S&P 500 or the Russell 2000 indices to capture the common effects of market movements on the comovements of stock prices. The filtered time series reflects the two remaining influences: industry and firm-specific.

3.  Measure the correlations between the filtered TSR time series of the subject company and the filtered TSR time series of each candidate firm. The resulting measure is the partial or "industry" correlation; it can be used as the industry classification of the company of interest. The size of correlation indicates how closely the subject company's stock price movement is associated with that of each of the different peer candidates. It measures the degree to which the TSR of each of the other companies moves in concert with that of the subject company, independent of general market factors. It also reflects investors' assessments of the comparability of companies under review.

4.  Formally test whether the observed comovement measured by the industry correlation is meaningful or simply due to random errors. The industry correlation is an estimate based on historical comovements of any two TSR data series. Because the estimate is subject to statistical error, it is important to ensure that the observed relationship is not pure coincidence. If the likelihood of coincidence is low, we are confident that the observed relationship captures the effects of industry fluctuations. Companies that pass this test at the conventional levels of statistical significance are selected as potential PSA peers for the subject company.

## (c) Case Illustration

We have used this PSA-based methodology to develop peer groups (for incentive compensation purposes) for numerous organizations across many industry sectors. As an illustration of the outcomes of this process, we will revisit the case of our client company HiTech. Exhibit 9.5 shows a list of 18 PSA-selected peer companies for HiTech based on monthly stock price data over the period from November 1999 to May 2003. In addition to the company identified, the table lists the

---

[12]Longer time periods provide more observations on stock price movements that should enhance the quality of statistical estimates. However, the effects of important structural changes in industry dynamics or how individual companies respond to industry and market conditions may be lost if prior history has too much weight in the analysis. The three- to five-year period allows us to examine particular windows of time within that interval to test the stability of the relationships uncovered. Such testing is a critical part of the PSA-based methodology.

**Exhibit 9.5** Comovement of Stock Prices Reveals How Investors Group Companies

| Company Name | SIC Code | SIC Description | Industry Correlation | Likelihood of Coincidence | Total Correlation |
|---|---|---|---|---|---|
| HiTech 10 | 3674 | Semiconductor & Related Device | 0.54 | 0.00 | 0.72 |
| HiTech 7 | 3577 | Computer Peripheral Equipment, NEC. | 0.49 | 0.00 | 0.60 |
| HiTech 9 | 3827 | Optical Instruments & Lenses | 0.49 | 0.00 | 0.68 |
| HiTech 13 | 3825 | Electronic Measurement & Test Instruments | 0.48 | 0.00 | 0.66 |
| HiTech 16 | 3674 | Semiconductor, Related Device | 0.43 | 0.01 | 0.65 |
| HiTech 17 | 3674 | Semiconductor, Related Device | 0.43 | 0.01 | 0.62 |
| HiTech 3 | 3674 | Semiconductor, Related Device | 0.42 | 0.01 | 0.60 |
| HiTech 18 | 3661 | Telephone & Telegraph Apparatus | 0.40 | 0.01 | 0.58 |
| HiTech 15 | 3674 | Semiconductor, Related Device | 0.39 | 0.01 | 0.60 |
| HiTech 12 | 3577 | Computer Peripheral Equipment, NEC. | 0.36 | 0.02 | 0.52 |
| HiTech 5 | 3663 | Radio, TV Broadcast & Communications Equipment | 0.36 | 0.02 | 0.50 |
| HiTech 1 | 3825 | Electronic Measurement & Test Instruments | 0.36 | 0.02 | 0.53 |
| HiTech 8 | 3661 | Telephone & Telegraph Apparatus | 0.36 | 0.02 | 0.55 |
| HiTech 11 | 3674 | Semiconductor, Related Device | 0.36 | 0.02 | 0.54 |
| HiTech 2 | 3674 | Semiconductor, Related Device | 0.33 | 0.03 | 0.60 |
| HiTech 2 | 3674 | Semiconductor, Related Device | 0.33 | 0.03 | 0.60 |
| HiTech 6 | 7370 | Computer Programming & Data Process | 0.31 | 0.05 | 0.50 |
| HiTech 14 | 3572 | Computer Storage Devices | 0.31 | 0.05 | 0.55 |

*Source:* Mercer Human Resource Consulting.

four-digit SIC industry code and associated industry description, industry correlation, likelihood of coincidence, and overall (or total) correlation.

The total correlation measures the degree of comovement of each company's monthly TSR with HiTech's, including the effects of general market movement. This value usually ranges from 0 to 1. For example, one interpretation of the value of 0.72 for the correlation between HiTech and HiTech 10 is that the two stock prices move together 7 out of 10 times. Those movements in the same direction can be the results of investment decisions reflecting both market and industry conditions. After we pull out, statistically, the effects of general market movements, we see that the remaining correlation drops to 0.54. This implies that out of the 7 comovements, about 5 are caused by industry-specific factors. In other words, the market factors account for only 25 percent of the total comovement of the stock prices. As can be seen, the differences between total correlation and industry correlation vary widely across 18 PSA-selected companies. Note, too, that the partial correlations of all 18 companies are statistically significant at or below the 5 percent level.[13]

How do we know that the PSA-selected peer group is better than one selected on a different basis? Since the purpose of this exercise is to distinguish systematic from unsystematic sources of variation in stock performance, it makes sense to see

[13]The analysis has been conducted on a total of 102 companies spanning nine four-digit industries. Only 18 survived the hypothesis test that no comovement exists between the stock prices of the subject company and the other individual companies.

how much more industry-driven variation in stock performance can be captured by the PSA-selected peer group. The more industry-specific variation that can be explained, the more information is being extracted from stock price movements about common risks. Let us take the case of HiTech once again. The company provided us an initial list of 30 competitors or industry "peers." Using an industry performance index based on the 30 client-designated companies, the PSA analysis showed that only 11 percent of HiTech's total TSR volatility is attributable to fluctuations in this peer performance index. On the other hand, using the 18 company PSA-selected peer groups, the industry component accounts for 28 percent of the TSR variation, a more than 150 percent jump in explanatory power. (See Exhibit 9.6.) The significant improvement in capturing industry fluctuations shows that the PSA-selected peer group helps to better differentiate the effects on stock performance of common external factors from those factors specific to the firm.

One advantage of this selection process is that it makes use of hard, factual evidence and therefore can minimize biases arising from management's subjective decisions about the comparator group to use in incentive pay. If executives know that their pay depends on how their companies stack up against peers, they may have incentives to choose relatively poor performing companies as the comparator group. Reliance on a formal process of peer group selection based on historical patterns of interdependence can enhance investors' confidence in management compensation structure and increase the credibility of management's assessment of the company's relative performance.

**Exhibit 9.6**   The PSA-Determined Peer Group Better Explains HiTech's Volatility than the Company Peer Group

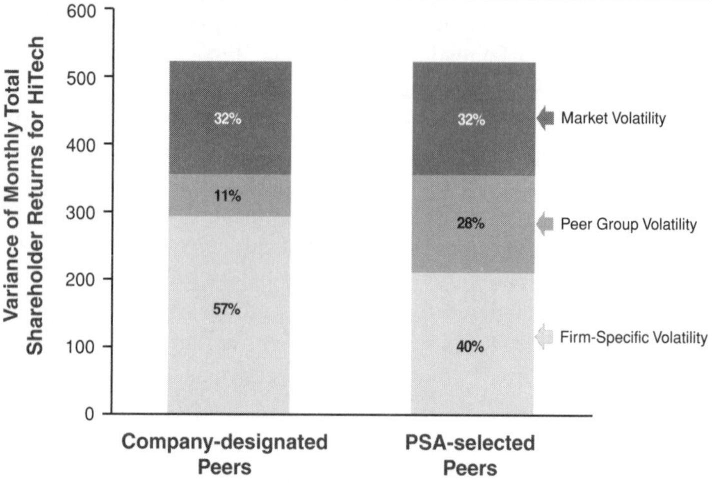

*Source:* Mercer Human Resource Consulting.

## (d) Management Perceptions vs. Market Realities

The PSA methodology tracks the pattern of investment decisions made with respect to comparable companies, as revealed in stock price movements. Sometimes the results of such an analysis are at odds with how management perceives the company and the sector(s) in which it operates.

For example, we recently undertook a peer group selection assignment for a large national retail organization. Two peer groups were assessed. The first, provided by the client, included only large retail organizations; the second, developed using the PSA methodology, included some additional medium-size regional retail organizations. Compared to the first peer group, the performance of the second group was able to explain far more of the fluctuations in the company's TSR, an increase to 42 percent from 29 percent. The significant improvement suggests that investors viewed the smaller retail organizations as comparable companies to our client. In the very least, the performance of these companies reflected some of the same external market dynamics that were affecting our client's performance. The underlying message, in effect, was that those smaller retailers as a group form a prospective competitive challenge to the industry position of this company, something of which our client's management had been aware but had not viewed as significant.

A similar case involves one of the large Canadian banks (CanBank). We were commissioned to select an appropriate peer group for use in the company's executive incentive program. The leadership was concerned that the small group of Canadian banks was not a sufficient basis for judging relative performance. The peer group had to be expanded. The prevailing view was that this particular bank was most comparable to U.S. regional banks, since there were similarities in business strategy.

We evaluated the full complement of Canadian banks and U.S. money-center and regional banks, calculating the comovements of CanBank's and the other banks' TSRs over the period from 1994 to 1998. As expected, all the other Canadian banks showed a significant industry correlation with CanBank's TSR. On the other hand, among the U.S. firms, only the money-center banks' TSRs displayed significant comovement with CanBank's. None of the U.S. regional banks passed the test. In fact, this really should not have been surprising. An examination of CanBank's balance sheet asset structure revealed that it was very much like that of U.S. money-center banks. It held significant foreign assets. In contrast, few foreign assets showed up in the balance sheets of U.S. regional banks. This distinction had special relevance at the time.

The global financial crisis in 1997 had had a significant impact on the performance of banks with high global exposure. Because of similarity in the asset holdings of CanBank and U.S. money-center banks, these global events had similar effects on their stock prices, which showed up in significant comovement among them. U.S. regional banks suffered much less during the global financial crisis because their asset structure had minimum global exposure. Thus the hard facts of the marketplace simply could not sustain the views of CanBank's management.

As these examples illustrate, changes in stock prices contain information about investors' expectations concerning both industry dynamics and company performance and growth potential. Therefore, the analysis results speak to the strategic position of a company and the success (or failure) of management efforts to influence investor perceptions of what the company is and what it is becoming. This kind of unvarnished feedback from the marketplace is particularly useful to companies that are trying to transform themselves through acquisitions or changes in product/service mix, or simply changing their brand image. The results of this analysis can reveal whether investors are responding to management initiatives or whether legacy dominates.

Of course, investors may be wrong in their judgments. Sometimes brand images and history are hard to shed. But as these perceptions nonetheless drive movements in stock price, they are important for management to understand and influence. Incentive compensation needs to recognize management's success (or failure) in its "influencing" role. That is another reason why a capital market perspective has an important role to play in peer group determination.

## 9.6   MEASURING RELATIVE PERFORMANCE— RISK-ADJUSTED MEASURES

### (a) The Basics

Once a peer group is established, there are a variety of ways to measure relative performance. The simplest is rank order. We helped design a long-term incentive (LTI) plan for a global natural resources company based on this approach. The plan's payout is linked to the company's standing relative to a group of 15 natural resources peer companies in terms of TSR over a three-year performance period. Its LTI payout is 100 percent, 66 percent, 33 percent, or 0 percent of base salary if its TSR is in the top quartile, above the median, and in the third quartile, respectively. A key advantage of this approach is simply familiarity. The approach is very popular among compensation professionals as a means to benchmark compensation levels and pay-performance relationships.

Alternatively, the comparisons can be made against a peer group performance index, with the awards made if, and only if, the company's performance surpasses the index. The comparison can be made simply in terms of the percentile standing against the index or can factor in the actual spread between the subject company's performance and that of the index.

This latter approach is more complex in that it requires the construction of a peer group performance index. A central issue here is how much to weigh the performance of individual companies in calculating the performance index. There are several different possibilities. One could weigh all companies equally. A more common approach is to use market capitalization or value weighting. For example, the S&P 500 index is a weighted average of the performance of the 500 largest companies publicly traded in the U.S. stock exchange markets, where the weights reflect the relative market value of each firm. This is also the procedure mandated by the Securities and Exchange Commission for reporting performance against peers where customized indexes are used.

An alternative approach commonly used in a PSA analysis relies on what we call "correlational weighting." Consistent with the underlying peer group selection method, it uses the relative correlations of the subject company's TSR with its peers' TSR as weights for each peer company in the index.[14] Peer companies of high correlation with the subject company receive more weight in the index than peer companies whose TSR moves more independently (lower correlation). This procedure is statistically designed to maximize the ability to draw inferences about the strength of common external factors affecting firms similarly situated in the market. Unlike the value-weighted average index where there is a bias toward higher-performing peer companies, the performance of the correlation-weighted peer index is influenced heavily by the performance of peers most like the subject company from a capital market perspective, reflecting the idea that the common risks are more likely being picked up by the high-correlation peers than by those with low correlation. The more we can explain of systematic movements in a company's TSR, the better the estimates of firm-specific performance.

From the RPE perspective, the choice of the appropriate weighting procedures for constructing a peer group index depends on how much more information regarding the common risk factors the alternative indexes can capture. As discussed in the section on the validation of PSA-selected peer groups, the peer index that, when used in the PSA estimation, results in the best statistical fit (highest $R$-squared statistic from linear regression) to the performance data is generally the best candidate.

A number of U.S. companies have introduced either rank-order RPE or comparisons against a performance index in their executive long-term incentive plans. These include Bristol Myers Squibb, ChevronTexaco, Ford Motor Company, General Motors, Motorola, Pfizer, and Wyeth, just to name a few.[15] These companies have implemented incentive plans that link LTI payouts to TSR, earnings per share, or other financial performance measures assessed relative to peers.

[14]This approach to weighting companies is inspired by R. Antle and A. Smith, "An Empirical Evaluation of the Relative Performance Evaluation of Corporate Executives," *Journal of Accounting Research* 24 (1986): 1–39.

[15]This information is drawn from a review of these companies' most recent proxy statements.

## (b) Alternative Measures of Relative Performance

More sophisticated forms of RPE involve comparing a company's actual TSR to some measure of "expected" TSR, based on market and industry conditions. In effect, such measures make adjustments in actual TSR performance to reflect the level and sources of risk associated with the company's shareholder return.

The risk classification methodology discussed earlier provides a reasonable basis to develop such alternative performance measures. From the investor's point of view, economic value is created when stock price returns exceed the cost of capital. From the executive's point of view, value is generated when actual returns exceed those expected after adjusting for industry and market performance (i.e., when company-specific returns are positive). This difference has implications for how one measures and motivates executive performance.

If investors want to motivate executives to deliver economic value, then a tighter link between executive rewards and company-specific performance should be established. Using the PSA methodology, this company-specific performance can be estimated by directly comparing a company's actual TSR for any given period to an estimate of the TSR that would be expected based on industry or market conditions, or both, during the same period. Two categories of measures are required to develop this estimate:

1. Indices of market and industry performance
2. Estimates of a company's sensitivity or responsiveness to these indices—their market and industry betas—derived either from public sources or from PSA estimation using the customized peer group

Once the betas are known, it is not difficult to estimate where the company's TSR should be, given how the market and the industry actually have performed. This information provides a benchmark for comparison that properly accounts for risks over which management has little control.

But which performance benchmark is appropriate? This question can be addressed by looking the risk profiles of the subject company derived from the PSA analysis. If the market factors dominate the systematic component of TSR volatility, the benchmark should be established against market conditions alone. If the systematic variation in TSR is dominated by industry fluctuations, the performance benchmark should be established based on industry performance. Otherwise, the benchmark should be chosen as the combination of both market and industry performance.

Adjusting for risk can be accomplished in several ways. Next we review a few of the more sophisticated measures of relative performance that can be used to better distinguish company vs. managerial performance.

***(i) Differential Shareholder Return*** We used this approach as part of an executive compensation assignment for the natural resources company mentioned earlier. The company (NatCo) was considerably more diversified than most of its peers. By virtue of that fact alone, its performance tended to be in the second quartile of its industry. (There are always pure plays in some sector of the industry that will be doing better than their more diversified counterparts.) Does this mean that the company' management should forever be judged as second-quartile performers? Obviously not.

Although diversification may reduce performance compared to some peers, it also changes the level and composition of risks faced by the company's shareholders. The real issue, then, is how these factors balance out. The net value to shareholders can be measured using PSA-based estimates of what we call the company's "differential shareholder return" (DSR). DSR is defined as actual TSR in a given period minus the expected TSR given market and industry conditions during that same period. The latter is measured as the sum of market beta times TSR on the market performance index and industry beta times TSR on the industry performance index, or

$$\beta_m P_m + \beta_I P_I$$

Exhibit 9.7 shows the DSR measure for NatCo and other companies in its peer group.

**Exhibit 9.7** Distribution of DSR Varies Considerably in the Same Industry

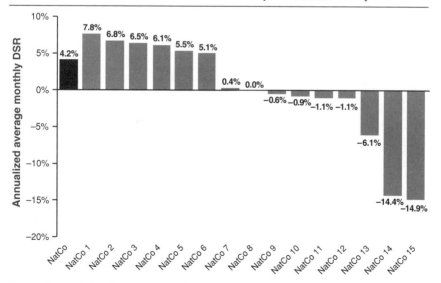

*Source:* Mercer Human Resource Consulting.

The vertical axis measures the annualized monthly DSR. Note that DSR is positive for NatCo. The company generated more returns than what would be expected, given how the market and industry performed and the company's historical sensitivity to both indices. In other words, the company-specific component of return is positive. The company is still in the second quartile of performance using this measure, which means the reduction in risk from diversification was not sufficient to offset the lower absolute return it generated compared to some of its peers. Still, in using this measure, executives would have strong incentives to make strategic decisions and manage operations in a way that optimizes value. Indeed, when the LTI plan payouts are linked to this measure of performance, a tighter link between executive rewards and actual management performance is established.[16]

*(ii) Return to Risk*    Another, simpler but related measure of relative performance that can be used to assess executive performance is the return-to-risk ratio (RTRR). This measure of "risk-adjusted" TSR indicates how much return a stock generates in a given period for one unit of externally driven volatility. It is calculated by dividing the company's average TSR by that part of TSR volatility jointly driven by market and industry fluctuations. By gauging TSR relative to its associated systematic risk, the measure, in effect, adjusts for risk and offers the prospect of apples-to-apples comparisons of performance against equivalent peers.

We recently used this approach to examine the performance of FTSE 100 companies over the period from 1999 to 2001. Our goal was to see if adjusting for risk materially changes the performance ranking of executives compared to those based on TSR alone. Exhibit 9.8 shows some of our findings. Take ARM Holdings as an example. Its stock generated an annualized TSR of 90.3 percent over the period from 1999 to 2001, while its TSR volatility (standard deviation) was 85.8 percent. Of that volatility, 73.7 percentage points were accounted for by fluctuations in the general market and industry indices. Thus, its return-to-risk ratio was 1.2 (90.3/73.3). A value of 1.2 indicates that for 1 percentage point of volatility, ARM Holdings generates 1.2 percentage point returns. In general, the higher the ratio, the better the executive performance.

---

[16]A variant of DSR is what we call incremental shareholder return (ISR), which captures changes in DSR over time. This measure is most pertinent in turnaround situations where it would be unrealistic to expect management to achieve positive DSR within the relevant time period. In distressed companies, the primary need is first to stem the hemorrhaging of value so that investor confidence can be restored. Only after this is accomplished is there any hope of returning to a state of value creation. Rather than throw in the towel on incentives and risk losing the top executive talent needed to achieve the turnaround, distressed companies can use ISR in their incentive programs to focus executive attention on this goal. Incentive payouts, therefore, would be keyed to improvements in DSR, that is, to reductions in the loss of value. This is more realistic than waiting for stock price to recover sufficiently for underwater options to become viable once again.

**Exhibit 9.8**  Performance Rankings of Top FTSE 100 Companies Change Once the Riskiness of Their Returns Is Taken into Account

| Company | Sector | TSR | Ranking | RTRR | Ranking | Volatility | Ranking | Systematic Risk | Ranking |
|---|---|---|---|---|---|---|---|---|---|
| Arm Holdings | Information Technology Hardware | 90.3% | 1 | 1.2 | 8 | 85.8% | 87 | 73.7% | 88 |
| Man Group | Specialty & Other Finance | 57.2% | 2 | 10.9 | 1 | 30.4% | 27 | 5.3% | 1 |
| Smith & Nephew | Health | 39.2% | 3 | 3.7 | 3 | 33.7% | 41 | 10.6% | 4 |
| Capita Group | Support Services | 36.5% | 4 | 1.4 | 7 | 46.1% | 74 | 26.8% | 52 |
| Celitech Group | Pharmaceuticals | 33.9% | 5 | 1.5 | 5 | 56.2% | 83 | 22.3% | 30 |
| Amvescap | Specialty & Other Finance | 32.7% | 6 | 0.7 | 16 | 50.9% | 81 | 46.8% | 84 |
| Anglo American | Mining | 32.6% | 7 | 0.9 | 13 | 41.2% | 64 | 38.0% | 75 |
| Shire Pharmaceuticals | Pharmaceuticals | 32.2% | 8 | 4.2 | 2 | 42.5% | 67 | 7.7% | 2 |
| Royal Bank of Scotland | Banks | 31.4% | 9 | 1.5 | 6 | 29.6% | 24 | 21.6% | 27 |
| Next | Retailers, General | 29.4% | 10 | 1.1 | 9 | 38.7% | 56 | 25.9% | 46 |

*Source*: Mercer Human Resource Consulting.

The adjustment of TSR for systematic risk produces changes in the performance rankings of these companies. AMVESCAP and Anglo American are in the top 10 of TSR performance but drop from that grouping when using RTRR. Their ranking change reflects the higher level of systematic risk they experience (i.e., for a given level of systematic risk, they generated less shareholder return than those in the top 10 based on RTRR).

## 9.7   MECHANISMS FOR INTRODUCING RPE IN STOCK-BASED INCENTIVES

So much of long-term incentives are delivered through stock-based rewards that it behooves us to consider how the principle of RPE might be applied in this context. After all, if pay for performance in executive compensation is effectuated by granting ownership rights or potential claims to ownership, it might seem on the surface that relative performance is a nonstarter for the bulk of incentive compensation. Owning stock necessarily means being subject to the vicissitudes of stock price fluctuations. Is there any way around this?

To some extent there is. With respect to stock options, one compelling method for implementing RPE is to index the strike price to changes in market and/or peer group performance. Under so-called performance indexing,[17] the exercise price of the option would periodically adjust automatically to changes in the performance of the selected index. To the extent that a rise in a company's stock price can be attributed reasonably to a rise in the S&P 500 or to industry developments, the strike price would rise as well to avoid windfall gains. Only that part of the increase that is beyond expectations would convey value to the affected executives. In a down market, similar adjustments would be made to insure that options do not automatically go underwater, simply by virtue of systematic market forces. This would lend stability to option programs and effectively diminish the inefficient and costly lottery aspect of traditional stock options.

It is easy to see how PSA can support this kind of price adjustment mechanism. The performance indices and associated betas estimated through PSA provide the essential components of a price adjustment mechanism. They allow us to estimate both systematic and unsystematic performance, to capture in hard quantitative terms a measure of investor expectations. In this way, the option exercise price can be pegged to the unsystematic component of TSR, filtering out, to the extent desired, those movements that are explained by changes in the business environment. Companies could determine as a matter of policy how much system-

---

[17]For a more detailed exposition of performance indexing, see Haig R. Nalbantian, "Performance Indexing in Stock Options and Other Incentive Compensation Programs," *Compensation and Benefits Review* (September/October 1993): vol. 25, 25–40.

atic risk they wish top executives to bear and reflect that proportion in the formulas by which they adjust exercise price.

There has been much talk about indexed options for a while now, but few companies actually have implemented them.[18] This is largely due to accounting considerations that have made it costly for companies to adopt them (see Chapters 7 and 8). Under Accounting Principles Board Opinion No. 25, an option whose exercise price can change over time is subject to unpredictable and uncontrollable variable accounting, something companies have wanted to steer clear of. This is changing, as the Financial Accounting Standards Board is moving to require fair value expensing of options at the time of award. The bias against indexed options could disappear. In that event, this incentive vehicle could become far more prevalent and do a lot to stem the real cost of option programs, including the pressures for dilution.

There are some additional plan designs that can incorporate relative performance measures. Companies could link the size of option grants or the vesting of outstanding options to some measure of relative performance, say relative TSR. So, for example, a program could be devised with the provision that only if certain relative performance thresholds are achieved would grants be made, with larger grants provided as the distance from threshold grows. In this way, options grants or options vesting are effectively sharing true value created, rather than merely redistributing existing shareholder wealth. The benefits in terms of dilution should be clear.

Finally, relative performance could also be used as the basis of cash incentives. RPE-based cash incentives could be introduced in place of stock options. Or, they could be used in tandem with stock-based programs as a form of insurance to offset partially the risk exposure inherent in executive and all employee stock ownership.

## 9.8 CONCLUSION

Pay for performance is under pressure mostly because of problems experienced with stock-based programs. The view that stock and stock options in particular are an easy, virtually costless way to deliver incentives to executives has given way to a recognition of the high costs that simplistic pay for performance programs often impose on shareholders. These costs are manifest in such things as dilution, unwanted turnover, manipulation of accounting data, skewed strategic decisions, and significant instability in incentive compensation programs.

---

[18]As of this writing, only a few companies, such as Level 3 Communications and RCN Corp., implement indexed option plans for their executives. In their plans, executives are rewarded only if the firm's stock performance exceeds that of the market represented by the S&P 500 index.

No one can doubt any longer that considerations of risk need to be front and center in the design of incentive compensation programs. Relative performance evaluation—in one form or another—offers a practical way to deal with such problems. Its benefits are compelling: RPE improves a company's ability to determine the effectiveness of its management team and help tighten the link between executive pay and true executive performance. It improves the efficiency with which risk is distributed between shareholders and employees and helps ensure that decisions are not skewed by executive attitudes toward risk rather than by a clear determination of shareholder interests. Finally, it can help stabilize incentive programs over the business cycle or in the face of major industry transformation.

But RPE poses challenges as well. There are data-gathering costs to deal with and the potential to introduce new sources of uncertainty in rewards due to errors in measuring relative performance. There also may be incentives for executives to choose a peer group with an eye toward compensation rather than competitive realities. And even objectively determined peer groups may be unstable, due to changes in industry and market conditions. Finally, no one can ever discount concerns about complexity. It is easy to track stock price of one's own company. Sophisticated measures of performance lack such transparency and could alienate those involved as well as add to administrative costs. Communicating how such measures are derived is always daunting, sometimes irredeemably so.

Clearly, companies need to balance the benefits with the challenges before taking the road toward RPE. Fortunately there are now concrete tools like PSA that can help them objectively assess these trade-offs.

In our view, the potential gains from RPE make it worthwhile for companies to undertake such an assessment. What is at stake is the ability to bring economic rationality to decisions about incentive compensation and thereby deliver stronger performance incentives at lower cost to shareholders. In this way, RPE opens the door for companies to create value by truly paying for performance.

# Chapter 10

# New Executive Compensation Model

**Michael J. Halloran**

Significant marketplace changes are occurring that are having a profound effect on the design of executive compensation programs in companies throughout the United States and abroad. Other chapters have discussed current perspectives on executive compensation plan design from various stakeholders, ranging from management to the board to shareholders. The continual and frequently changing effects of accounting rules have also been discussed. In this chapter, a framework for the new executive compensation model is outlined that is intended to serve as a reference for the architects of executive compensation programs as they rethink current program design.

## 10.1 PROGRAM OBJECTIVES

Any revision or redesign of existing programs begins with an examination of program objectives. This section reviews how fundamental aspects of program objectives, ranging from competitive positioning through pay for performance, will be addressed in the new executive compensation model.

### (a) Competitive Positioning

One significant shift in the compensation model will be in the area of competitive positioning. Various surveys indicate that over half of companies position their executive compensation program at the median or above. And one-third of companies target the upper quartile or above. This situation has fueled a ratcheting effect of executive pay levels over the past 7 to 10 years.

There is growing pressure for compensation committees to anchor programs closer to the market median, especially in the area of targeted incentive opportunity. Actual performance levels then will yield payout levels that will be significantly above or below the median, providing a stronger pay for performance correlation.

Variations in salary levels will have some impact on pay positioning as companies with conservative salary postures set higher incentive targets and those with aggressive salary postures set somewhat lower incentive targets. These changes are predicated on an expectation that companies, with oversight by their compensation committees, will continue to focus on desired levels of total compensation and then set specific objectives for the mix of the elements within their overall package.

## (b) Peer Group Trends

The use of peer groups also will change. In many sectors, the number of direct peers has shrunk due to industry consolidation. In addition, the availability of data on peers has decreased as many competitors are now often part of a larger organization or of a foreign entity and may no longer share data or participate in surveys on a regular basis. The definition of peer also needs to be expanded. Many companies now realize that they are recruiting from and losing good people to companies other than direct competitors.

Consequently, many companies and their compensation committees are finding that part of the answer to fair executive compensation is found by comparing executive pay levels to companies with similar performance as defined by growth rates, return on investment or shareholder returns, and other measures. (See Chapter 9 for a discussion of peer selection and analysis.)

These trends will lead many companies to use a threefold approach to establishing a peer group for benchmarking purposes:

1. Industry peers, consisting of companies with the same or similar product lines
2. General industry peers, reflecting companies of similar size, complexity, and possibly close in geographic proximity, recognizing some of the real-time sources and possible losses of executive talent
3. Peers with similar performance, as companies focus more on the assessment of the fair relationship between pay and performance

## (c) Pay Mix

Significant changes in the pay mix are not expected for senior executives. There is a general belief that the overall structure of executive pay levels has reached an optimal level, given company size and performance considerations. Many critics in fact believe that overall executive pay levels are higher than is necessary or appropriate.

The growth in base salary levels will continue to be moderate for the foreseeable future. Targeted annual incentive levels have remained stable for the past few years, and growth had been moderate in the late 1990s. Levels of long-term incentives escalated significantly in the 1990s. However, the increased concern over dilution levels from stock-based plans, the potential expensing of options, and growing scrutiny of executive pay levels will lead to a leveling off if not a modest decline in the area of long-term incentives.

These trends indicate a slowing in the growth of the targeted overall executive compensation package, recognizing that actual results will vary significantly from the targeted structure. These trends also indicate that the mix of pay should not change in any meaningful way (see Exhibit 10.1). Total pay levels for senior executives will continue to be made up mainly of incentive-based compensation, and long-term incentives will represent at least two-thirds of the overall incentive structure at target.

## (d) Role of Equity

Equity-based incentives, predominantly in the form of stock options and stock grants, will continue to play a prominent role in executive pay packages. (See also Chapter 8.) Most strongly believe that equity incentives are a cornerstone of a highly successful, entrepreneurial-based U.S. economy. There are, however, several changes to the ways in which companies view equity compensation that will impact how it is used in the future.

**Exhibit 10.1**  Program Objectives

| | Today's Programs | Tomorrow's Programs |
|---|---|---|
| **Competitive Positioning** | Large Majority "Above Average" | Salary Targets Vary<br>Incentive Targets at Median |
| **Peer Group** | Direct Industry Competitors | Diverse Peers<br>• Similar Industry<br>• Similar Characteristics<br>• Similar Performance |
| **Pay Mix** | Heavy Incentive Emphasis | Heavy Incentive Emphasis *(no change)* |
| **Role of Equity** | Frequent Megagrants<br>Largest Part of Package | Few Megagrants<br>Largest Part of Package<br>Moderation in Size |

- The use of large megagrants of equity (typically stock options) has been declining in the past several years, as the excesses in the overall system are minimized. This trend will continue and is expected to have a dampening effect on practices at the higher end of the range.
- Given the size of equity grants in recent years, many companies are at dilution levels considered optimal to perhaps high in the eyes of many shareholders. Thus the usage may slow somewhat as dilution levels come more into line with levels more acceptable for shareholders.
- As discussed later, the typical long-term incentive program of the future likely will have a higher cash element.

Nonetheless, equity-based incentives will continue to represent the largest element in executive long-term incentive packages. Companies and shareholders always will believe that a meaningful incentive focused on growth in shareholder value is a critical component of a total compensation package.

## (e) Stock Ownership

It is generally expected that senior executives should own company stock, and over 40 percent of major companies have formal executive stock ownership guidelines. Although this percentage is expected to increase, it is unlikely that an overwhelming majority will establish stock ownership guidelines. The main reasons are twofold:

1. Many believe that mandatory ownership levels are not compatible with desired levels of personal financial diversification.
2. Many companies have numerous programs that enable executives to accumulate company stock. For many executives with long-term service, the natural accumulation of company stock often far exceeds reasonable stock ownership standards. Thus a typical ownership guideline may well encourage executives to sell stock down to the guideline level.

Typical ownership levels required for executives will increase somewhat. The common standard of 5 times base salary for a chief executive officer (CEO) may well increase to 7 to 10 times salary with a longer time frame in which to meet the guideline. With the decline in share prices in the past few years, a growing number of companies are revising their guidelines to mandate owning a specific number of shares, rather than having to meet a set dollar amount, so that guidelines can be calibrated and administered in a more stable fashion.

## (f) Pay for Performance Relationships

Significant changes are expected in how companies and compensation committees will view the pay and performance relationship. In the future we will see a much more rigorous assessment of the relationship between pay levels and performance. A typical part of a compensation committee's ongoing due diligence will include:

- An assessment of a company's three- to five-year performance, focusing on both shareholder return and key financial metrics. These results will be used to assess the appropriateness of the relative level of total compensation over this same period.
- An analysis of a company's annual financial performance, focusing on the key financial metrics in the annual incentive plan, relative to performance on the same metrics by similar companies. These comparisons will be used to test the degree of difficulty in the annual goal-setting process. Should the goals appear to have been too difficult or too easy to achieve based on peer company performance, it may become more common for discretion to be applied.

If data for a viable competitor group are not available, comparisons will be made relative to a broader group of companies with similar size and complexity.

## 10.2   BASE SALARY

### (a) Role in Overall Program

The growing use and size of long-term incentives in recent years has reduced the proportion of the overall executive compensation package delivered in base salary. In most large to mid-size companies, base salary currently makes up from 40 percent to as little as 10 to 15 percent of a typical executive's total compensation package. This is generally not expected to change much in the future.

Neither is the role of base salary expected to change much in the coming years. Base salary generally will continue to serve as the anchor point for many aspects of the overall program, such as annual and long-term incentive awards, employee benefits (e.g., 401(k) plans and life insurance), and stock ownership requirements, all of which are nearly always expressed as a percent of base salary.

Given expected low inflation and a continued emphasis on incentive pay, growth in salary levels overall at the executive level will remain moderate (e.g., 3 to 5 percent) for the foreseeable future. Any meaningful increase on an individual basis will be achieved either via promotion or job changes.

### (b) Process for Setting Levels

In the mid- to late 1990s, most companies adopted a market-based approach to establishing salary levels for their executive positions. This extremely focused approach relies mainly on the use of market survey data to identify competitive salary levels for similar positions.

The greatest change in the process for setting salaries relates to a heightened focus on performance. In the past, it usually took three to five years or more to move an executive's salary from somewhat below a fully competitive level to the identified market rate (i.e., from the minimum to the midpoint of the salary range). Today, current expectations for high performance have altered the traditional executive-employer relationship. Many companies expect, if not demand, executives new in the position to reach a level where they are fully performing in the job within 18 to 24 months, if not sooner. With the performance bar now raised, the quid pro quo from the executive's standpoint is that the salary level for the job should match the full market rate in the same 18- to 24-month period. This has changed how salaries are administered at the executive level. Most companies now establish an accelerated schedule for moving an executive's salary in sync with performance expectations. This is a critical issue in ensuring a fair total compensation package, since most incentives are tied to base salary.

## 10.3  ANNUAL INCENTIVE PLAN DESIGN

### (a) Award Opportunity and Mix in Overall Package

The portion of the overall executive compensation package represented by the annual incentive has remained relatively stable for the past few years in most industry sectors. No significant upward movement is anticipated. At the CEO level, the annual incentive represents about 10 to 15 percent of the overall total compensation package at target and 20 to 25 percent for the next several levels of key executives. In years of strong performance, a typical program will provide up to 200 percent of the target award for performance considered outstanding. No significant change in the award opportunity at the higher performance levels is anticipated.

### (b) Performance Measures

Ideally, annual incentive plan measures are those most indicative of the successful execution of a company's business strategy. The selection of the performance measures is, therefore, a critical step in the design of an effective plan. As the focus on pay and performance increases, a key challenge is for companies to ensure that the right measures are being used. (See also Chapter 2.)

Several key guidelines should be followed in selecting the right performance measures:

- Measures should be consistent with the company's overall business strategy.
- Measures should have a high correlation with increased shareholder value over time. Several analytical tools are available to help companies identify those measures with the highest correlation to increased shareholder value. In

addition, investment analysts provide an independent view of the metrics used to value companies in a given industry.

- In most cases, some combination of growth and return measures should be considered. Nearly all companies strive to grow, and the incentive plan measures should reflect that. However, growth in earnings, sales, and so on can be achieved through moderate or heavy investment. A measure that captures return on the investment in the business is usually critical in the eyes of most investors.

- The use of a return on investment measure requires careful selection of the investment definition. For example, a return on equity measure would be meaningless in a company where most of the capital invested in the business is in the form of debt.

- Fewer is better. Studies indicate that a focused executive team will produce consistently better results. Aligning the team around a small number of metrics will increase line of sight and achieve a better overall understanding of the key areas of emphasis for the company.

- Strive for transparency. The continuing changes in accounting rules make for a very soft foundation for incentive plan measurement. Many companies today face a myriad of year-end exceptions and potential exclusions or add-backs to their financial results. Measures that use inputs that are readily tracked in the company's financial systems are of the greatest value in incentive plans.

- "Cash is king." Most leading financial experts believe that cash-based incentive plan measures should be used. Many companies, however, do not manage the business exclusively on a cash basis, and significant changes to internal reporting systems plus an extensive education effort to raise management awareness are needed before any sizable shift to cash-based measures occurs. Yet discounted cash flow valuation metrics consistently are shown to be most accurate over time, and it is expected that the use of cash-based measures will grow in the near future.

## (c) Setting Financial Targets

The current spotlight on executive pay for performance focuses squarely on the process of setting financial targets. In recent years controversy has revolved around the apparent disconnect between the size of annual incentive awards and the perceived (and often real) low level of financial performance that occurred. Correcting this disconnect will be one of the most important roles for boards and compensation committees in the future.

In order to establish fair yet challenging financial targets, five steps should be taken:

1. *Examine company performance relative to competitors.* Is the company outperforming or underperforming? Is performance improving or deteriorating relative to others facing similar business conditions?

2. *Review macroeconomic trends* regarding such factors as inflation, costs of raw materials, and government regulation and determine how changes and trends in these areas will aid or hinder a company's ability to perform.

3. *Review investor expectations.* Today the valuation of a company is impacted by shareholder expectations, and developing an understanding of these expectations will enable proposed targets to be reviewed with an eye toward how outsiders view the company's prospects.

4. *Consider standard benchmarks*, such as a company's cost of capital. High-performing companies consistently produce returns in excess of their cost of capital or continue to improve their returns. Goals should be assessed in light of whether an acceptable return will be achieved or if improvement in the returns will occur.

5. *Analyze the strategies inherent in the business plan.* Are tactics in place to achieve the plan effectively, or is the plan too optimistic? Conversely, is the inherent performance at a significantly lower or slower growth level than in prior years, or at a level that is noticeably different from what is expected within the industry?

In the end, compensation committees will be asked to exercise judgment in approving goals with a fair degree of difficulty. Many considerations just mentioned have been a part of the typical business planning process, but frequently have not been used in establishing incentive plan goals. This approach should yield fair and defensible goals.

## (d) Establishing Leverage

Setting the leverage or award curves also entails challenges. Guidelines for setting the minimum or threshold levels as well as the maximum performance levels (where a maximum exists) follow.

- *Threshold/minimum:* Based on all considerations, what level of performance is deemed acceptable for the year? As pressure grows to meet Wall Street expectations, thresholds typically are set relatively close to the target (e.g., 5 to 10 percent below the target). In years of relatively slow growth (e.g., 5 to 7 percent growth), thresholds typically are set no lower than results in prior years. Since most think that threshold performance should yield a meaningful award, companies generally provide awards of 50 percent of the incentive target for threshold or minimum financial performance. Assuming performance at threshold is 90 percent of the target for the year, the resulting leverage would be 5 percent additional incentive for each 1 percent of incremental performance against plan.

- *Maximum/outstanding:* The setting of this level also has been greatly influenced by the intense pressure to meet Wall Street expectations. Many companies think that exceeding annual financial targets by a large degree does not create any significant value for shareholders unless the added performance is sustainable. Thus, the gap between target and maximum/outstanding has narrowed.

Key considerations in setting this performance level include:

- What is the higher end (i.e., top quartile) of industry performance for the given measures?
- What is the economic sharing of the increased financial performance level with the executive team? A fair sharing of the additional financial results in a range of 10 to 30 percent is generally considered reasonable. These percentages can vary depending on special circumstances.

Most companies use a maximum, and this practice will continue as a means of balancing the general imprecision in any goal-setting process. For those that do not use maximums, the incentive program typically is calibrated along a percentage sharing concept so that the percentage is either fixed or declines as performance accelerates.

### (e) Aligning Pay and Performance

A much stronger pay and performance alignment of annual incentive plans will result from these changes. Overall, companies and compensation committees will strive to ensure that top-quartile annual incentive awards are provided only when the company's financial results are clearly in the top quartile. Conversely, performance clearly in the lower quartile will result in few if any incentive awards. Although cases of turnarounds always require special treatment, the norm will be a more strongly aligned pay for performance structure that shareholders feel provides a fair treatment of management and investors.

### (f) Award Allocation

The determination of individual executive awards has evolved into two philosophical camps. Each perspective is valid and will continue to be followed by a large number of companies in the future.

***(i) Financial Results Only***   In an era where investors focus strongly on the company achieving its financial business plan, many companies tie the entire bonus award to the achievement of the company's financial targets for the year. Although the compensation committee may use discretion when warranted, the incentive determination process has become an all-encompassing process of producing financial results. These organizations often are known for strong teamwork and a collaborative management spirit and generally believe that the key executive group represents the best talent the company has in each area. Thus individual performance differentiations are not necessary. To the extent that a particular executive is not pulling his or her weight, the general approach is to replace the executive rather than deliver a series of negative messages through lower bonus awards (which generally cannot be done in an incentive structure based exclusively on financial results).

*(ii) Mix of Financial and Individual Results*    Alternatively, a significant number of companies believe that part of the incentive should be used to reward the achievement of individual goals. Thus the incentive program is used to differentiate among the executive team. Given the heightened pressure today to achieve financial results, these companies nevertheless believe that achieving specific nonfinancial goals and differentiating among performance within the executive team are critical to the company's success.

These companies typically weight nonfinancial goals at 20 percent to 35 percent of the target award and fund the nonfinancial part of the incentive program in nearly any economic environment, creating the ability to provide the awards if the goals are achieved. Many plans, however, do have certain financial performance thresholds that must be met or this portion will not be funded. These thresholds sometimes can be at a dramatic level (e.g., no funding if a loss is incurred) and may be funded only partially if performance falls short of a required rate of return or other similar hurdle (e.g., no funding if ROE is below 6 percent).

## 10.4   LONG-TERM INCENTIVES

### (a) Eligibility

Participation in long-term incentive plans will change if, as expected, the Financial Accounting Standards Board (FASB) requires an expense for stock options. (See Chapter 7.) As companies focus more closely on the cost of all long-term incentives, one means to expense management will be to reduce the number of participants.

These changes will occur in two ways:

1.   Reduce overall participation (i.e., fewer levels of management or fewer salary band levels will be eligible). This reduction will inevitably impact the lower levels of participation.

2.   Apply more rigorous performance standards to determine who will receive awards. Thus, for example, although the categories of eligible employees may not be reduced, only 50 percent of employees in certain categories would receive awards, compared to the 90 to 100 percent who received awards previously.

Eligibility for certain types of incentive vehicles also may change. Some companies will expand the use of restricted stock, while others will limit stock options to senior level executives. This change is discussed in more detail in the following sections.

## (b) Stock-Based Incentives

Another change if the FASB requires the expensing of stock options will be in the types of stock-based incentives used as well as the groups eligible for these incentives. Even without stock option expense, there is a shifting landscape in terms of the type and mix of stock-based incentives used for executives.

Overall, a new long-term incentive model will evolve where many companies will use two or three stock-based vehicles on a regular basis. (See Exhibit 10.2.)

*(i) Stock Options*   Grants of options will continue as a regular part of the long-term incentive program for many companies, especially in the technology sector (Microsoft's elimination of its stock option grants notwithstanding). Nonetheless, stock options are widely recognized as an imbalanced incentive vehicle. There is

**Exhibit 10.2**   Changing World of Long-Term Incentives

| Today's Programs | | | Tomorrow's Programs | |
| --- | --- | --- | --- | --- |
| Focus/ Rationale | Plan Type & Weighting | | Plan Type & Weighting | Focus/ Rationale |
| Increased Stock Price Cost Effective | Stock Options (80%–100%) | | Stock Options (25%–50%) | Increased Stock Price |
| | | | Restricted Stock (25%–50%) | Retention and Stock Price Growth |
| Retention and/or Longer-Term Financial Performance | Restricted Stock and/or Performance Plan (0%–20%) | | Performance Plan (20%–40%) | Longer-Term Financial Performance |

significant incentive and retention value when the options are in the money, but the retention value disappears rapidly if the options are underwater (i.e., the current stock price is below the exercise price). With increased stock market volatility comes the greater likelihood that any stock option grant will be underwater for a longer part of its term, impacting its overall effectiveness.

At the same time, major investors want to see some portion of long-term incentive plans tied to increased stock price. Thus the long-term incentive program of the future will continue to include a significant stock option component, with a typical weighting of around a third of the total long-term package and possibly more. Given the heavy reliance on stock options by many companies, this will be a dramatic shift. However, if expensing of options is mandated, the strong economic advantages that options currently enjoy over other vehicles will be diminished if not eliminated.

*(ii) Restricted Stock*    Companies traditionally have used restricted stock as a retention device. Critics maintain, however, that the typical restricted stock grant that vests based on the passage of time (i.e., service-based vesting) has no real performance aspect other than continued tenure.

Yet in the current reassessment of stock-based vehicles following the recent stock market decline of 2001–2002, companies have taken another look at the positive aspects of restricted stock. The fact that restricted stock has a high perceived value in the eyes of participants and is always in the money (it can grow or decline in value on a real-time basis) has led many to conclude that restricted stock can be an effective incentive over and above its retention value. As it always has value, restricted stock provides a better balance than the more one-sided stock options.

Thus we expect that the stock-based incentive programs of many companies will contain a meaningful component of restricted stock, with a weighting of up to one-third or more in the overall package. Although an expense is required for restricted stock, the likely requirement to expense stock options would narrow or level the playing field for this vehicle as a choice relative to options. With proper communications, restricted stock can become an effective incentive as well as a retention vehicle.

*(iii) Performance Shares*    Companies have used performance shares to link long-term financial performance with stock price performance. However, the requirement for an expense coupled with variable accounting for any changes in stock price has discouraged many companies from using this vehicle.

Ongoing developments may lead to increased use of performance shares. One development is the more level playing field that will be created by the expected expensing of stock options and the desire to attach performance requirements to restricted stock grants for those who want to address one of the perceived negative attributes of service-based restricted stock. Another factor driving the expected growth in performance shares and other long-term vehicles tied to financial performance is the increased desire by many companies to adopt incentive vehicles that focus on the achievement of longer-term financial results. The long-term program of the future is expected to contain a meaningful weighting on the achievement of financial goals independent of stock price performance, providing a balance in the overall program between stock price performance and financial performance. A weighting of at least 25 percent and possibly greater would be an anticipated middle-of-the-road result.

*(iv) Cash Incentives*   Many expect the use of long-term incentives tied to the achievement of specific long-term financial goals to increase. Management teams are responsible for producing a growing, profitable enterprise and generally have direct control over the financial results of a company. This concept of direct control contrasts sharply with the innate volatility of stock markets, where a company's share price at any point in time many not reflect a company's true value.

This perspective will lead to an increase in two common types of long-term plans:

1. *Performance units or cash:* Awards in cash or units (with an assigned dollar value) are payable based on a company's performance over a multiyear period against specific financial or strategic goals. These awards are payable independent of stock price performance. The cash awards subsequently can be used to pay taxes on the exercise of stock options or the vesting of restricted shares, giving the liquidity that may allow an executive to retain company shares.

2. *Performance shares:* As discussed, contingent shares are awarded, with the final number earned based on the company's performance over a multiyear period against specific financial or strategic goals. The final award value is a function of both the number of shares earned and the stock price at the end of the period. Many companies will pay the final award in cash. Although the award value is dictated by the stock price, thus blending long-term financial results and stock price results, the cash award allows the liquidity cited earlier, and provides a balance in the overall long-term program.

   It is projected that cash-based long-term incentives will constitute up to 25 percent or more of the overall long-term package. In addition, programs tied to multi-year financial results can present a tangible balance to the decisions made annually with respect to achieving of short-term incentive award targets. This is unlike the less direct (but implicit) tradeoffs expected to be made by management teams between achieving short-term financial goals or investing for longer-term growth that hopefully will be realized in a higher stock price.

## (c) Performance Measures beyond Stock Price

The expected growth in long-term plans tied to multiyear financial results will result in a greater focus on measures of financial performance. The earlier discussion of annual incentive performance measures outlined key considerations for selecting the proper performance measures. (See also Chapter 2.) Most of those principles apply to the measures used in longer-term performance plans as well. Key considerations for long-term plans include these areas:

- There should be a focus on shareholder expectations. How do investors view the balance between growth and return?
- Earnings growth is a critical component that should be captured in the measurement system.
- For capital-intensive industries, a return on investment measurement usually is needed. Only companies earning a very strong return on investment relative to their cost of capital should consider ignoring this measure.
- A maximum of two measures should be utilized, in order to optimize the focus of the management team.
- Given the difficulty of multiyear goal setting, the use of peer group performance or other relative measurement indices should be considered.

## (d) Measurement Periods

The range of practices regarding long-term incentive measurement periods has narrowed considerably. We may see some change in the area of stock options, but little change is expected for longer-term performance plans.

*(i) Stock Options*   Ten-year terms have been the typical length. However, most expect that any valuation methodology associated with stock option expensing will have the term of the options as a key metric. In an attempt to manage or reduce the cost of options, companies may want to reduce the option term to five to seven years.

*(ii) Performance Plans*   A large majority of plans currently have three-year performance periods, in part due to practical considerations: Most consider two years to be too short but have difficulty setting credible goals beyond three years. Thus the three-year measurement period should continue to be the predominant period for measuring long-term financial results, although if business cycles continue to shorten, a two-year period may become more viable.

It has also become very common for long-term performance plans to be established in rolling or overlapping fashion. For example, at any point in time an executive may be involved in three multiyear (usually three-year) overlapping performance periods (i.e., 2002–2004, 2003–2005, 2004–2006). The advantages to this approach are:

- Companies have the ability to reset the long-term financial goals each year.
- New award opportunities can help offset prior plans where the goal achievement might be missed or to add additional motivation if the company is on track for outstanding results for prior periods.
- The retention aspect is quite strong, with the potential forfeiture of three potential awards at any time.

The rolling three-year structure is expected to remain very common in the coming years.

### (e) Vesting and Holding Periods

The vesting periods used by companies for their long-term incentive plans are not expected to change much from current practices in the early 2000s.

*(i) Stock Options*   Most option grants vest over a three- to five-year period. This length is unlikely to change much unless any mandated method of expensing stock options provides a significant bias toward shorter or longer vesting. In all cases, the company strives to strike a balance between retention (i.e., longer is better) with perceived value (i.e., shorter is better).

*(ii) Restricted Stock*   The three- to five-year vesting period also is currently very common with restricted stock, although the length on average is longer than with stock options. As a larger portion of the long-term package is expected to be delivered in restricted stock, the proportion of companies using long vesting is expected to increase.

Although it is unlikely that the overall vesting period will extend beyond five years (due to the impact on perceived value), it is expected that a larger portion will vest over years 3 to 5.

With respect to holding periods, there has been much debate regarding the virtues of requiring senior management to own company stock. The debate also has extended to the advantages of requiring executives to hold any shares acquired through incentive plans, especially stock options, for a certain period of time.

### (f) Pay and Performance Alignment

The prior paragraphs have described the programs of the future as having a more balanced focus on both stock price (through stock options and restricted stock) and financial performance (through greater use of long-term performance-based plans). This increase in focus on longer-term financial performance will raise the pay for performance alignment of long-term incentives and moderate some of the dysfunctional results that can occur due to stock market volatility and timing differences.

Although many believe that management teams ultimately are measured by the company's stock price performance, such teams have the most direct control over a company's annual and longer-term financial results. A greater focus on long-term results will bring the incentive structures closer to reflecting a view that a growing number of investors espouse: Management delivers financial results and markets value companies.

## 10.5  EXECUTIVE BENEFITS AND PERQUISITES

Executive benefits and perquisites represent a fairly small portion of the total value available, although supplemental retirement programs can be sizable at some companies. Looking at the future, the structure of these programs will change in these ways.

### (a) Supplemental Retirement

Greater disclosure requirements are expected from the SEC, as many believe that the value of supplemental retirement arrangements, particularly in companies with defined benefit pensions plans, is quite substantial. As companies continue to move away from defined benefit pension plans, the use of supplemental retirement plans will shift toward programs that allow executives to participate in "shadow" 401(k) or defined contribution plans without the imposed government limits. However, a substantial portion of the value derived in these plans is based on an executive's own contributions. Thus the company-provided portions will be relatively small.

As most companies believe that long-term incentive plans should form the greater portion of an executive's wealth creation, the emphasis on these programs generally will overshadow the value of most supplemental retirement plans.

### (b) Other Executive Benefits

Programs relating to other executive benefits, where they exist, are generally modest in value and cost. No significant changes are expected.

### (c) Perquisites

The use of perquisites has leveled off and possibly even declined in recent years as the IRS has tightened its rules regarding the taxability of various perquisites. The most prevalent perquisites provided today are financial planning, tax preparation, and annual physicals. Most companies no longer provide company cars or car allowances and have rolled the value of these perquisites into base salaries. Club memberships other than for business purposes also have declined.

Greater disclosure requirements for perquisites are expected from the SEC due to the recent media coverage of significant perquisites provided to several prominent, recently retired senior executives. Such requirements will cause additional downward pressure on the use of significant perquisites. Overall, no real growth in value is expected.

## 10.6   ROLE OF THE COMPENSATION COMMITTEE

Recent corporate scandals, new board governance regulations, and heightened scrutiny of executive compensation have changed the ways compensation committees are structured and operate. (See Chapter 4.)

In the future compensation committees will:

- Increase their focus on the overall relationships between executive pay and performance
- More rigorously assess the degree of difficulty of incentive plan goals
- Increasingly examine the appropriateness of the various performance measures used in the executive incentive plans, focusing on the linkage among business strategy, company valuation, and the measures used
- Reexamine compensation philosophies, with particular emphasis on the validation of programs targeted at the upper percentiles
- Discussion potential plan changes in more depth, with multistep review processes allowing full dialogue around program changes prior to committee action

These changes will improve the overall governance process related to executive compensation and will allow for greater transparency for the investor.

## 10.7   SHAREHOLDER EXPECTATIONS

In the past several years, shareholders have become more interested participants in the executive compensation arena. This interest is not limited to the smaller yet vocal shareholder activist groups. Larger institutional shareholders of all kinds (pension funds, insurance companies, investment management companies) now include executive compensation issues in their overall assessment of a company's investment prospects. (See Chapter 6.)

A more transparent linkage between executive pay and performance will increase understanding and confidence in the appropriateness and viability of executive compensation programs. More important, investors will be better able to judge which programs are designed to focus on growing shareholder value, by using appropriate performance measures, setting fair but rigorous goals, and establishing a balance between stock price movements and financial results. Finally, the level of accountability will be raised at all levels, providing the overall system with greater integrity.

# Chapter 11

# Outside Director Compensation

**Peter J. Oppermann**

## 11.1 INTRODUCTION

Without question, the focus on corporate governance has put directors in an intense spotlight. New legislation and regulations from the stock exchanges discussed in other chapters have been aimed, most directly, at directors and how they carry out their role as representatives of shareholders. Not surprisingly, the job of a director has become much more demanding, fraught with additional risk, with actions of directors coming under close scrutiny.

It is with these and other issues as background that director compensation has been changing. While director compensation has been evolving for the past 10 years or so, more recent history has seen, if not a revolution, then a significant uprising. And the most significant changes are likely to come over the next few years.

This chapter covers those issues that have and will influence how directors are compensated, discusses the reactions and newer designs that have emerged recently, and lays out a template for designing a reward strategy for directors.

## 11.2 FACTORS INFLUENCING CHANGES IN DIRECTOR COMPENSATION

### (a) Increased Time Commitments

Probably the greatest impact on directors and their compensation is the increased amount of time that they will spend on board and committee matters. Some of this increase is coming from regulatory changes, some from internal controls, and some from the general focus on board activities in general.

Specifically, members of the audit committee, who used to meet no more than other committees, have seen the demands of their positions increase geometrically. Demands include:

- Meeting at least quarterly to review the quarterly audited financials, prior to both the chief executive officer (CEO) and chief financial officer (CFO) certification required under the Sarbanes-Oxley Act. Although regulations do not require these meetings, audit committee review appears to be a prudent move to provide another layer of review and assurance to the investing public.

- Meetings to discuss and review the nonaudit work of the company's auditors. Prior to Enron, the extent of the relationship between an audit firm and its client, outside of the traditional audit work, was disclosed in the company's proxy, represented by the total fees paid for non–audit-related work. This work typically was funneled through the CFO or others within a client, but not through the audit committee. It was typical for the committee to both ask and question the fees involved after assignments were completed, but not typical to approve the hiring of the auditor for the work. Times have changed. The audit committee now must approve all work done by the auditor prior to the auditor being hired. In addition, it is now typical for the audit committee to hire the auditor directly, with input from the CFO. Past practice would have had those roles reversed.

- While at least one member of the audit committee must be certified as a financial expert, other members also must have financial savvy and add value to the committee's work. In some cases, that means additional education to ensure that committee members understand the more complex transactions and changing regulations regarding such issues as pension accounting, stock option accounting, and purchase accounting, all of which are changing or having a greater impact on corporate profits.

Although the audit committee is the most heavily impacted, the chair and members of the compensation committee also are dealing with issues of greater complexity and sensitivity. Four issues have significantly increased the time spent by the compensation committee:

1. Pending changes to stock option accounting are forcing companies to rework entire compensation and especially executive compensation programs. Option accounting knowledge is no longer the purview of just auditors. As companies move toward different compensation programs, compensation committee members are being asked to understand and approve compensation plans that they have never been exposed to in the past. Performance-based restricted stock, performance-based option vesting, and the related accounting for these types of plans are new, and require more time and study by these compensation committee members.

2. With the focus on pay and performance relationships, directors are being asked to understand how the performance measures selected for use in incentive plans relate to shareholder value. In addition, they are asking for more and more proof of this relationship before and after plans are put in place.

3. In addition to pay for performance, directors are spending time on such issues as severance and contract issues, as shareholders are increasing their scrutiny of these forms of payment.

4. The committee now must hire the outside compensation consultant used to review and comment on executive pay issues. While not a time-consuming issue, the committee's involvement in this process has increased their time commitment.

The role of the corporate governance committee is evolving, but the addition of another committee to the directors' process undoubtedly will cause directors to spend more time fulfilling their duties.

## (b) Greater Demand for Qualified Directors

A second influence on director pay is the increased demand for qualified directors. This is not to imply that current directors are not qualified. Rather, many of those who are currently qualified and in demand will have to spend more time on board duties and therefore will be able to be members of fewer boards.

This is especially true of board members who are currently executives, especially CEOs in their own companies. Due to recent reforms in corporate governance, the typical executive now must spend a significantly greater amount of time preparing for board meetings, audit committee meetings, preparing for the quarterly sign-off on the financial statement (for the CEO and CFO), and keeping up with changes in stock exchange and Securities and Exchange Commission (SEC) regulations. And that is just for duties as a board member in the company in which he or she works. The time commitment for executives who are insiders is as great or greater than for outside board members. With that additional time commitment, executives have less time available for outside board memberships. Consequently, executives who are now on multiple boards are having to cut back their involvement to spend time on their own companies. Starting in 2002, many high-profile executives who were members of up to six outside boards resigned from half to focus on their own companies and on fewer boards.

There is no evidence that any resignations by insiders or outsiders has anything to do with the level of compensation offered by any organization. However, it would not be inconceivable for a board that paid below-average compensation to have its compensation program questioned by shareholders if any board members were to resign before the end of their terms. Consequently, companies must have a sharper focus on the levels of compensation paid not just in their industry but within a larger universe of companies of similar size to ensure that compensation for current directors does not become an issue.

In addition to executives who are reducing their board roles, the mandate that some committees be comprised solely of outside directors have forced some boards to add to their outside directors just as this pool of qualified individuals is starting to shrink. However, this increase in demand is not due to the fact that there are too many insiders on corporate boards today.

Based on the Mercer 350, a database of 350 companies with revenues in excess of $1 billion, the average mix of inside vs. outside directors is about two insiders to nine outside directors. This fact would seem to indicate that there are enough outside board members to generally satisfy the mandate of all outside members on the audit and compensation committees. However, as those figures are just averages, we can assume that some companies have fewer outsiders than insiders or fewer outsiders than the average. In fact, in 19 companies, insiders make up 40 percent of the boards. At least from this sample, there would appear to be a demand for additional outside directors to replace some insiders.

### (c) Regulatory Changes

An additional factor influencing the increased demand for qualified directors is the requirement within the Sarbanes-Oxley Act that at least one member of the audit committee be a certified financial expert. Many executives exist who would qualify, but many audit committee chairs do not, and will have to be replaced. The demand for these individuals will definitely increase, and there will have to be a new source of expertise to fill these positions.

### (d) Board Performance

The focus on corporate governance has encompassed the performance of the board, its committees, and the individual directors as well. Each committee must create a charter that defines its role, responsibilities, and the expectations of its members. With the requirement that each committee annually evaluate its performance against that charter, directors will be more cognizant of both their own and the committee's diligence.

The demand for experience, outside the experience needed for the audit committee, will increasingly become a part of the demand for directors.

### (e) Establishing a Lead Director

Through 2001, less than 3 percent of companies in the database of 350 large U.S. companies had lead directors. In 2002, that number increased to over 13 percent. Anecdotal information indicates that this trend is increasing dramatically. A lead director typically takes on the role as the "lead" independent director, setting up meetings of all nonmanagement directors, being the key contact with the CEO, and possibly having a key role in one aspect of governance. This role may be overseeing changes in internal controls or in a poor performing business unit, or ensuring that all corporate governance procedures are being followed. This position is not the nonexecutive chairman of the board, but a new role that will take on greater importance as more director involvement becomes needed due to changes in legal and regulatory rules.

In some companies, lead directors are rotated among all board members, with no one serving more than one year. In these cases, the argument can be made that since all directors share in the increased responsibilities, no additional monies are needed as compensation. However, more companies have identified one individual as the lead or presiding director, and have assigned additional responsibilities and duties that are in direct response to the Sarbanes-Oxley Act.

## 11.3  CURRENT COMPENSATION

A review of the current state of director pay helps to put the changes in compensation in perspective.

### (a) Cash Compensation

*(i) Retainer*   Almost all companies in the studies pay an annual retainer to directors, a practice that has been consistent over time. Company size is the major determinant of retainer amounts. However, the increase in retainer attributed to company size is nowhere near the increase in CEO salaries attributable to size. (See Exhibit 11.1.)

Retainers in 2002 increased over 2001, with the median increasing from $35,000 to $40,000. Although that amount is not a large percentage increase, for comparison, the increase the prior year was only $1,000. It seems that cash for directors is increasing in relation to their workload.

**Exhibit 11.1**   Median 2002 Annual Retainer by Company Size

| Revenue | Annual Retainer |
| --- | --- |
| $1.0–1.99 billion | $25,000 |
| $2.0–$4.99 billion | 34,500 |
| $5.0–$9.99 billion | 40,000 |
| $10.0 billion + | 50,000 |
| **All Companies** | **$40,000** |

*Source:* Mercer Human Resource Consulting.

Stock has become common in the retainer portion of compensation programs. Only a small percent of companies pay the entire retainer in stock; almost 40 percent, however, pay part in cash and part in stock. In the administration of these plans, the equity portion is most often stated as a dollar amount, with the number of shares changing year to year based on the stock price at the time the retainer is paid. This arrangement results in a smaller number of shares paid when the stock price increases and helps to shelter directors from year-to-year market fluctuations. These awards generally are made in one of three ways:

1. *Unrestricted shares,* with the cash portion used to pay any taxes due on receipt, making the retainer a true equity award. These shares also may be paid quarterly.
2. *Restricted stock,* with a one- to three-year vesting.
3. *Deferred stock,* with payout deferred until retirement.

## (b) Meeting Fees

Retainers vary by company size, but meeting fees are fairly consistent by company size and industry, generally between $1,000 and $1,500 per meeting. The practice of paying board members a fee to attend a meeting has two purposes: to induce directors actually to attend meetings and to differentiate pay for those who contribute more than for those who contribute less. Interestingly, during 2002, the median meeting fee did not increase from the $1,500 fee common in 2001. Apparently the increase in directors' pay in 2002 was more in recognition of the increased amount of time they spent on company business outside of meetings.

## (c) Committee Pay

Fees for committee membership and committee chairmanship are common in all industries and company revenue ranges. More than half of the companies Mercer surveyed pay a retainer for committee chairpeople, and over 80 percent pay a fee to all board members for attendance at meetings. This practice is intended to further the idea of equal pay for equal work, with directors receiving different pay based on the amount of time they spend on company business and the amount of responsibility they shoulder. Committee work and committee chairs involve substantially more time than mere board membership, and in some cases greater fiduciary responsibility, requiring larger compensation packages to help induce participation. The size of the retainer paid for committee chairs, however, ranges from $2,000 to $8,000, with most between $3,000 and $5,000. Committee fees range from $480 to $1,350, with the vast majority of companies paying $1,000 per meeting. The differentiation of committee and chair work is not great, and considering the spotlight turned on members of the audit, compensation, and nominating committees by shareholder groups, the compensation may not justify the responsibility. Changes in the coming years are likely.

The total amount of cash paid for both board and committee service obviously depends on the number of board meetings and committee memberships and meetings a director may participate in. Exhibit 11.2 gives examples of total annual compensation by company sales/revenues.

## (d) Equity Compensation

As stated earlier, the most noticeable trend and the element that has had the greatest impact on directors' compensation is the use of equity in the form of options, restricted stock, or stock units.

Equity in directors' compensation programs usually is used in any of three ways:

1.   As a stand-alone grant, with the primary purpose of tying a portion of compensation to shareholder returns. In most cases, options are used for this purpose.
2.   As a substitute for some other form of compensation, usually retainer, meeting fees, or committee chair fees or retainers.
3.   As the basis for increased stock ownership by directors.

*(i) Stand-Alone Grants*   The use of stock options as an add-on to existing cash programs is very typical, with the majority of companies now having stand-alone plans. Stock grants now comprise the majority of director's pay. (See Exhibit 11.3.)

Not surprisingly, nonqualified options are the core long-term vehicle, granted under a shareholder-approved plan, generally granted with a fixed number of options each year and possibly a larger number granted on joining the board. Vesting usually is short, typically one year, with the only controversy being how far

**Exhibit 11.2**   2002 Median Total Annual Cash Compensation (TAC) by Size

| Revenue | Annual Retainer | TAC |
|---|---|---|
| $1.0–1.99 billion | $25,000 | $49,000 |
| $2.0–$4.99 billion | 34,500 | 54,000 |
| $5.0–$9.99 billion | 40,000 | 66,750 |
| $10.0 billion + | 50,000 | 74,000 |
| **All Companies** | **40,000** | **59,100** |

*Source:* Mercer Human Resource Consulting.

**Exhibit 11.3**   Stock Grants to Directors

|  | Percent of Companies | | |
| --- | --- | --- | --- |
|  | 2000 | 2001 | 2002 |
| Stock for Directors Overall | 94% | 95% | 96% |
| Stock Options | 75% | 77% | 79% |
| Unrestricted Stock | 36% | 36% | 39% |
| Restricted Stock | 28% | 27% | 28% |
| Deferred Stock | 27% | 25% | 26% |
| Other | 1% | 1% | 2% |
| Multiple Award Types | 58% | 62% | 59% |

*Source:* Mercer Human Resource Consulting.

past a director's retirement or resignation a director is allowed to exercise the option. In a few cases, there is no limit other than the term of the option. The rationale is that the director's influence on company performance extends beyond the time he or she serves on the board, and the director should recognize the rewards for a period of time. Most companies, however, do not extend the exercise period beyond one year.

The percentage of a director's total compensation that comes from stand-alone equity plans varies by industry. Those industries that typically compensate executives heavily in equity follow that trend with directors. (See Exhibit 11.4.)

**Exhibit 11.4**   Total Direct Compensation by Industry

|  | Equity % of TDC[1] |  | Equity % of TDC[1] |
| --- | --- | --- | --- |
| Electronics, Electrical Equipment | 72 | Commercial Banking | 55 |
| Computers, Office Equipment | 72 | Transportation | 55 |
| Scientific/Photographic Equipment | 71 | Chemicals | 53 |
| Diversified Financials | 68 | Food, Beverages | 53 |
| Health Care, Pharmaceuticals | 66 | Industrial, Farm Equipment | 53 |
| Insurance | 64 | Utilities | 50 |
| Retailers | 64 | Forest, Paper Products | 45 |
| Metal Products | 62 | **All Industries** | **59** |

[1]Total direct compensation (TDC) is the sum of total annual compensation plus long-term incentives, including the value of grants in the form of restricted stock, unrestricted stock, deferred stock, and stock options (valued using a binomial option pricing model). Includes equity stock retainer.

*Source:* Mercer Human Resource Consulting.

Although the increase in annual compensation for directors does not increase that dramatically with company size, the size of equity awards does leverage the total compensation package in larger companies. (See Exhibit 11.5.)

*(ii) Substitute for Other Compensation*    A second reason for using equity in directors programs is as a substitute for another form of compensation. If equity is used as a substitute for cash, three methods are most typical.

1. Paying the entire cash compensation in stock, typically options or restricted stock
2. Paying part in cash and part in stock
3. Deferring part of compensation in stock or deferred stock

Although it is not typical practice, the use of stock options only to compensate a director for service has a powerful attraction for some companies and their shareholders. It says to shareholders that the directors are willing to be rewarded for the direction and the decisions made by the management they oversee. Further, it says that the directors that this organization wants on its board are willing to accept the consequences of their decisions and are not joining just to receive a compensation package or recognition as a board member.

Although there are benefits of paying directors entirely in stock—tying directors to enhancing shareholder value, and increasing director share ownership—some concerns accompany this course of action. With options, there is a real chance that directors will focus more on the short-term performance of the stock, to increase the value of their options, and not on the long-term, where the greater potential gain could be realized. A simple way around that objection might be to vest the options over a three-year period, the term of their directorship, or to have the vesting based on the stock price reaching a certain level, with vesting in effect accelerated from a longer period, say six years.

Another concern is evident whenever options are granted: What happens when the price of the stock declines? A director typically receives options each year. If

**Exhibit 11.5**    Median Total Compensation by Company Size

| Revenue | Total Annual Compensation | Total Direct Compensation |
|---|---|---|
| $1.0–1.99 billion | $49,000 | $85,272 |
| $2.0–$4.99 billion | 54,000 | 105,300 |
| $5.0–$9.99 billion | 66,750 | 132,300 |
| $10.0 billion + | 74,000 | 155,000 |
| **All Companies** | **$59,100** | **$128,530** |

*Source:* Mercer Human Resource Consulting.

the price continues to decline over a period of time, then the real value of the options is much less than any model would show.

A second typical use of stock is paying in a combination of cash and stock. This type of arrangement allows companies to emulate the type of programs available to executives, that is, to have some of their compensation paid in a non-variable form and some in variable compensation. In our studies, about 25 percent of companies split the board retainer between cash and stock. Stock retainers typically take one of four forms:

1. Unrestricted shares, paid once a year
2. Restricted shares with one- to three-year vesting
3. Deferred stock with payout deferred until retirement
4. Deferred stock units, where the amount to be deferred is converted into units whose value rises or falls with the company's stock price; at the end of the deferral period, the amount is paid in stock

A third type of substitution is to defer part of current compensation into some stock vehicle, in effect deferring the receipt of some compensation until a later time, and (it is hoped) enjoying the appreciation in the stock price over that time. Half of the companies that Mercer studies offer this type of deferral. The most typical type is the deferral into stock units. The amount to be deferred and converted into units whose values then rise or fall with the company's stock price. At the end of the deferral period, the amount is paid in company stock. In offering deferral of retainer or fees in company stock or stock units, the company may offer an inducement to mitigate the risk of stock vs. the certainty of cash. A premium of 10 to 20 percent in the number of units or shares over the current value of cash may be offered for deferral into stock. Similarly, the number of options offered in exchange is increased by 20 percent over a Black-Scholes value to induce deferral.

## (e) Increasing Stock Ownership

Probably the most compelling reason for using stock in a director plan is to support a stock ownership policy for the directors. This trend of encouraging directors to own stock follows a similar trend for executives. The link between these two is important because it puts the directors in the same boat as the executives whom they oversee. The use of stock ownership guidelines is on the increase, growing from 1 percent to over 25 percent of companies surveyed in six years.

The importance of stock ownership by executives is not generally disputed; the amount, however, is. There is a central tendency to have guidelines that approximate three to five times the annual retainer. But as we said before, annual retainer does not increase as rapidly as the size of a company, so the amount of ownership required for a small company may be similar to the ownership in a large company. The amount of ownership therefore might be related to some measure of capitalization or to the amount of total compensation (retainer plus meeting fees) for the director.

## (f) Coping with Volatility

Between receiving over half the value of their compensation through stand-alone equity grants, usually options, possibly receiving stock as part of a retainer, and having the ability to defer other forms of cash into equity, the volatility of the stock market can cause havoc with directors' compensation programs. To be sure, the voluntary election of stock or stock units as a replacement for cash or the choice of deferring cash into some form of deferred equity can enhance the competitiveness of some pay programs. And those choices are the individual directors'. But some choices are available to help lessen the effects of this market volatility over time.

With most stand-alone stock option grants expressed as a specific number of shares, the value of option grants declines when the market value of a company's stock declines. Instead, a company can delineate the option grant as a Black-Scholes value, say $30,000. If the price declines in one year, more options are granted; if the price increases the following year, fewer options are granted.

If a company were to grant a fixed dollar amount of shares as part or all of its retainer, price fluctuations would result in higher numbers of shares when the price falls, but fewer when it rises. If this plan was coupled with a typical option plan that grants a fixed number of options each year, then an increase in price one year would not reduce the number of options. Options would increase in value when fewer shares of stock were being granted as part of the retainer. The opposite is also true.

## (g) Pay for Performance Programs

True pay for performance plans are few and far between in director compensation programs. Less than 5 percent of companies that Mercer studied had plans for directors that were based on performance. They fall within these areas:

- Stock options based on the extent to which the company reached a certain level of performance the prior year
- Performance-contingent vesting (vesting occurs upon the company reaching a performance hurdle)
- Performance-accelerated vesting (vesting accelerated from a service date to an earlier date based on performance)
- Performance units
- Performance shares
- Annual incentive

Interestingly, all of the companies that have these pay for performance plans use them in addition to typical options or restricted stock plans.

## (h) Special Situations

Frequently, directors are asked to take on specific tasks or responsibilities that go beyond the normal scope of board participation. These special services could include special assignments or inspection trips made on behalf of the company, additional meetings involved with mergers or acquisitions, or other special meetings as representatives of the company. In most cases, compensation for these services comes in the form of cash payments, typically $1,000 to $2,000 per day or per meeting. This would be the case of extraordinary board meetings, as well, where the number of meetings exceeds the normal 12 or so meetings. Such extraordinary meetings usually are not rewarded through stock grants or option awards, although the ability of directors to choose the form of payment would apply to these fees.

## (i) Non-CEO Chair

The concept of a company having an employee non-CEO chairman is not unusual in the world, with Great Britain having these arrangements as the regulatory norm. In the United States, less than 10 percent of the companies studied have a nonexecutive chair, and the range of compensation for this position is wide. Most receive compensation under a special arrangement in amounts that can range from $25,000 to over $3 million per year, based on the time commitment and the chairman's prior experience. The median is $230,000. As part of these arrangements, the non-CEO chair receives stock or options typically granted to other nonemployee board members, and sometimes in an even larger amount than those directors. Former CEOs who move on to the role of chair are paid more than twice as much ($205,000 vs. $420,000) as those who were not CEOs prior to becoming board chair. That amount is usually within 10 percent of the current CEO's compensation.

Compensation for an employee chairman, however, is substantial and is at median 75 percent of the current CEO's total compensation. At median, total compensation for an employee non-CEO chair was $1.8 million. Interestingly, both salary and total cash compensation equaled 100 percent of the current CEO's compensation, but lower or missing long-term arrangements reduced the total compensation to the 75 percent figure. The non-CEO chair position, while not new in corporate America, may continue to increase in importance as a balancing factor to the role of CEO.

## 11.4  TRENDS

Although the typical compensation structure probably will not change dramatically, the one-size-fits-all program of retainer, fees, and equity will have many more variations. Meeting fees for both board service and committee membership will change as the way in which a board conducts its business changes. No one really believes that a director who makes millions of dollars a year as the CEO of a public company is only worth $1,500 per board or committee meeting, especially as these meetings become longer and longer. Further, significant work is needed in preparation for meetings, and median or typical meeting fees do not reflect that. Some companies that compensate for time spent in meetings may increase meeting fees substantially to recognize that fact; one company studied increased fees based on meeting length. Those companies that differentiate pay between a face-to-face meeting and a telephonic one may have to create a new level of pay if videoconferences begin to replace meetings.

Consequently, we see companies moving away from the pay per meeting to the pay for membership concept. Committee retainers will become more prevalent, and the recognition that board membership may not mean just attendance at meetings may result in an increase in board retainers. Critics of corporate boards identify individuals who do not attend at least 75 percent of board and committee meetings. In the future, with greater demands on time, actual attendance at meetings may not be a good indicator of director quality, and compensation will need to reflect that reality.

Committee chair retainers will increase for both the audit and to a lesser extent the compensation committee chairs, to reflect the additional work that these committees and especially their leaders will have going forward. In 2002, the retainers for these positions were $10,000 and $5,000, respectively, numbers that will undoubtedly increase as more companies report 2003 changes in their programs.

Shareholder interests are reflected in equity grants, but must be appropriately balanced with the governance role of boards. Some clients and the media have raised the concern that too heavy an emphasis on equity leads to negative behavior by executives and the board. Exhibit 11.6 shows how the compensation mix has changed over the past six years.

**Exhibit 11.6**   Change in Compensation Mix over the Past 6 Years

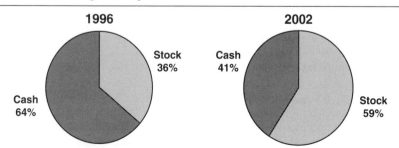

*Source:* Mercer Human Resource Consulting.

The emphasis on pay for company performance, as reflected in stock, may be too high if directors, like executives, are allowed to capitalize on that performance in the short run, rather than over a longer period of time. Balancing stock options with full-value shares would help to alleviate that concern and is a common practice among the Mercer 350. To add some consistency and long-term focus to equity grants for directors, we suggest:

- *Denominate option grants as a value,* reviewing their value every two or three years. If the price of the stock decreases, more shares are granted, but the value remains the same.

- *Denominate full-value shares as a number of shares.* If the price drops, so does the value, and if the price increases, the value increases as well. When coupled with value-denominated options, this program provides a good balance of risk and opportunity. The value of the overall program does not fluctuate dramatically, but contains an appropriate reward for an increasing stock price.

- *Vesting options at the end of the three-year term.* Full-value stock should vest at retirement from the board. Vesting options at the end of a typical three-year term allows the executive to increase share ownership or create cash from any increase in value. There is no perceived focus on short-term performance. Vesting full-value grants at retirement removes any perception that long-term performance is being sacrificed for short-term stock price movement.

- *Implement stock ownership guidelines* equal to a multiple of the amount of equity awarded annually. Allow two three-year terms for the executive to reach the level of required ownership. As companies move toward changing their plans to include more retainer and fewer meeting fees, a more appropriate measure of ownership will be how much these executives hold in relation to how much opportunity they receive. Restricted stock or units would be counted as ownership.

- *Pay for the role of lead director will continue to evolve.* The range of pay is substantial, from $10,000 to over $100,000 per year, reflecting the amount of time and importance that companies place on the role and especially on the person. The great variance probably reflects a difference in the importance that companies place on the position and the value that may be placed on the specific individual in the job. With such increased responsibilities, individuals who serve as lead directors probably will not be active executives but retired. Compensation would more than likely be totally cash or full-value stock, reflecting the fact that this job is not one of increased long-term impact but one of increased short-term time commitment.

The market for specific skills in directors makes it essential for companies to hold on to their directors who have those skills. Companies that need those skills the most—those that are poor performers or are going through a restructuring—will find it increasingly difficult to attract good directors. The directorship of an organization that is essentially sound and has little risk is attractive. But a company that is a risk, one that involves significant time and oversight, might not be able to compete in the director market. A CEO might take the job in such an organization with appropriate safeguards and appropriate rewards. The compensation for directors in such organizations might have to mimic the CEO's, with significant equity for upside performance and significant cash for the time involved. Unfortunately, these organizations might find it difficult to structure such a plan, with shareholders not looking to spend more for management or directors who presided over poor performance.

## (a) A New Approach

A few large companies have moved toward a total compensation approach, one with fewer elements and a holistic view of board compensation. Based on the competitive analysis completed as part of the compensation strategy development, companies look at the total value of the compensation package for peer companies and split that value into cash and stock components. Each element is viewed as follows.

Retainers for board service are an appropriate mechanism for compensating directors for their availability and participation in the board process. However, the use of meeting fees for board service may not be the most appropriate method for compensating directors for participation. With the typical meeting fee at approximately $1,500, directors are not attending meetings because of the financial reward for their attendance. And $1,500 does not represent the value that the company receives for a director's participation. With the frequent participation of meetings by telephone, the concept of "attendance" at a meeting has a different meaning than it once did. Therefore, some companies are moving from paying for attendance to paying for contribution. Instead of paying meeting fees for board meetings, companies determine the annual amount of meeting fees it would pay based on a historical number of meetings, or a planned number of meetings for the year, and pay that amount in cash retainer.

The same concept can be applied to committee fees. Many companies are for the first time differentiating the chair roles for audit and compensation committees, but not other committee chairs. In most cases these roles are being compensated with retainers, not additional fees.

As directors have increasingly received stock options, restricted or unrestricted stock, or units as part of their compensation, shareholders have begun to ask just how much of this stock-based compensation is eventually turned into ownership. As with executives, shareholders want to see directors with some skin in the game when it comes to their own pay. Stock ownership guidelines have been instituted in about 25 percent of the larger companies in the United States, according to a review of the Mercer 350. The increase in director compensation from this change will begin to manifest itself with changes in how companies deliver stock-based compensation and how the rules for vesting and holding stock will be designed to make real share ownership easy for directors to attain. In the case of companies that have approached compensation from a total compensation view, some have changed their equity program to one of restricted stock units, with no options granted as part of the regular compensation program. The vesting of these restricted units is usually not until retirement from the board, or later, which ensures that no component in the compensation plan encourages short-term thinking because of too much emphasis on short-term stock performance. If a director wants to replace some of the cash retainer with options, he or she is usually given the opportunity to do so. That decision, however, is the individual director's, not the company's.

The mix of cash and stock is typically between 40 percent cash/60 percent stock and a 50 percent/50 percent ratio. This ratio also ensures that directors have a vehicle to accumulate stock but are not using cash compensation in order to reach stock ownership levels. A valid criticism of plans that have too much compensation tied to options and not enough cash is that directorships are only for the rich. Given the need for directors to come from new sources of talent, this type of plan would not attract all viable candidates.

## 11.5 DEVELOPING AN OUTSIDE DIRECTOR COMPENSATION PROGRAM

Mercer suggests that companies follow a six-step model in setting up their compensation programs.

### (a) Total Reward Strategy

Establish a total reward strategy and guiding principles for outside directors that reflect the way the board expects to conduct its business. The total reward strategy should identify the types, role, level, and mix of each compensation element that will be used. Companies also should define a peer group/competitive market to use for purposes of benchmarking total compensation levels and mix, as well as assessing pay for performance relationships. The peer group should be comparable to the company with respect to key scope indicators—revenues, assets, market capitalization, business mission/services/characteristics, and long-term performance indicators, such as return on equity and total shareholder return.

### (b) Provide Competitive Compensation

Provide total direct compensation levels—retainers, per-meeting fees—and target long-term incentive opportunities that are competitive with market medians, unless there is a compelling business case for positioning well above or below market medians. Use variable compensation—long-term incentive compensation—to provide upside opportunity for achievement of long-term performance results.

### (c) Establish Ownership Guidelines

Emphasize ownership by making equity worth about half of the total compensation package through equity grants, payment of retainer in shares, and/or mandatory/ voluntary deferred compensation vehicles. Use stock ownership guidelines—three to five times annual equity compensation, with six years to reach the guideline—to demonstrate commitment to shareholders.

### (d) Balance Options with Full-Value Awards

Use a balance of stock options and full-value awards—unrestricted stock, re-stricted stock—for equity grants. Stock options reinforce a focus on shareholder value creation. Full-value awards are effective for purposes of attraction/retention and encourage a perspective beyond short-term stock price appreciation. They also help mitigate the effects of market volatility. Consider providing equity grants with a mix of 50 to 60 percent of the estimated present value coming from stock options and 40 to 50 percent coming from full-value plans.

### (e) Use Retainers for Committee Chairs

Use higher retainers to compensate committee chairs for the additional responsi-bilities in audit and compensation committees. Chairs of other committees should receive more modest retainers.

### (f) Limit Benefits

Limit retirement and other benefits/perquisites that are not performance related.

## 11.6  CONCLUSION

Changes in director compensation always have been evolutionary. Meeting fees reflect an old tradition of paying directors by check when they came to a meeting, in many instances as an incentive to attend. Little work was done outside meetings, but board retainers took care of any time commitment not covered by meeting fees. Equity was added when shareholders wanted directors to have the same tie to their own interests. When security laws were changed, allowing directors to de-termine the amount of options or stock they themselves should receive, and not re-quiring shareholder approval, few companies reacted. The year 2002 has been a wake-up call to directors, and corporate governance is now the focus of every company and its directors. If past practice is any predictor of the future, change in compensation will be slow. But some long-term trends might involve:

- No meeting fees, but large cash retainers
- Equity grants, both options and full-value stock equal to no more than half the total compensation
- Significant restricted stock grants for members with key responsibilities as chairpersons of committees
- Annual performance reviews for individual directors and committees, with the results published in the company's proxy statement. Annual pay for performance is not appropriate for boards, but the performance of individual members is appropriate for shareholders to know and understand. However, this type of disclosure must wait until the processes of board assessment have been embedded in the new corporate governance reforms.

# Chapter 12

# Board Assessment: Designing a Process that Is Meaningful, Practical, and Engaging

**Beverly A. Behan, Mercer Delta Consulting**

## 12.1 IMPORTANCE OF BOARD ASSESSMENT

"To assess or not to assess" is no longer the question for boards of major U.S. companies. Now that the New York Stock Exchange (NYSE) requires boards and their committees to conduct annual self-assessments, a more relevant question is "Should we do only the minimum required for compliance, or is it worth investing in a more ambitious approach that has the potential to improve our overall governance?"

The answer is that when it comes to board assessment, doing just the bare minimum means squandering one of the best opportunities one will ever have to genuinely improve the way the board works, both as a team and together with the chief executive officer (CEO) and senior management. Assessment is one of the most powerful interventions available for turning a good board into a great board—one that is constructively and effectively engaged, that genuinely adds value for the CEO and the management team, and that provides strong corporate oversight.

A *de minimus* approach to board assessment—merely recycling a survey used by another board, for instance—will not substantially improve a board and actually might create some risks. A poorly designed and executed board assessment process can destroy trust, erode credibility, and shatter essential working relationships.

## 12.2   RISKS AND OPPORTUNITIES

### (a) Major Risks

Conducting an assessment is, in itself, an intervention with the board, and it can have either a negative or a positive impact. More specifically, poorly designed assessment processes raise two major risks:

1.  *Damage to board dynamics:* Board assessments can surface exceptionally delicate issues. Without a well-planned process, these issues can be raised in ways that produce heated arguments and exacerbate rifts within the board or between the board and management.
2.  *Erosion of credibility:* Conversely, if sensitive issues are raised and then swept under the rug, directors will view the process as a sham. That can seriously hurt the credibility of everyone responsible for the board assessment process.

### (b) Potential Benefits

Although it requires significant thought and effort, effective board assessment offers real benefits:

*   *An accurate check on the board's "pulse":* Some CEOs believed they had excellent relationships with their boards, only to be taken completely by surprise when these same boards fired them. Corporate secretaries and chairs of governance committees will describe their board as "ahead of the curve" one day. The next day a member of that same board may say, "I'm on three boards and this one is not up to snuff with the others, but no one seems to want to face up to that. I'm seriously thinking of getting off this board." Regular and effective assessment can tell the CEO and board leaders what the directors are pleased with and raise red flags before problems turn into crises. This type of process does not rely on assumptions and wishful thinking; instead, it provides concrete data on how the board is working together.
*   *A "safe" way to surface and discuss board issues:* A sound assessment process gives the CEO and other board leaders a chance to assess where the board stands before deciding how to proceed with key issues. Understanding the lay of the land in the boardroom almost always makes it easier to navigate important and challenging issues. An effective process enables the board to talk about issues without the CEO or any one of the board members having to lead the discussion, which can increase the candor of discussions while preserving political capital.

One CEO said, "For about a year, I wanted to raise the issue of recruiting more directors with industry experience onto the board. I felt sure this issue would make several board members defensive, so I held off. To my surprise, they raised this issue themselves in the course of the assessment and tasked the nominating committee to develop a list of board candidates with exactly the kind of experience I felt we needed—all without my having to be the heavy on this."

- *Increased ownership and accountability:* A process that incorporates input from each board member and the chair/CEO builds commitment and a shared sense of responsibility for addressing the priorities that emerge from the assessment, which is rarely achieved from a superficial process. A more thorough approach, which requires the active engagement of the board and CEO as a group to discuss the results, leads them to agreement on how the board is operating and what it can do to improve.

An experienced board member of a consumer services company shared this during his first board assessment: "I've served on this board for nearly 10 years, and this is the first time I've really sat down and thought about how we have been working together. We've never really talked about that—our discussions always focus on how we are addressing everything on the always overloaded agendas. Now that I've spent some time thinking about this, there are definitely some things we could do better. It also made me think about why I joined this board in the first place—I seem to have lost sight of that somewhere between all the meetings and the calls."

- *More effective boards and CEOs:* This is the ultimate payoff. The data collected for a well-designed assessment can dramatically change how a board uses its time, how it works with the CEO, and how the board and the CEO work together to focus on the organization's real priorities.

## 12.3 VIEWING BOARD ASSESSMENT IN CONTEXT

### (a) Assessment as a Lever

Rather than looking at board assessment as an isolated regulatory requirement, it is critical to think about it in the larger context of building a truly effective board. An effective board assessment can be used as a lever for creating a board that both meets legal obligations and becomes a source of added value for the company. Moreover, it is wrong to think that only poorly performing boards should spend time on assessment. Typically, the better the board, the more useful a robust board assessment process can be in helping it discover new ways to enhance performance. The best boards constantly look for opportunities to raise their game, and effective board assessment is one of the best tools available to help good boards get even better.

## (b) The Board as a Team

Frame thinking about board assessment by viewing the board as a team. Traditionally, boards were groups of people who assembled periodically and behaved quite ritualistically. Other than ratifying management's proposals, in many cases there was little real work for them to do.

All of that has changed. Today there is a great deal of real work to be done in the boardroom and an unprecedented degree of visibility and accountability. To meet these demands, the board must begin to truly function as a team—a set of people who work together to accomplish specific objectives they could not achieve separately. That definition sounds simple, but it implies that many boards will have to start thinking about their roles and responsibilities in fundamentally new ways.

Viewed in this context, the board assessment process should be designed to help optimize the board's ability to work together as a high-performing team. Start by identifying areas of current strength and opportunities for improvement. The process itself should serve as a team-building exercise for the board rather than a process that most board members view as going through the motions with little real utility.

## (c) Degree of Board Engagement

There are five general types of boards, each one functioning at a different level of engagement (see Exhibit 12.1). It can be useful to consider where a board currently is operating within this model and where it has operated over the years. Is it operating at the appropriate level of engagement, or is it either underengaged or micromanaging? Consider how the board assessment process can be used as a tool to move the board in a particular direction to achieve a more appropriate level of engagement or to reinforce and capitalize on the current level of engagement, if that is more desirable.

## (d) Board Building

Our framework for developing effective boards involves a detailed process that helps reshape not only the structure of the board but also the fundamental nature of a company's corporate governance. (See Exhibit 12.2). Board assessment plays a vital role in two phases of this process:

1.  *Taking stock of the board:* A comprehensive, diagnostic assessment—designed, executed, and interpreted well—can provide a natural starting point for board building. The assessment process envisioned is markedly different from what

**Exhibit 12.1** Degree of Board Engagement

| "Passive" Board ↔ | "Certifying" Board ↔ | "Engaged" Board ↔ | "Intervening" Board ↔ | "Operating" Board |
|---|---|---|---|---|
| • Functions at discretion of CEO<br><br>• Limited activity and participation of board<br><br>• Limited accountability<br><br>• Ratifies management preferences | • "Certifies" to shareholders that: CEO is doing what board expects; management is capable of taking corrective action when needed<br><br>• Emphasizes outside/independent directors; meets independently without CEO<br><br>• Stays informed of current performance; designates external board members to evaluate CEO<br><br>• Establishes orderly succession process<br><br>• Is willing and able to change management to be credible to shareholders | • "Partners" with CEO to provide insight, advice, and support to CEO and management team on key decisions and implementation<br><br>• Also recognizes ultimate responsibility to oversee CEO and company performance; dual role of guiding/supporting and judging the CEO<br><br>• Board meetings characterized by useful two-way discussions of key issues/decisions facing the company<br><br>• Board members need sufficient industry and financial expertise to add value to decisions<br><br>• Time and emphasis spent on defining role and behaviors required of board members and on boundaries of CEO/board responsibility | • Typical mode during "crisis" situation<br><br>• Board becomes intensely involved in discussions of key decisions facing the organization and in decision making<br><br>• Frequent and intense board meetings, often called on short notice | • Board makes key decisions; management implements<br><br>• Not uncommon in early start-ups where board members selected to "fill gaps" in management experience |

**Exhibit 12.2**   Board-Building Framework

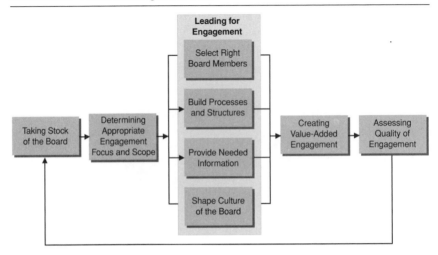

*Source:* Mercer Delta Insight, *Beyond Compliance: The Challenge of Board Buildings,* 2003. © Mercer Delta Consulting LLC, 2003.

is happening at many companies and again brings up the issue of doing the minimum required to achieve compliance. If the goal is compliance, then it is fine to simply generate a checklist or quick survey. But if the goal is to improve the quality of governance, much more is required.

It is essential that the CEO and board leaders, typically including the nominating and corporate governance committee, work together on the key decisions that will shape the assessment. They need to determine what topics will be explored, what data will be collected, how data will be collected and by whom, how feedback will be shared with the board, and how to act on the feedback.

These issues go to the heart of the CEO-board relationship, and the process of designing the assessment presents an ideal opportunity to build engagement and understanding. Indeed, taking stock of where the board is today is a vital step in determining where it is headed tomorrow. The results of this diagnostic process will be used to frame the priorities and actions throughout much of the board-building process.

2.  *Assessing quality of engagement:* The assessment process also plays a role in the last step of the board-building framework. It is, in essence, the feedback loop that provides the board with useful information about the impact of initiatives taken in board building—changes made to the board's composition, processes, and culture. This information allows the board to make necessary adjustments as it learns from experience.

Typically, successful boards find it useful to conduct both ongoing and more intensive, periodic assessment. Ongoing assessment involves building in measures of processes that can help the board make appropriate corrections as work progresses. This might involve regular short board surveys to test directors' perceptions of effectiveness or progress in addressing priorities, or incorporating a "How are we doing?" discussion in the executive sessions at the end of each board meeting. At a minimum, boards should evaluate their process at least once a year, as required in the new NYSE rules.

However, at times it does make sense to go back and take a deeper look at all of the issues, beginning with the work of the board and its degree of engagement on issues such as corporate strategy, CEO succession, and the like. It can be burdensome—and frankly unnecessary—to do an in-depth analysis every year, but it is certainly worthwhile every few years. A more comprehensive assessment can be particularly helpful the first time the board assesses itself, providing a useful road map for identifying and addressing its priorities. Progress along that path can be monitored over time by less comprehensive pulse checks.

In Mercer Delta Consulting's work with boards, we sometimes hear concerns about the amount of time that a more comprehensive assessment process will require, particularly now that board members are facing unprecedented demands. We understand that concern, but we have found that most directors are willing to invest whatever time is needed if they find the assessment process to be both engaging and useful. One company, for example, asked us to design an assessment that included interviews only with the board's executive committee. Before long, word got around to the other board members that the directors we had interviewed had enjoyed the discussions and felt that important issues were being addressed. The other board members felt left out and demanded to be interviewed, too. Instead of feeling relieved that their time was spared, they wanted to participate in the process.

Despite their busy schedules, directors almost always are willing to continue their interviews past the allotted time so they can make their points and provide examples. In one instance, a board member refused to interrupt his interview to take an urgent call from a well-known Fortune 100 CEO, asking his assistant to "Tell him I'll call him back; it won't be that long. This interview is fun, and I'm on a roll here."

In most cases where directors cite busy schedules as an excuse to avoid or cut short the assessment interviews, their real concern is that the process will unearth some particularly sensitive issues that could poison the board's dynamics. That is a legitimate concern. However, a well-designed assessment provides a constructive way to confront "the moose on the table"—a metaphor for addressing the unpleasant but unspoken issues that often lie at the heart of a group's concerns.

## 12.4   BOARD ASSESSMENT PROCESS

### (a) Achieving Real Value

A board that assesses itself by checking off a few boxes and concluding "We're okay" might satisfy the NYSE requirements, but will have little else to show for its effort. The real value of a board assessment lies in engaging board members in thinking about and discussing how the board does its work and in finding ways to make the board even more effective.

The general counsel of a large public company recently told us, "Our board assessment was so good that we had no issues." Maybe so; some boards are, indeed, in pretty good shape. But more often than not, a perfect score actually indicates either a poorly designed process or a board that simply has disengaged. Effective designs for board assessment typically surface three to five major issues, generate good discussion about them, and yield useful ideas for improving the board's performance. Boards that are appropriately engaged tend to raise more issues, because they generally strive for continuous improvement.

### (b) Five Questions to Address

There are five fundamental questions to address as the assessment process is designed. Each one represents a crucial fork in the road; together, the answers will shape the process and determine its effectiveness. It is preferable to consider them all and develop a game plan before getting started, rather than trying to redesign the process on the fly.

1. *Is it possible to get the board to buy in before the process starts?* It is one thing for a board to accept that assessment is required; it is quite another for members genuinely to believe the effort is worthwhile. So it is essential to involve directors right from the start in designing their own process, beginning with goals and assessment criteria. There are some thorny decisions to be made: How will confidentiality be assured? Who will collect the data? Who will see the results? Will the committee assessments be done separately or as part of the overall board assessment, and will noncommittee members have input into them? Directors need to play a role in shaping the assessment in ways that will convince them of its legitimacy and value.

2. *What topics will be explored?* A crucial aspect of the design is to reach a shared understanding of the issues to be assessed. These might range from board structure and work processes to quantitative measures of corporate financial performance. In addition to broad issues, there may be particular topics a board has focused on in the past year that would benefit from a pulse check. The challenge most often is to develop a list of topics that is neither too sparse nor too tedious, one that creates useful discussion and covers topics

that board members feel are critical in assessing their effectiveness as a governing body and as a working team.

3. *How will the data be collected?* Will the data gathered be quantitative or qualitative, or a combination of both? Surveys are useful in evaluating perceptions and are invaluable in tracking progress over time, but they have their limits. Individual interviews tend to unearth richer data and underlying concerns, forming the basis for excellent board discussion and yielding highly productive results. Real-time assessments can surface insights about performance in a format that also can serve as a beneficial team-building exercise. (All three of these approaches are described in detail later in this chapter.) The selection of a methodology—whether alone or in combination—represents a major choice point in the design of the assessment process.

4. *Who should conduct the assessment?* Using internal staff is less expensive; in addition, insiders, with their knowledge of the organization and its board members, may raise the board's level of comfort. Yet an outside third party might bring more expertise in assessment methodologies and be perceived as more candid and objective. We once worked with a board that had used internal resources to conduct board assessment for three years before our involvement. One component of the assessment, a survey that tracked year over year, was markedly different the year we were part of the process. When this was discussed with the board at the feedback session, board members confessed that they had been much more candid with "outsiders." Consequently, some important areas not previously identified were discussed and addressed.

   Each choice carries its own drawbacks and advantages, but one word of caution: The market is flooded with vendors selling packaged assessments, checklists, and surveys. They might help you to comply with the NYSE rules, but they will not provide you with the real benefits of effective assessment and actually might increase the risk of experiencing the hazards discussed earlier.

5. *How will feedback from the assessment be handled?* This is probably the single most important component of the process; it will go a long way toward determining whether the process succeeds or fails. Deciding who will share the feedback with whom, in what settings, and under what conditions are all critical choice points. Even more important is the design of the working session with the board where feedback results will be presented and discussed. Determine beforehand, rather than in the heat of the moment, how to constructively manage challenging or sensitive issues that might arise so that they are acknowledged and dealt with—not swept under the rug or allowed to fester.

   It is not enough for the assessment to raise touchy issues; to be successful, it also has to be seen by directors as a process that helps them resolve the issues. For example, one board's self-assessment raised concerns about a "two-tiered board"—one level consisting of the full board, the other including only members of the executive committee, which met twice as often as the board and therefore was seen as better informed and more actively engaged.

The issue was aired during the feedback discussion, and it was agreed that in the future, all matters would be brought to the full board either through meetings or conference calls whenever possible, and the executive committee would be used only for emergencies.

## 12.5   THREE APPROACHES TO EVALUATION

### (a) Choice of Methods

The best board assessments involve some combination of both qualitative and quantitative data. Mercer Delta's work with boards, for instance, usually involves three approaches: surveys, one-on-one interviews, and real-time group self-assessments. All three of the approaches develop questions and discussion topics based on information gathered from the corporation's articles, bylaws, corporate governance guidelines, board committee charters, and criteria for nominating directors. (See Exhibit 12.3.)

### (b) Quantitative Self-Assessment: Survey Approach

In this approach, board members complete a written survey that asks them to rate the board's performance on a variety of dimensions, using a numeric scale. The data from the completed surveys are evaluated and compiled in a report that generally includes analysis of both numeric scores and summaries of any write-in questions. The report forms the basis of the working session with the board where feedback from the assessment is discussed, areas for improvement are identified and prioritized, alternatives are debated, and the best path for improvement is determined.

A survey is a straightforward, standard practice that most board members are familiar with. A major advantage of using a quantitative assessment is the ability to perform comparisons and track the board's progress over time. Surveys also can be designed to ensure anonymity and give board members flexibility because they can be completed at their convenience. The value of questionnaire formats often is maximized when used in combination with one of the qualitative approaches.

### (c) Qualitative Self-Assessment: Interview Approach

Confidential interviews with each board member are useful for gathering in-depth insights about the board's performance. Typically, a list of interview questions is distributed to board members in advance. While the structured questions provide some uniformity in terms of topics covered, an interview format enables directors to raise issues that go beyond the questions. Notes from the interviews are compiled and analyzed by key themes, which typically are summarized in a report. As

**Exhibit 12.3** Three Approaches to Board Evaluation

The most robust assessments use a combination of these methods, rather than relying on a single approach.

| | Quantitative: Survey | Qualitative: Personal Interviews | Qualitative: Real-time Assessment |
|---|---|---|---|
| **Description** | Board members complete a written survey, rating board performance on a numeric scale; results are discussed by full board in feedback sessions. | One-on-one interviews are conducted with each board member; results are discussed by full board in feedback sessions. | Trained facilitator leads a group discussion of the full board; session summarized in report for future use. |
| **Strengths** | • Participants are familiar with this straightforward standard practice.<br>• Can be completed at a participant's convenience.<br>• Can track a board's progress over time.<br>• Feedback sessions often focus on generating additional information and insights to supplement the survey data.<br>• Anonymity can be ensured. | • Participants become engaged in the interview process; most find it interesting and even enjoyable.<br>• Information tends to be more detailed and complete than what a survey gathers, which is helpful in fully understanding the issues, setting priorities, and developing plans to address them.<br>• Feedback sessions tend to be highly engaging.<br>• Anonymity can be ensured. | • Participants find the process energizing, engaging.<br>• Critical thinking is heightened because views are shared with everyone and participants can question each other.<br>• Generates consensus on priorities and support for plans to address them.<br>• Requires no preparation by participants.<br>• Serves as a team-building exercise.<br>• Most effective when there is a high degree of trust and openness among board members. |

with the survey format, the results are presented in a working session with facilitated discussion.

Interviews can be designed to protect the anonymity of participants, particularly if a third party is used to conduct them. When anonymity is ensured, candid discussion is generated in a format that surfaces a rich pool of commentary. Because this approach typically generates far more detailed and complete information than is possible with quantitative assessment, it allows interviewers to delve deeply into complex issues. Consequently, the working sessions to discuss results tend to be interactive and engaging, and the detailed data are useful in setting priorities and considering alternatives.

### (d) Qualitative Self-Assessment: Real-Time Approach

In the real-time self-assessment, a third party trained in the method leads a group discussion of the board of directors. The session involves direct, probing questions and full engagement of all directors in a group setting. Our experience shows that critical thinking is heightened if board members are together when asked questions and have the opportunity to hear other opinions and even question each other. This kind of process typically generates consensus from the board members and support for steps that need to be taken in response to issues that are raised. A report that summarizes the session can be used in subsequent working sessions with the full board to discuss results and future actions.

The group discussion can be an effective and efficient means of surfacing rich dialogue. It works particularly well in situations where there is a high degree of trust and openness among board members. These facilitated sessions require no preparation by directors and are consistently seen as engaging and energizing by participants. Moreover, the process itself typically serves as a team-building exercise for the board, which also can be beneficial.

### (e) Combining Approaches for Maximum Impact

Those new to board assessment typically select one of the three methodologies—most commonly the survey—and use only that approach. More sophisticated boards have learned to combine approaches and tailor them to their specific needs, which allows them to view the board through somewhat different lenses and capitalize on the benefits of each approach. Here are examples:

- A high-growth Nasdaq company decided a board assessment process could be beneficial, even though it was not obligated to do it. It used a survey, followed by a group discussion. The survey indicated there were concerns about information, board leadership, and corporate strategy. However, it was not until the group session that the real issue was uncovered: The company had undergone a series of acquisitions that had transpired so quickly that board members were worried they had not been able to evaluate the deals sufficiently. The CEO, however, said the board impeded his momentum in deal making. Their discussions led them to a consensus that the board needed a deeper understanding of the company's strategy in order to make quicker decisions about possible acquisitions. Without the group self-assessment, it is unlikely they would have reached a resolution as quickly as they did.

• Another company we worked with arose from the merger of two predecessor companies of approximately equal size. The board, which was composed of members from each original firm plus directors new to the company, had worked together about 18 months when it embarked on its first assessment. Members combined a survey and personal interviews to collect the data, which revealed that although the board had made significant progress in integrating the cultures, there were still marked differences between the two sides. The survey data indicated that the working relationship of the chairman and CEO was an area for improvement. However, it was not until the in-depth interview data were added to the mix that the reasons for these differences surfaced.

The current chairman's role at one of the predecessor organizations was very hands-on. It was entirely different at the other predecessor organization, where the CEO had come from. Consequently, the level of involvement that the chairman considered appropriate on the basis of his prior company seemed like micromanagement to the CEO, who came from a very different model. Understanding these different frames of reference helped both individuals to reshape their roles and improve their working relationship. The survey data by itself could not have surfaced these underlying issues in a way that provided this level of understanding.

## 12.6  FEEDBACK—A CRUCIAL STEP

### (a) Make Decisions at the Outset

As indicated, the feedback portion of the overall assessment process is perhaps the most crucial. Decide at the outset how the feedback will be delivered and by whom. Even if a third party facilitates the board's working session to discuss the feedback, the real leader or leaders of that session are in fact the chair of the corporate governance committee and/or the chair of the board. As such, they need to be aware of factors and dynamics that are likely to come into play during this discussion.

### (b) Consider Emotional Responses

People walk into board feedback sessions with various emotions and preconceptions that can be more intense than those normally found in similar situations involving other groups. After all, boards tend to be made up of individuals at the height of their professions who are not used to getting performance reviews—even if it is a review of a group they belong to. If not managed well, these feelings—particularly anxiety, defensiveness, and fear—can get in the way of effective communication and hinder board members' ability to identify and solve problems. (See Exhibit 12.4.)

Not all feelings are negative, however. Some directors look forward to board feedback sessions with enthusiasm; they see an opportunity for raising critical issues, solving problems, and initiating change. They view the assessment process as a means of breaking through the patina of gentility that cloaks most boardrooms to enable long-overdue discussion of important issues.

This was the case with the board of a global company in the services sector when its assessment raised issues surrounding succession. Although a primary concern because the CEO was approaching retirement, it had not been addressed directly until the feedback session. Although board members unanimously endorsed the choice of an internal candidate to become the new CEO, the board's discussions led to a series of initiatives to address other succession issues such as mentoring of the candidate and the future of other members of the executive team.

## (c) Be Aware of the Boardroom Environment

When delivering board assessment feedback, be sensitive to the potential negative dynamics, build on the positive dynamics, and establish an environment that helps direct energy into appropriate actions that will enhance the board's effectiveness. One needs to create a boardroom environment in which there is:

* *Motivation to work the assessment results:* Board members need to feel that addressing the issues surfaced through the board assessment will be worthwhile. If the perception is that the assessment process is nothing more than going

---

**Exhibit 12.4**  Emotional Responses to Feedback

---

These emotions must be recognized and managed in order for a board to get the full benefit of feedback during the assessment process.

**Anxiety:** People do not know what to expect. The ambiguity regarding what will happen and how the board and individual board members are going to react causes people to be anxious.

**Defensiveness:** Anticipating the possibility of negative feedback, people show up ready to defend themselves or the group.

**Fear:** People worry about the consequences of giving candid feedback, causing some to hedge their observations and leave the real issues lurking just beneath the surface.

---

© Mercer Delta Consulting, LLC, 2003.

through the motions with no real desire to find out what the issues are, there will be scant motivation to dig into the feedback and do something with it.

- *Assistance in using the assessment results:* People need to fully understand the key issues and themes surfaced in the process. For example, if an assessment indicates dissatisfaction regarding corporate strategy, it is important to understand the nuances: Do board members feel the corporate strategy is not right for the company? Are they concerned about implementation? Or is the real issue that they want to be more involved in reviewing and developing the strategy? Without knowing what the real issue is, it is impossible to resolve the problem.

- *Appropriate power:* Boards should limit their actions to governance issues— even if management issues arise. And once priorities are set, they need the resources to address them. Such resources may include access to outside advisors; the ability to put these items on board and/or committee agendas; and access to the CEO or other members of senior management, as appropriate, to discuss the issues and develop approaches.

## 12.7   VARIATIONS ON THE BOARD ASSESSMENT PROCESS

### (a) Customization Can Be Beneficial

Some boards have customized their assessment processes, adding an assortment of bells and whistles, such as data on senior management's perspectives on the board's effectiveness, assessments of the chair (or lead director) and the board committees, and a review of board minutes.

### (b) Management Evaluation of the Board's Effectiveness

Although a board assessment typically involves input by the board members themselves, some boards want to know how management thinks they are doing. Does the board actually add value for them as senior managers? What do they see as the most valuable contributions by the board? What, if anything, would they want to change in terms of how the board and management interact?

A high-profile media company included in its assessment a set of questions to be completed by seven senior managers who regularly worked with the board and attended its meetings. A comparison of results showed that the average scores the board gave itself on several components differed dramatically from the scores given by senior management. Some differences came as a surprise; on several issues, management clearly felt the board was adding more value than the board thought it was. The nominating and corporate governance committee and a subset of the management group that had participated in the assessment process met to discuss the underlying issues and themes that were raised. At the session, both the board and management decided to make some changes, which, within a year, had a positive impact on the board and its working relationship with the management team.

### (c) Assessment of the Chair of the Board and/or Lead Director

In the United States, the vast majority of public companies—more than 70 percent of the Standard & Poor's 500—combine the roles of chair of the board and chief executive officer. These two roles, however, are very different. An individual can be an outstanding CEO but a poor chairman and vice versa. Recognizing this, some boards feel it is useful to evaluate the CEO separately in his or her role as chair of the board, either as part of the annual CEO evaluation or as a component of the annual board assessment.

The three approaches to gathering board assessment data just discussed can be used effectively in designing assessment of the chair. First, a number of questions must be answered: Who will lead the process, review the data, and provide feedback to the chair—the chair of the compensation committee, the chair of the governance committee, or someone else? Is there value in using a third party to collect data? Will employee directors serving on the board be asked to provide input into the chair's evaluation, or will this input be limited exclusively to outside directors? How will results of the chair's assessment be shared with board members?

If the board has a nonexecutive chair (someone other than the CEO serving as chair of the board) or a lead director, it might be useful to assess his or her effectiveness. In these circumstances, the question of who will assume leadership for the process and deliver the feedback is sometimes even more difficult. This responsibility typically falls to the chair of one of the key board committees that the nonexecutive chair or lead director does not lead. While the role of presiding director is becoming more prevalent, it is typically too limited in its scope to warrant a separate assessment. However, the effectiveness of executive sessions of the board and the leadership of those sessions should be included in the board assessment, providing feedback on the presiding director's performance.

### (d) Assessment of Board Committees

Prior to the new NYSE rules, a separate evaluation of each board committee was relatively uncommon even among those boards that annually evaluated board performance. Most commonly, questions about board and committee structure and perhaps a few questions about each committee's performance would have been incorporated into the board assessment process. However, now that NYSE rules require an annual assessment of the performance of board committees, more comprehensive practices are developing. Committee assessments can be done either as part of the board assessment or independent of it.

A key consideration is whether to incorporate feedback from both committee members and nonmembers into the process. Committee members are the only ones who can observe how the committee operates from within. However, the full board receives regular reports from each committee, including committee recommendations to the board. Most board members who do not serve on a particular committee form impressions about the effectiveness of the committee from this information. This perspective can be very worthwhile for the committee to incorporate into its assessment.

### (e) Review of Board Minutes

Some boards find a review of minutes helpful. The review explores how the board actually spends its time and compares this with how the board feels it should spend its time. For example, if board members feel strongly that CEO succession and executive development are a board priority, a review of board minutes over the past year can indicate how often the board discussed this issue. A similar review can be a useful component in committee assessments.

## 12.8 DIRECTOR PEER REVIEW—THE EXTRA STEP

### (a) Potential Value

Although not a regulatory requirement, many boards have begun to incorporate director peer reviews into their assessment process because of their potential value. The Conference Board's 2003 Blue Ribbon Commission on Public Trust and Private Enterprise recommended a three-tier board evaluation process, which includes an assessment of the board as a whole, the performance of each board committee, and the performance of each individual director.

### (b) Recognizing the Benefits

In a typical peer review process, board members provide structured feedback on each of their fellow directors. Some benefits include:

- *Professional development:* Feedback becomes increasingly rare at higher organizational levels. Consequently, directors receive very little—if any—feedback on their performance other than isolated comments such as "That comment you made today was right on" or "I really think we've got to be careful about beating a dead horse." A structured director peer review process provides a comprehensive perspective on a director's overall contribution—identifying both areas of strength and opportunities for development. The feedback from a peer review typically is helpful to a director's professional development on all boards he or she serves on.

- *Enhanced board performance:* Board members typically use peer feedback to leverage their strengths and address developmental opportunities, which ultimately results in better performance of the board as a whole. Noticeable improvement often follows a peer assessment simply because the director has been made aware of a need for change—often for the first time. Even when board members disagree with feedback, most find it useful.

- *Team-building:* Destructive board dynamics are a risk—especially if the peer review process is poorly designed and/or badly managed. If done well, however, peer review can foster board team building by providing a forum for board members to reflect on both individual contributions and how they work together.

## (c) Keeping It Constructive

Because peer assessment takes evaluation from a group to an individual level, anxiety tends to increase. Most board members are highly accomplished, many have not had a performance review in years, and many might be happy never to have one again.

We have one piece of advice to ensure that a peer review is beneficial, not alienating: Keep it constructive. For example, one board member we interviewed in the course of a peer review had been seething over the boardroom behavior of three fellow directors for years and welcomed a forum to give them a piece of his mind. Once he had finished letting off some steam, however, we began to ask him more probing questions about the behavior he had described. In every case, there was a rich kernel of constructive feedback hidden beneath the venting that preceded it. The feedback to the three individuals focused on the constructive suggestions instead of personality issues. Consequently, it was relatively well received by the three board members, even though it was by no means positive.

## (d) Designing a Process

Because of its sensitive nature, the design and implementation of the peer review warrant even more care than other aspects of a board assessment. Three areas, in particular, require careful consideration:

1. *Identifying objectives:* Sometimes a peer review is solely for professional development of individual directors, which allows board members to become comfortable with the process before attaching consequences to the results. Board members tend to treat their peers' feedback seriously, even when it is purely developmental. In extreme cases, low scores have prompted resignations; more generally, a noticeable improvement in performance can be ex-

pected. Since the proposal of new governance legislation, peer reviews are being used increasingly by the nominating and corporate governance committees to help them make renominating decisions.

2. *Collecting data:* We typically recommend a combination of quantitative and qualitative approaches. It is particularly helpful to conduct confidential interviews when the process is first introduced, which allows directors to be more candid and more expressive than they can be with a survey. Use of a third party to collect and analyze the data helps ensure both candor and confidentiality—both essential to a successful process.

3. *Providing feedback:* Results often are used to shape developmental opportunities for the board as a whole or for individual directors, and improvement can be measured yearly.

If the review is developmental, feedback usually is summarized in writing and given (typically by a third party) directly to each participant. If quantitative data is collected, a comparison of each director's individual score with the average score of the entire board is provided. Individual meetings or phone calls are suggested if sensitive or challenging issues emerge in an assessment.

If the assessment is part of the review for renomination, decide at the outset who will see the results: the chair of the nominating and corporate governance committee or the whole committee, the chair of the board or the full board. Typically the nominating and corporate governance committee or its chair receives a summary of the results shortly after the full results are provided to each director. If results suggest performance and renomination concerns, the committee discusses how to handle this, and the chair schedules individual meetings with the appropriate board members.

## 12.9  SUMMARY

Now that many boards are obliged to conduct an annual assessment, most want to do it right—creating a process that is meaningful, practical, and engaging. A comprehensive and effective board assessment is one of several critical components of an overall process to move beyond legal compliance to a more purposeful effort to improve a company's governance.

To maximize its effectiveness, the assessment process must be designed and implemented thoughtfully and thoroughly, with careful attention paid to goals, topics to be explored, data collection, and feedback. This process can mean a significant investment of time and effort—not only to create and execute the process itself but also to address appropriately the issues that surface during the evaluations and feedback sessions. Even so, it is an opportunity that should be embraced, not squandered, especially when one considers its true potential as a significant leverage point to turn a good board into one that is truly outstanding.

# Chapter 13

# Creating Value with Communication*

**Lea L. Peterson**

Organizations in recent years have worked hard to redesign their executive pay programs to align rewards more closely with shareholder interests and realize more value for the millions paid to top executives. Emerging from this overhaul is a reemphasis on pay for performance, executive accountability for results, and responsible pay management. Similarly, there is now more emphasis on communication, driven by the need to improve business performance, comply with enhanced disclosure requirements, and implement substantive program change. More and more organizations recognize that communication can help to create value. This is particularly true when communication is viewed as more than a vehicle to inform executives about their pay programs and performance targets. Communication has the most impact when used as a facilitator of organizational change, a behavior motivator, and a means to focus and engage key leaders.

Responsible executive pay communication:

- Articulates the business outcomes valued by the board and expected by shareholders
- Focuses management energy and behavior on the priorities important to creating value
- Communicates the rewards program in the context of the organization's values, code of conduct, business objectives, and other drivers of enterprise success
- Clarifies the links among pay, business outcomes, and personal performance.
- Integrates all components of pay into a comprehensive view of the total rewards package

*The author wishes to thank Mercer communication principals David Jackson, Terri Ehrenfeld, Rod Fralicx, Debra Slappey, Debra Besch, Scott Williams, and Joseph Loya for their thoughtful contributions and thorough peer review.

- Translates technical plan details to ensure easy assimilation and thorough understanding
- Provides personalized information about wealth accumulation to build long-term commitment and improve perceptions of value
- Reinforces the right behaviors through periodic, not just one-time, communication in the context of a broader change process
- Engages leaders in conversations about goals, performance, and rewards
- Provides ongoing performance feedback against defined enterprise and individual metrics
- Measures the impact of communication for continuous improvement

This chapter outlines *Communication for Impact*™, Mercer's approach to ensuring responsible executive pay communication. It discusses:

- The dependency of effective executive rewards design on good execution
- Research findings about executive views related to performance and rewards
- The unique needs of the executive audience
- Specific ways to create a responsible communication strategy for executive rewards
- The importance of personalized communication
- The challenges of communicating in today's regulatory and shareholder environment

## 13.1   COMMUNICATION LEVERAGES PLAN DESIGN

With the amount of public attention today on executive performance, rewards, and behavior, no organization can afford to ignore communication. Chapter 6 deals with communication issues related to external audiences; this chapter provides the internal view. Without effective communication, executive rewards will simply not achieve the desired impact. To help drive organizational change—improved performance at the individual and enterprise levels, ethical behaviors, and a common focus—communication must be well planned, executed, and sustained. It must be an ongoing process, not a one-time event.

It starts with communicating the basics about the rewards program. A well-designed compensation plan that is silent will have little impact. Say nothing about the objectives behind program design or the process used to determine the metrics, and the program will have less clarity and credibility. Communicate only at implementation and payout, and you will miss opportunities to maintain momentum and to reinforce key messages throughout the year. Deliver details of a multimillion-dollar executive pay program with only a sketchy, generic memo or a technical plan document, and executives may question the program's value and be confused about the personal impact and the actions needed. A communication vacuum speaks loudly and is guaranteed to create problems, such as misalignment, confusion, fractionation, and frustration.

There is plenty of evidence that, even in well-managed organizations, communication gets short shrift. It is often seen only as:

- Information sharing, rather than behavior change
- The dissemination of explanatory materials, rather than a four-dimensional process that includes listening, involving, leading, and informing, as shown in Exhibit 13.1
- The final step prior to implementing a new plan design, rather than integral to the redesign process, when there is a need for consensus building, audience research, anticipation of issues, and strategic communication planning

**Exhibit 13.1**   Mercer's LILI™ Model
The Four Dimensions of Communication

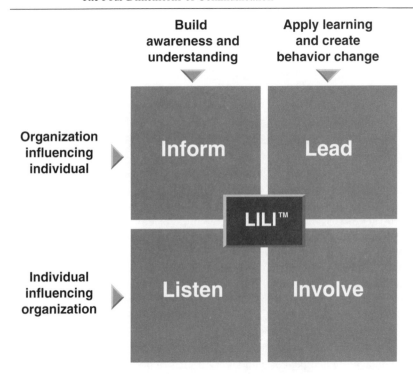

*Effective executive communication is more than just one-way information-sharing. It includes listening, involvement, and leadership communication strategies as well.*

Communication can offer more value. Clear and consistent communication of corporate values, strategic objectives, performance metrics, and behavioral expectations, in addition to communication of the rewards themselves, can enhance the motivational power of executive rewards, improve perceptions of value, and build the bridge between organizational imperatives and individual executive actions and results. Research and involvement strategies can help to ensure well-targeted messages, effective plan design, and engaged leaders. In addition, pay programs will be ineffective in attracting and retaining talent unless their value is well understood and appreciated. This takes ongoing, interactive, and personalized communication, rather than just the distribution of event-specific communication material, as the remainder of this chapter will describe.

## 13.2   MERCER STUDY RAISES CONCERNS ABOUT EXECUTIVE VIEWS

Important and surprising senior management views about compensation emerged in Mercer's recent *What's Working*™ study, initially conducted in the United States and now implemented in 16 countries globally. (See Exhibit 13.2.) Although results on all compensation-related items are generally more favorable for senior managers than for other employees, the low senior management scores on some items should be of concern. Most organizations are not effectively communicating to senior managers about performance and rewards. Consider the following:

- Although leaders who responded feel a strong sense of commitment to their organizations (82%) and say they understand how their pay is determined (87%), less than half (46%) are personally motivated by their organization's incentive plan.
- Although 71% say they have clearly defined performance goals and objectives, and 69% understand how their performance is evaluated, only 54% get informal, regular feedback on performance, and only 45% receive any coaching. In fact, 39% say they haven't had a performance appraisal in the last year.
- Only half (53%) of the senior managers who responded say their organization does an adequate job of matching pay to performance. One-fourth (24%) do not feel their performance is rewarded when they do a good job.
- Thirty-five percent have some question about whether they're fairly paid given their performance, and 38% question whether they're competitively paid.

Given the importance of the senior management audience, the amount spent on executive compensation, and the influence of the management group on the attitudes of employees at large, these scores bear further analysis. Clearly, there seems to be an issue with the motivation power of incentive plans—more than

**Exhibit 13.2**   What's Working™
                   A 2002 Mercer Study of People at Work*

* In 2002 Mercer surveyed a statistically valid sample of 2,600 U.S. workers on their attitudes and perceptions about their job, organization, work environment, and compensation. You may access the complete study results at www.mercerhr.us/whatsworkingstudy.

half of the senior managers in the study say incentives do not influence their performance. This may be due to a plan design that's flawed, or to misalignment with business needs or, more likely, to poor communication.

Senior managers also receive less performance feedback than they expect, and would perhaps benefit from (and welcome) more consistent formal and informal feedback and coaching related to their individual performance.

Given that the majority of respondents say they understand how their pay is determined, it is surprising that over one-third feel unfairly paid from an internal and external standpoint. Some of this negative feeling about pay can be discounted, since people generally tend to respond more negatively to survey items related to compensation. Nevertheless, survey results indicate a need for better communication and suggest that organizations have some retention risk with their executive workforce.

The results overall suggest an underinvestment in the communication of executive rewards, particularly incentives, and in one-on-one performance-related communication. With the significant amount of time and money spent on incentive and other compensation plan design and the importance of executive alignment in increasing shareholder value and pursuing the enterprise's business objectives, companies cannot afford to tolerate poor communication. They do their executives, shareholders, and themselves a disservice. Effective compensation communication provides executives with the information and exchange necessary to understand performance expectations, links between corporate and personal goals, actions needed, performance metrics, rewards, and risks. In an era when high-performing talent is in great demand, good communication can help to ensure that talented performers, especially those at the executive level of an organization, are well informed about their total rewards value and opportunity and how their personal compensation ties to business success.

## 13.3   WHAT'S UNIQUE ABOUT EXECUTIVE COMMUNICATION

It is a common fallacy that, because executives are astute business managers, they do not need as much communication as do other employees. The fact is that they need just as much communication, if not more, because their accountability is broader, their compensation package is more complex, their time is at a premium, and they are important spokespeople on compensation and performance for the rest of the organization. The enterprise relies on their focus, energy, judgment, and leadership to generate results for shareholders. There are also serious personal financial implications if an executive misinterprets plan provisions or makes uninformed choices, such as on deferral or investment opportunities.

As for any other audience, it is difficult to generalize about the communication preferences and needs of an executive audience since it is not a homogeneous group. Plans vary among management levels within an organization, and there are distinct differences and emphases based on industry, geography, and other variables. It is not uncommon to have a multi-component program of options, performance shares, and restricted stock for the top executives, for example; stock options and/or restricted stock plans for the next tier and for mid-managers; and different programs for executives outside the home country where the business operates. Some programs may cut across all geographic boundaries. In addition, eligibility for equity and other incentive plans often extends through all management ranks, sometimes to all employees, requiring broad communication of short- and long-term equity and other incentives to a very diverse population Within each organization, the needs of each group eligible for stock, incentives, and other rewards should be carefully evaluated as part of the communication plan. The plan should also identify what must be core and consistent in all communication and what must be tailored to the audience.

That said, there are some important considerations when communicating to senior management audiences about executive pay. Consider these characteristics:

- In many ways, executives are an audience of one. Each executive's compensation package is linked to his or her individual leadership role, potential influence on business outcomes, and specific short- and long-term business goals. Like other employees, executives look to their rewards to provide a measure of what's in it for them. The most effective communication is specific to the individual.

- Senior managers are usually well versed in the business issues facing their organization, so it is typically not necessary to spend a lot of time explaining the basics of shareholder value or financial metrics to the executive suite. As communication moves down the executive ladder, however, lower-level leaders will need more business education and more "line of sight" between business requirements, performance expectations, metrics, and rewards.

- Executives may be savvy and sophisticated on the business front, but many have surprising knowledge gaps about the workings of their executive compensation plans and the underlying financial concepts, such as the potential long-term value of their total rewards and the risks if performance does not measure up. They may have a clear sense of business measures but variable understanding of complex incentive and equity plan provisions, especially related to issues of taxation.

- Many deferred compensation, stock, and other equity arrangements offer complex choices, with serious short- and long-term financial implications for participants. It is crucial that executives understand the implications of their choices if they are to realize the full value of their total rewards package.

- When executives want information, they want it soon, if not immediately. Plan administrators scramble to answer questions and respond to executive queries about their plans. Providing on-demand information that executives and their financial planners can access through web sites, modeling tools, and other communication vehicles that are always accessible can diminish the need for such administrative support—but only if these sites are easy to navigate, comprehensive, and intuitive for the user.

- When they receive compensation plan information, most executives read what is in plain language and hand the technical plan documents to their financial planners. The latter materials serve a purpose—they meet plan reporting requirements, provide some litigation protection, and serve the needs of the secondary audience, financial planners. But they are usually difficult to decipher and provide no motivation or inspiration value. Given their time constraints, executives have little patience with lengthy treatises whose careful study will still not lead to understanding. They prefer quick highlights, followed by details in plain language.

- Clear communication to executives reaps benefits far beyond that small audience. They are collectively responsible for the rest of the organization. Executives have a dual perspective—they view compensation not only from a personal standpoint, but also as a tool to motivate their direct reports and other employees. Equipping them to understand their own plans and the links to business strategy helps them communicate goals, rewards, performance expectations, and measures more clearly and effectively to their own reports, who in turn follow suit. Good communication to the top serves to role-model the communication process that should cascade to all employees.

- Finally, each executive is important to the success of the enterprise. Although a small proportion of the population, senior managers are an audience worth a communication investment. Organizations realize a clear return on investment from ensuring that this group is focused on the right set of objectives, performance requirements, behaviors, and metrics and understands the returns that are at stake for the business and themselves.

Executives share many communication needs in common with other employees. They also have unique needs because of their roles; the scope and complexity of their compensation arrangements; and board, shareholder, and public scrutiny of their performance. They are like other employees, but with less time, more distraction, more responsibility, and more at stake financially. Organizations can make their executives' jobs easier, realize more motivation power from their well-designed compensation program, and enhance business results by communicating effectively throughout the goal setting, performance management, and rewards cycle. The next section begins to describe how.

---

**Illustration**

A highly acquisitive, globally dispersed holding company implemented new executive pay programs, including stock options, to bring multiple acquired companies with disparate cultures together at the executive level through common goals tightly linked to individual rewards. Because of the organization's ongoing, aggressive growth strategy, its success was predicated on quickly acclimating new leaders to the drivers of corporate success, motivating these leaders to focus on key performance targets, and retaining them despite the significant organizational change. Creating one leadership community would be a powerful way to create shareholder value. To target newly acquired, hired, or promoted leaders, many of them unfamiliar with performance-based pay plans, the company provided a toolkit to educate them about the total program, the mechanics of stock options, and the value of the awards. It also used this as an opportunity to focus all leaders on the specific actions that would optimize business performance. The communication plan included key messages about business strategy, cultural integration, and program goals; introduction of the new measures of business performance and how those measures were expected to drive stock performance and subsequently the value of the options and other rewards; personalized individual grant information with a calculator tool to model value over the long term; and an interactive process to invite discussion and answer executive questions. Feedback from the discussion process was used to shape ongoing communication. The result was greater collaboration to achieve corporate business targets, lower-than-expected turnover, and greater "line of sight" between business performance and rewards.

## 13.4 WHAT WORKS WITH EXECUTIVES

Effective communication does more than educate executives about their rewards programs—it helps drive the behaviors important to enterprise success. Communication should provide perspectives on the executive behaviors and actions needed to:

- Meet business objectives
- Get full value from the compensation package
- Manage and communicate pay
- Motivate performance among employees in their respective groups

The communication plan should anticipate what executives should *get, support, and do* to meet business objectives, take advantage of their financial opportunities, provide communication leadership, and make responsible pay decisions.

Responsible executive compensation communication is not just about distributing plan information. It provides the following:

- *Context:* Organizations design their executive rewards to support goals linked to creating shareholder value, whether through a focus on economic value added (EVA), total business return (TBR), earnings per share (EPS), stock price, or other similar objectives. In addition, there is a set of values and a code of conduct, stated or implicit, that govern behavior. Rewards should be communicated in that business, performance, and cultural context, in the language of the enterprise, and the communication should provide a "line of sight" between the executive's actions and business outcomes.
- *Clarity:* Without clear communication, the best plan design is unlikely to motivate performance or influence behavior. The communication should shed

light on what's important and what's required to succeed. In terms of plan detail, there is no doubt that executive compensation plans are complex, as is the related tax information. The communication should translate legal documents for the layman; be clear, crisp, focused, and relatively short to respect executive schedules and preferences; and provide a personalized view of plan impact on each individual. Executives should, at a minimum, be able to explain to their financial planners how the plans generally work and have some understanding of the short- and long-term risks and opportunities.

- *Cohesion:* An executive's compensation consists of multiple short- and long-term components—cash, equity and other incentives, special benefits, and perquisites. Together, these plans provide tremendous wealth potential, but the full impact is lost if each component is viewed in isolation. Synthesizing the many discrete parts into a cohesive total rewards perspective helps the executive not only to remember the many components, but also to understand the intent of each plan and appreciate the full value of the package, which is greater than the sum of the parts. Ongoing communication about total rewards is also important if executives are to (1) see the connection between business performance and their rewards and (2) remember to revisit their choices periodically with regard to investment selections, the timing of payouts, annual reenrollment in certain supplemental plans, and so on.

The most effective executive compensation communication focuses on a core set of strategic enterprise messages that are reinforced in all conversations, materials, and other communication about goal setting, performance, rewards and results. It breaks through the clutter of information overload with highly customized, personalized content, along with enough program detail to satisfy financial planners as well as executives. It facilitates speed of understanding through clear, simple writing; graphic displays of information; and time-saving electronic compensation statements and modeling tools. It provides plenty of opportunity for executive participation in the development of goals, measures, and performance targets at the front end; feedback against established metrics along the way; and results at the end of the performance cycle. Finally, it equips executives with effective performance and pay administration tools and guidelines to manage compensation and communication for employees within their own spans of control.

---

**Illustration**

The CEO of an investment firm wanted to send important signals to executives about changes to the business strategy. To focus them on new performance targets, corporate officers and other business unit leaders were invited to participate in interactive sessions to develop business scorecards at the corporate and division levels. The scorecards included financial, customer, people, and process objectives, initiatives, targets, and measures. This early communication exchange among key leaders was effective in building consensus for the new incentive plan design based on the scorecards. It facilitated understanding, buy-in, and action. Executives were engaged as a team, and clear links were established between the business strategy, executive performance, and incentives. Subsequent communication focused on progress toward that strategy and consequent rewards. Engagement made the difference.

## 13.5   HOW TO COMMUNICATE FOR IMPACT

In Exhibit 13.3, Mercer has outlined a six-step approach, called *Communication for Impact*™, for developing an effective executive communication strategy. The sequence of context assessment, articulation of the change agenda, strategy development, implementation, measurement, and reinforcement allows an organization to diagnose its communication needs, build an implementation plan on a solid foundation, and execute against a well-defined roadmap. The strategic communication planning process should begin early in the rewards design process and be an integral part of compensation development and planning, not a totally separate exercise, although it may run on a separate track with dedicated resources and focus. To communicate executive pay plans with impact, follow these guidelines:

### Step 1: Context Assessment

- *Look at the big picture.* Identify and document the historical and current business, stakeholder, cultural, and environmental issues that will affect implementation of a specific rewards program in your unique organization. Anticipate executive perceptions about the program.

**Exhibit 13.3**   Communication for Impact™
Mercer's Methodology for Strategic Communication

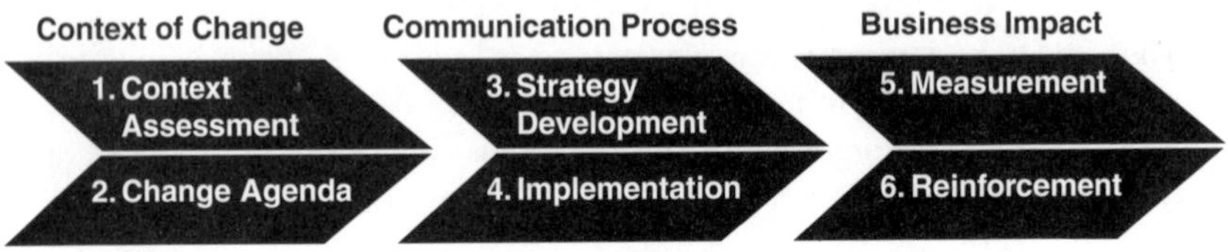

## Step 2: Change Agenda

- *Scope out the change.* Assess the extent, depth, and type of change that the executive rewards program will herald and drive. If you are overhauling your incentives, for example, what is motivating that change? The board? Regulatory requirements? A change in business strategy? The need to reduce costs or realign distributions to high performers? Think in terms of behavior and organizational change, not just information exchange. On what do you need executives to take action? What do you expect them to do differently? Thorough context assessment and documentation of the change agenda will serve as a guide for all those involved in developing and implementing the communication strategy, as described next.

## Step 3: Strategy

- *Identify audience needs and communication issues.* Anticipating how you will face an audience with messages about your new plan design is always a good filter for determining or fine-tuning executive pay design. Profile the executive audience to anticipate current perceptions and likely responses to the change. Segment the audience groups that will need targeted communication.
- *Conduct research.* You may need to conduct some research—executive interviews, focus groups, or surveys—at this or an earlier stage to diagnose the issues thoroughly from an audience standpoint. Research can be used for many reasons—to engage stakeholders early in the change process, capitalize on their ideas, capture their views, build consensus, signal change, begin the education process, and/or encourage constructive debate, about the plan design or the communication or both. The learning from this process can help to ensure that the final plan design can be effectively communicated and will be well accepted and understood.
- *Set communication objectives.* Objectives should ensure executives can *get, support, and do* what is needed over the short and long term. These should be SMART communication objectives: Specific, Measurable, Attainable, Realistic, and Tangible.
- *Develop key messages.* Create a core set of messages in the language of the enterprise to serve as the framework for all communication and to cascade in conversations, presentations, and media. The messages should clearly articulate the total rewards perspective, the purpose of each component, details about the performance expected, how the plans will work, and the targeted rewards contingent on performance. Consider not only what must be said and how it should be said, but also how the multiple audiences will hear and interpret the messages. Look for other conflicting messages—sources of interference—in the organization that will color executive views about what is being said.

- *Create a communication plan.* Determine the appropriate communication channels, measures of effectiveness, tools, and schedule. Plan for an advance communication process with key decision makers and other stakeholders to build consensus and avoid surprises. Also plan for communication after the program's introduction to clarify, reinforce, and report on results. Keep in mind that effective communication will require more than just one-way information sharing. As illustrated in Exhibit 13.1, the plan should include engagement and listening strategies, as well as opportunities for the CEO or chairperson to be a visible spokesperson for any changes to executive compensation and to discuss their significance for the business and intended impact.

### Step 4: Implementation

- *Develop a comprehensive project plan.* Executive pay plans are often designed and deployed under very tight schedules, sometimes with urgency, and often with public visibility. As for any critical initiative, communication strategy and plan development and implementation should be rigorously project managed to ensure flawless delivery—on time, on budget, and with high impact. At a minimum, there should be a project plan with a schedule of defined deliverables, assigned owners for each task, and an assessment of risk if the communication plan is not met. As shown in Exhibit 13.4, the project

**Exhibit 13.4**   Mercer's Project Management Approach

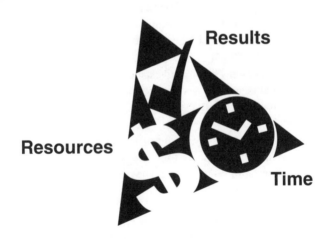

*Results, resources, and time must be prioritized, planned, and balanced for successful communication implementation.*

plan should factor in three critical drivers of project success—*results, time, and resources.* Balance the results required against the time and resources—both people and budget—available for implementation. Each driver affects successful execution of the communication plan, and you will need to decide which should take priority.

## Step 5: Measurement

- *Evaluate effectiveness.* Build a scorecard to track communication results based on the SMART objectives established in Step 3. Since the communication is likely to be supporting a change process, not just implementation of a new pay plan, measure results over time, not just after program implementation. Do executives *get it, support it, and do it*? Did the messages get through? Is information translating into changed behavior? Are people taking appropriate actions? Has the communication had the intended business impact? Do executives understand and value the total rewards package? Based on the success measures established earlier, evaluate what did and did not work and what needs revision or recommunication.

## Step 6: Reinforcement

- *Provide feedback.* It goes without saying that executives, like other employees, should receive both formal and informal performance feedback—not only related to the quantitative results they already see in routine financial reports but also to the qualitative results that can affect business achievement, such as relationships with internal and external customers and leadership style and effectiveness. Provide the executive audience with feedback related to personal performance and business impact. Communication should incorporate and differentiate the performance criteria used for salary management versus incentive plans, which are often different. The plan payouts and other rewards should not come as a surprise but should instead be seen as a direct consequence of executive actions, with direct correlation to shareholder results.
- *Recommunicate.* Communication of executive rewards at the time of new program implementation is critical but insufficient to motivate long-term behavior or culture change and ongoing commitment to the organization. Messages need to be reinforced, data needs to be updated, performance results require regular dissemination, and success needs to be celebrated. The best techniques for regular updates and reinforcement include leadership discussion and correspondence initiated by the CEO or another top leader, as well as web-based tools for personal and organizational and compensation management.

**Illustration**

An entrepreneurial, decentralized consumer products company wanted to tie the pay of executives to achievement of its global growth objectives through the use of stock options and other executive rewards and to implement stock ownership requirements. Without an understanding of the potential long-term value of the total package, the new design would be ineffective as a motivational tool and there might be resistance to the ownership levels required. After research with a sample of the 300 executives affected, the company decided that communication would need to be highly personalized to be effective. The company implemented an executive web site to present complex executive compensation information, relate that data to business results, and provide frequent updates to support decision-making and financial planning. Web site postings included tax notices, estimates of stock option value, administrative forms, projections of wealth accumulation for retirement planning, and other modeling scenarios. All of this data was personalized for each executive, and there were links to administrator sites. Executives were able to access information from any computer at any time and allow direct access by their financial planners. Key messages about the business were updated and reinforced in the display of each executive's personal compensation package, with clear links made to the achievement of growth objectives.

## 13.6  THE IMPORTANCE OF PERSONALIZATION

Compensation cannot be communicated effectively without personalization. Written material and general presentations can go only so far. There must be dialogue about the performance expected and evaluated. There should be a translation of business strategy into specific individual goals and actions and of general compensation plan information into the potential short- and long-term impact for each executive. What actions does each executive need to take? How do an executive's goals and performance measures convert to a potential payout? How do the multiple components of base and variable pay, equity, and other incentives, benefits, and perquisites integrate into a total package? And what is the total value of that package for the executive in the short and long term? Dozens of individual pay and benefit plans, perquisites, and services contribute to total rewards, making it difficult for executives to appreciate the total value, much less the competitiveness, of the package, as the results of the *What's Working*™ research in Exhibit 13.2 show.

Give executives what they need to manage their financial relationship with the company. Integrate the components of pay for each individual. Beyond discussing the package with executives, provide online solutions, not just print materials, to give them quick access to information on demand. A well-designed rewards web site for executives can serve as the gateway to their personal account balances, with data from multiple plan administrators integrated in one site, displayed graphically, and often refreshed. It should include general information about executive pay plans and services, transaction capability, and modeling tools to project long-term accumulation and the impact of investment fluctuation. In effect, this online toolkit enables executives to:

- **Learn** about programs, get answers to their questions, and view their annual compensation, equity holdings, total rewards picture, and future accumulated wealth—at the point when they have the interest in, or need for, the information.
- **Plan** for the future with interactive tools to project the potential payouts of short- and long-term incentives, track rewards against performance measures, meet ownership guidelines, model equity value and tax impact, project future wealth, and plan for retirement.
- **Do** transactions, including enrollment, election changes, adjustments in investment direction and mix, requests for help, and other actions.

Best-in-class web sites of this kind take full advantage of current available technology to save executive time and build appreciation of total rewards value. (See Exhibit 13.5 for an illustration.) Many executives today want to manage all aspects of their finances online and appreciate ready access to personalized, focused information and resources at their point of need and interest.

When new compensation plans are introduced, particularly those requiring complex choices, executives also appreciate access to a financial counselor. Hotlines can be set up so that counselors have electronic access to executive profiles and compensation data, as well as plan information, so they can respond quickly with answers to most questions.

**Exhibit 13.5**  A Personalized View of Total Rewards

---

A total rewards web site allows executives to view their annual compensation as well as their accumulated wealth across all components of pay over time. The following web page provides an example of values at one point in time, but data would be refreshed and updated regularly.

| **My Pay and Benefits for [Year]** | **$784,750** |
|---|---|
| Annual Salary | $500,000 |
| Incentive Compensation paid in [year] | $200,000 |
| Dividend Equivalents paid in [year] | $20,000 |
| Perquisites | $14,600 |
| Retirement and Benefit Company Costs | $50,150 |

| **My Equity Grants for [Year]** | **$1,550,000** |
| --- | --- |
| Stock Options (present value at time of grant) | $950,000 |
| Restricted Stock | $600,000 |
| **My Accumulated Wealth** | **$8,694,230** |
| Employee Retirement Plan | $122,500 |
| Savings Plan | $167,080 |
| Stock Options | $4,300,650 |
| Restricted Stock | $3,254,000 |
| Deferred Compensation | $850,000 |

## 13.7  COMMUNICATION CHALLENGES IN A TOUGH ENVIRONMENT

In executive and employee circles alike, uncertainty is on the increase and trust is in decline. Economic and regulatory unknowns about executive pay have distracted boardrooms and executive meeting rooms. Many stock options are under water, fewer options are available, incentive pools continue to shrink, and salaries are frozen. Higher performance is demanded for business turnarounds, and shareholder scrutiny of executive compensation is not likely to abate. Executives spend more time now wondering about their future financial prospects and security, while memories of the lucrative stock grants and incentive payouts of the past still linger. And there are no guarantees that things will ever return to "normal". An environment of this kind poses special communication challenges. Here are a few principles to keep in mind:

- *Expect skepticism.* A normal response to a significant change is resistance, particularly when change sets higher performance bars, imposes new limits on financial rewards, or takes away plans that are familiar. Executives will certainly read between the lines to discover any "hidden agendas" in the plan design and will not hesitate to voice their opinions of the change. Communication messages must be clear, direct, and complete. The communication process must allow for discussion, surface and resolve any areas of confusion, and identify for further consideration any components that do not resonate well.
- *Assume all communication is public.* Some materials become part of required government filings, proxies, and other investor communication. They will certainly be shared externally with financial planners and discussed with family. Whether labeled "confidential" or not, assume that information about your executive pay plans will be in the public domain and will create strong impressions of your culture, values, standards, and commitment to creating shareholder value—among customers, investors, government officials, and others.

- *Avoid silence.* When times get tough, some companies go silent, even with top tiers of leadership. Underwater stock options are a good example. On many issues, it is far better to take a proactive stance, for example, reminding managers of the long-term nature of their rewards or the business strategy that will help to turn the situation around. Communicate a point of view rather than leaving the communication vacuum to be filled by speculation. If the direction is unclear and decisions are yet to be made, acknowledge the issues, explain the decision process, and remind managers of the turnaround strategy. This in turn will give them a message platform to use with their own employees in response to questions.

- *Confront the tough messages.* Messages have changed. Equity values have declined, and many future equity-based plans will carry tougher performance requirements. The likelihood of option expensing will mean fewer shares for distribution. Company earnings and views about responsible executive pay may limit plan payouts. Corporate governance and accounting standards also impose new restrictions. None of these messages means more wealth for executives, unless results create more wealth for shareholders. Organizations must come to terms with and communicate these tough messages—the financial risks, the take-aways, and the benefit reductions and limits, along with any positive news about the upside opportunities. Executives will be motivated to higher performance if they feel targets are clear and achievable, are convinced that the enterprise can succeed and their contribution will make a difference, understand the value of their total rewards package, and understand what is at stake.

- *Equip executives to communicate.* Executives are an important audience to receive compensation communication, but they are also messengers and advocates for the organization's compensation philosophy and approach overall. As the LILI™ model in Exhibit 13.1 illustrates, it is important to inform executives about compensation matters in times of turbulence, but executives should also be involved in socializing communication messages and provide visible leadership to help focus and motivate their employees. Experience and research have shown that many executives are grateful for assistance in the task of communicating effectively and welcome training, support tools, and strategic partnering from communication and human resource professionals.

## 13.8 WHAT'S AT STAKE

Executives, like any other employee audience, are motivated to perform for and commit to an organization by more than just the rewards package. Affinity with the values and culture, enthusiasm about the organization's mission, alignment with corporate goals, and allegiance to peers—all factor into an individual's choice, regularly revisited and renewed, to stay with an organization.

**Illustration**

Due to the downturn in the economy, executives at a manufacturing firm saw their performance shares based on EPS dwindle in value. The organization was concerned that the plan would not offer suitable rewards and thus lose its power to retain key leaders. It decided to allow its 60 top executives to swap their performance unit entitlements from previous years for future long-term cash bonuses. A change of this kind was likely to create skepticism and suspicion, so communication was critical. In developing the communication strategy, the company reinforced the "line of sight" between company performance and individual rewards and strengthened executives' understanding of how they could drive business results and thus influence the value of their rewards. To help executives make well-informed choices, communication included historical data about stock price and EPS, an interactive calculator to help executives project company performance and compare the value of the two plans, and other information to facilitate evaluation of the exchange offer and timely choices. Using a strategy that enabled executives to model and evaluate with complete and personalized information dispelled the potential for resistance—59 of the 60 executives chose the new plan.

A professionally planned and executed communication strategy will define, clearly and unambiguously, what is required in terms of performance standards, positive behaviors, and ethical approaches in business, and what is at stake in terms of personal rewards and business impact. It will ensure that results and consequences are well understood and the right behaviors and activities are repeated and reinforced. It will also model the effective communication performance that all managers, especially executives, should incorporate into their day-to-day work as they explain compensation to their employees and communicate about other critical corporate topics.

Well-planned and well-executed communication can help to motivate executives to achieve higher levels of performance in line with shareholder interests, and keep leaders fully engaged over their careers as partners in driving business success. This is more likely to happen if communication considerations and planning are an integral part of the rewards redesign process. Communication should appeal both to the executives' commitment to advancing the organization and to their desire for personal advancement and wealth. The *Communication for Impact*™ approach described in this chapter, and illustrated in Exhibit 13.3, will yield many benefits for the organization and its executives and help to ensure that the investment in executive rewards pays off in results for shareholders and executives alike. It takes both responsible executive pay design and effective communication to create that value.

# Chapter 14

# Role of the Compensation Consultant

## G. Steven Harris

Establishing competitive and responsible executive compensation levels and practices has never been more challenging. Compensation committees and senior management must have access to accurate information and sound advice to make proper judgments on compensation matters. Obtaining reliable information on pay levels, industry variations, best practices, and emerging trends is critically important in the wake of accounting scandals and new governance standards.

But simply reviewing what other companies have done in structuring executive rewards is inadequate. Compensation information must be properly collected, interpreted, and a perspective applied for it to be useful. This is the key role of the compensation consultant.

Much has been written about "pay out of control" and "excessive executive compensation" representing scant linkage with performance. And shots have been taken, some fairly and some unfairly, at consultants whose role is to advise compensation committees and management on executive pay matters. The compensation consultant should fulfill the role of trusted advisor in providing guidance on competitive and sound compensation practice. This chapter suggests, from the perspectives of both the user and the provider of compensation consulting services, how the role of consultant can best be accomplished and how pitfalls can be avoided.

## 14.1 IMPORTANCE OF AN INDEPENDENT PERSPECTIVE

### (a) Lens on Competitive Market

Collecting, cleaning, and compiling compensation information is an arduous task. Major compensation surveys take many weeks and staff hours to build. Even proxy pay information, which is readily available, represents a time-consuming and challenging task to build an accurate historical compensation picture across large company and industry groups. Although this information may be available to companies for a fee, seldom do corporate human resource staffs have the time or financial resources to invest in completing and purchasing the various surveys that comprise the database of major consulting firms. This wealth of pay information covers each component of compensation for virtually all executive positions, levels, and industries.

In addition to being the source for published pay studies that can be purchased by participants and nonparticipants, consulting firms typically conduct a number of proprietary compensation surveys that allow in-depth evaluation of pay practices. These in-house studies, often available for purchase in bound or software form, allow consultants ready access to substantial amounts of precise data. This wealth of information can be constructed in multiple ways and helpful in interpreting pay patterns.

Although broad industry studies form the data foundation for compensation program measurement, special studies can be invaluable in identifying pay trends and best practices. It may not be possible for a particular company to conduct an industry study due to the confidential nature of the information involved. But a third party can perform this role effectively and provide specialized pay information that otherwise would be unavailable.

There are many different ways to design and administer a compensation program. Some approaches, as we all have seen, work better than others. And there are pay programs that have delivered appropriate results in companies with sustained strong performance. These pay approaches, or best practices, have withstood the test of time, industry differences, and economic cycles. Specific studies have been conducted that explore what "best practice companies" do in compensation design and delivery that can benefit others. These insights can be invaluable in considering the wide array of possible approaches to pay program design.

## (b) Broad View of Sound Practices

Most compensation committee members and corporate staff responsible for pay design can cite examples of how a few other companies approach the topic. Committee members may sit on other compensation committees or have experience handling pay matters as chief executive officers (CEOs). Similarly, corporate compensation staff often network with their peers in other companies and learn how they tackle pay issues. These perspectives are valuable but generally incomplete.

A key aspect of the compensation consultant's role is to provide a broader perspective. Experience and knowledge gained across numerous corporate settings and challenges can be crucial in providing advice. These experiences can help the consultant focus efforts on the most relevant information and offer proven solutions to problems. As a third-party advisor, the consultant should be aware of relevant company information but be detached enough to see issues from the outside looking into the organization. Combining this broader view with an array of experience in developing sound compensation programs and a clear understanding of the company's situation allows consultants to deliver a valuable and independent perspective. The next section covers the process of maintaining independence in providing compensation advice.

### (c) Impact of New Legislation and Governance Standards

The pace and importance of change in governance practices that help ensure consultant independence is underscored by new legislative and governance standards. The U.S. Congress passed the Sarbanes-Oxley Act of 2002, which attempts to address the widespread concern that auditors' independence can be compromised by the magnitude of nonaudit services provided by the audit firms. This legislation applies not only to U.S.-based companies, but also to foreign companies listed on various U.S. stock exchanges and is discussed in Chapter 4.

The stock exchanges have passed new listing requirements that attempt, among other things, to address shortcomings in compensation committee membership, authority, and procedures (see Chapter 4). The New York Stock Exchange (NYSE) rules state that if a compensation consultant is to assist in the evaluation of director, CEO, or senior executive compensation, the compensation committee charter should give the committee sole authority to retain and terminate the consulting firm, including sole authority to approve the firm's fees and other retention terms. The Conference Board Commission on Public Trust and Private Enterprise in its report on this topic suggested it should be best practice for the compensation committee to retain any outside consultants who advise it, and the outside consultants should report solely to the committee.[1]

## 14.2   MAINTAINING INDEPENDENCE AND AVOIDING A CONFLICT OF INTEREST

A series of corporate and accounting irregularities recently have led to the collapse of several major corporations and, along with them, the reputations of prominent executives and board members. One common thread in these scandals appears to be a lack of truly independent, impartial advice to boards of directors and senior management. Although much of the problem has centered on audit firms and oversight of their activities, the need to eliminate questions surrounding independence of outside advisors reaches all third-party relationships where a potential for conflict of interest exists. Maintaining independence may be an issue across various consulting services, but executive compensation clearly represents an

---

[1]*NYSE Listed Company Manual.* Corporate Governance Listing Standards—Commentary to Section 303A(5), 2003. Conference Board Commission on Public Trust and Private Enterprise. Part 1: Executive Compensation. New York, NY, Sept. 17, 2002.

area where effectively addressing the potential for conflict of interest is needed. Next we cover key aspects of avoiding a conflict of interest and maintaining consulting independence.

## (a) Identifying the Client

One of the fundamentals of consulting is to identify clearly the client and the client's expectations for the business relationship. Although apparently simple, this consulting fundamental is not always easy to execute. However, it is an important aspect to avoiding a potential conflict of interest.

Traditionally consultants have been hired by management to advise companies on competitive compensation levels and practices. In this role the consultant worked closely with various members of the management team to collect information on the company's business strategy, key performance objectives, compensation philosophy, and current pay practices. As the competitive market picture was formed and contrasted with company information, the consultant developed findings and recommendations. Common practice was then to share the findings and recommendations with management and get their reaction and buy-in prior to making a presentation to the board's compensation committee. The professionalism and good reputation of the consultant and his or her firm were enough to assure that the advice rendered was independent. Management typically was the client, but the consultant attempted to balance the interests of management with that of the board and all shareholders. In many cases this approach worked well, and arguably it still can be effective for some companies today.

The new governance environment casts a different and still-changing light on the process of hiring and providing executive compensation consulting services. No one-size-fits-all approach exists to establishing a working relationship with a consultant. Some companies, as mentioned, continue to view the relationship as primarily between management and the advisor, with a requirement to meet periodically with the compensation committee and report on how the company's pay levels and practices compare to the competitive market. However, a growing number of compensation committees are taking to heart the new governance environment and requiring that they be the client and hire the consultant, who will then report directly to the committee and work with management to accomplish their role. This approach seems to be the most effective one to honor the letter and spirit of stock exchange rules and governance best practice. In addition to holding hire and fire authority over the advisor, the compensation committee should approve the consultant's work scope and fees generally—not just on matters over which the committee has direct responsibility.

## (b) Working Exclusively for the Compensation Committee

Some board members hold the view that regardless of who hires and fires the consultant, the true reporting relationship goes the way of the fees. In other words, if a consultant who reports to the compensation committee is involved in more work, thus greater fees, at the request of management than requests flowing from the committee, the consultant's allegiance will be with management. Following this logic, true independence cannot exist in the absence of an exclusive working relationship with the committee. Although few companies currently follow this approach, a growing number of committees hire their own compensation advisor to reinforce both the perception and the reality of independence in pay decisions.

The existence of a consultant working exclusively for the compensation committee can readily create the need for two advisors—one working for the committee and the other working closely with management but accountable to the committee. The committee's advisor in these cases does not routinely engage in substantial projects or cover the same ground as the consultant working with management. Rather, the committee's advisor reviews findings and recommendations from management and may provide a second opinion. Although having two separate consultants might produce images of dueling advisors debating endlessly the best approach to Black-Scholes calculations, the concept can work if approached and managed correctly.

Gathering and analyzing detailed company and competitive market information, and making corresponding recommendations, is best left to the advisor who puts in the time to learn and reflect on the subtleties that can distinguish between a successful or a failed pay program. Generally this person will be the consultant working regularly with management. The role of the committee's exclusive consultant then can be to review recommendations and supporting information and provide the committee with a written record outlining areas of agreement, disagreement, and, if needed, suggestions for alternate courses of action.

### (c) Ground Rules for Providing Advice

The steps and processes a consultant and client should follow to ensure independence will vary based on the nature of the role each is expected to fulfill. As outlined, the expectations may be different where an advisor works exclusively for the committee rather than working for the committee and management. The most typical working relationship involves management. Exhibit 14.1 offers detailed guidance on how the independence of a consulting role can be maintained where one consultant is engaged. These guidelines also could apply in situations where the committee, or even management, periodically brings in a second consultant to render specialized advice or to ensure the reasonableness of the primary consultant's advice.

### (d) Working Out of a Conflict

The nature of providing advice on executive compensation matters can give rise to a conflict of interest, regardless of the care taken and sensible guidelines followed to avoid such conflict. There can be different ways to view competitive pay

**Exhibit 14.1**   Principles and Process to Maintain Consultant Independence

---

1. *The consultant must establish a clear mutual understanding of the client reporting relationship and clarity of consultant role, and ensure that advisory duties are appropriate.*

   - For each consulting assignment, the consultant must identify whether the reporting relationship is to the compensation committee of the board of directors (the committee) or to management of the client organization.

   - The consultant should report directly to the committee on compensation work pertaining to the senior-most executive officer, the next executive tier, and other matters over which the committee has direct responsibility, and report findings and recommendations directly to the committee.

   - Where the consultant reporting relationship is to the committee, that body can initiate any potential engagement and have direct access to the consultant without the need for management involvement.

   - In support of the reporting role to the committee, the consultant should attend regular executive session meetings with committee members but without the presence of management for at least a portion of the session.

   - Where the consultant reporting relationship is to management, any recommendations pertaining to matters under the direct responsibility of the committee should be provided directly to the committee.

   - In assignments where the reporting relationship is to both the committee and management, the consultant should obtain an understanding among all parties of how the work will be conducted and the extent to which information can be shared.

   - The consultant must preserve the confidentiality of discussions with committee members and management held in or outside of formal meetings.

   - While the consultant's reporting relationship may vary across clients and assignments, the responsibility as an independent advisor is best performed and the client is best served if work is performed in collaboration with the committee and management in the interests of shareholders.

2. *The consultant should disclose all proper information to the company management and board to establish and maintain role independence and avoid the potential for a conflict of interest.*

   - The consultant should assume the responsibility to disclose the nature of material relationships between the client organization or direct business competitors and any part of the consultant's organization.

   - The consultant or another member of the consulting firm should be responsible for identifying the firm's relationships with the client or direct business competitor and for determining whether they are material, given the relevant facts and circumstances.

   - If the consultant is uncertain as to whether to disclose any such relationship or potential conflict of interest, the client should be given the opportunity to be informed and to pass judgment on whether independence is at risk.

**Exhibit 14.1**  *Continued*

---

- A process should be implemented to help maintain current knowledge of material relationships between the consultant and client or direct competitors for business.
- Any issues that surface regarding the consultant's ability to avoid a conflict of interest in performing the nature and scope of compensation consulting services should be discussed with the client organization.

3. *The consultant should provide documentation of his or her role, reporting relationship, and other information useful in substantiating independence and avoiding a conflict of interest.*

- An engagement letter or other written description of work to be performed should be provided that specifies the consultant's reporting relationship to the client (e.g., to the committee, management, or both), the scope of compensation work, and the process for reviewing and delivering findings and recommendations.
- A separate written agreement between the consultant and the committee describing the nature of the reporting relationship is desirable and considered best practice.
- The consultant should advise the committee to address relationships with consultants as part of its charter statement.

---

*Source:* Mercer Human Resource Consulting.

data, different peer comparisons used, and different approaches to goal setting that can mean the difference between a target incentive payout and little or no incentive award. Executive compensation can be a complex topic; different answers to a problem may exist, with each one having merit but none being fully correct. Perspective, emotions, and sometimes greed can enter into a decision process and endanger a consultant's independence. Although the best course of action is to avoid a conflict of interest from occurring, a consultant and client can take several steps to remove the conflict and reestablish independence.

1. *The consultant and/or client should admit that the consultant's role is in danger of losing or has already lost independence and that immediate action is needed.* Telltale signs may include ignoring information when it is at odds with the "desired" answer, or excessive involvement of the client in reformulating consultant findings and recommendations, or the client providing prepackaged solutions without giving the consultant the time or license to sufficiently validate or refute their appropriateness.

2. *The consultant should inform the client that consulting independence, and therefore the ability to provide advice, is being jeopardized.* This can be a very difficult step to take because it presents real risks to personal and financial relationships. But the risks are probably greater than they may seem. A conflict

of interest that is allowed to continue can lead to poor or self-serving decisions that risk the reputations of the consultant, consulting firm, client personnel, and the company. How this is best handled depends on the facts, circumstances, and personalities involved. But direct discussion on such a sensitive issue is naturally best, perhaps reinforced in writing to define clearly the problem and document the need for change.

3. *The consultant should recommend specific actions to be taken to remove the conflict and reestablish independence.* If possible, this should be done with step 2. For example, a recommendation may be made to provide the consultant's report under separate cover apart from management documents and to send the information several weeks in advance of the scheduled committee meeting. Doing this would allow ample time for board members to absorb the information, formulate questions, and request any additional analysis be performed prior to their meeting. Any recommendation to remedy the immediate independence issues should be coupled with a renewed understanding and agreement on guidelines for avoiding a conflict of interest in the future.

Because the identification of a problem with independence and the recommendation to solve it may not fall on receptive ears or may create new difficulties in the consulting relationship, the fourth step may be to terminate the consulting role. As mentioned, the risk of allowing a conflict to continue can be much greater than the immediate personal or financial considerations.

## 14.3   SELECTING A COMPENSATION CONSULTANT

Reasons to seek third-party assistance on compensation issues include access to relevant pay information and sound governance practices, tapping into additional staff resource and/or highly specialized expertise, and obtaining a broader and experienced perspective. There is no easy rating system to select a compensation consultant, where a 10 means a top-notch advisor, 5 or 6 connotes solid capability, and anyone below 3 is not chosen. Board members and executives must resort to other means in selecting an advisor. The world of executive compensation consultants tends to be small, so word of mouth can be effective in at least identifying possible candidates. Board member and executive relationships in other companies and input from human resource professionals can be effective in sourcing candidates. But what should one look for in selecting an advisor? These areas should be considered.

### (a) Capabilities and Experience

Although every company is to some degree unique, many aspects of a company's compensation program design and related challenges are probably not new. A bright but less experienced consultant can likely find a solution, but at how much time and cost? A highly experienced advisor may have had success in similar situations and, while more expensive per day, may represent a more cost-effective choice.

### (b) Industry versus Broader Expertise

There is no question that industry expertise is critical for a consultant to provide sound advice and counsel. However, real innovation, thought leadership, and competitive advantage often arise from being able to synthesize and apply concepts, ideas, and solutions from a variety of experiences and situations. It is this broader expertise and perspective that should be sought from all business advisors.

### (c) Relationship versus Defined Role

Most interactions with consultants begin within the context of a defined role, but sound advice and counsel are really the by-products of established relationships. In essence, it is the difference between hiring a vendor and engaging an advisor. A vendor may be able to assist the organization with an immediate and isolated challenge, but only through on-going dialogue, interaction, and learning can an advisor obtain the knowledge and perspective necessary to add value consistently to the organization.

### (d) Importance of Professional Standards

Never before has the importance of professional standards been more acute. Many of the issues cited earlier, such as maintaining independence, avoiding conflicts of interest, and working out of a conflict, need to be handled with the highest level of professionalism. Knowing that the consultant will do the right thing, every time, in any situation, should not be a luxury but rather a requirement. Although assessing professional standards can be difficult in the short term, consultants who consistently place client needs above their own demonstrate the foundation of sound decision making and the highest level of professional standards.

## 14.4  CRITICISMS OF COMPENSATION CONSULTANTS

### (a) Management's Advocate—Regardless of Facts or Circumstance

As mentioned, one of the fundamentals of consulting work is clearly identifying the client. Where senior management is the client, and sometimes even where the compensation committee is the client, a common criticism of compensation consultants is that they too often serve as ardent advocates for the management team.

In other words, their analysis and recommendations are biased toward the benefit of management despite the existence of contradictory facts and circumstances.

One component of this criticism hinges on the financial aspect of the consultant-client relationship. Compensation consultants may be perceived as beholden to management because they are concerned about collecting fees and providing other services. Or the criticism may be more emotional, questioning whether the consultant's desire to please overrides other considerations.

Both of these criticisms typically are aimed at vendors as opposed to advisors. Vendors may be more susceptible to these financial and emotional concerns because their work is primarily transaction-oriented and immediate financial outcomes are paramount. Advisors generally place a higher value on maintaining and growing the relationship itself than on the outcomes of the current transaction, and are more likely to avoid these potential concerns.

Compensation consultants need to behave and be perceived as business advisors. By taking a long-term view and developing a deep understanding of the client organization, they can maintain appropriate distance and objectivity. This further enhances the value of the services being provided and increases the likelihood of an ongoing, constructive client relationship.

## (b) Driving an Upward Spiral of Executive Pay

A common criticism of the compensation consulting profession is that compensation studies and recommendations automatically result in an upward spiral of executive pay. According to this argument, each time a company attempts to position its pay relative to the pay of other organizations, the benchmark is increased. For example, if a company desires to pay at the 50th percentile of a peer group, then adjusts its pay upward to achieve the 50th percentile of the peer group, the benchmark (50th percentile) rises for the next company that desires to pay at the 50th percentile of the same peer group.

Rather than being the cause of spiraling executive pay, keeping informed of prevailing market practices is a critical element in attracting, motivating, and retaining the highest level of talent needed to deliver superior results. Companies need to be informed of the market value or replacement value of the key positions within their organizations and then make thoughtful and appropriate decisions with respect to the incumbents in these positions and the overall financial strength of the organization. By considering changes in the market rate of compensation for critical positions, the skills and abilities of the incumbents in these positions, and the financial resources of the organization, sound and defensible compensation decisions can be made without artificially inflating pay levels.

The primary driver of any upward spiral in executive pay is scarcity. Just like any other product or service where demand exceeds supply, prices increase. In the context of executive compensation, the demand for great CEOs far exceeds the supply of great CEOs. And, many believe that the gap between the supply of and demand for CEO talent is only going to increase in the future. Under these circumstances, we should not be surprised to find an escalation in executive compensation.

Criticisms rather should be focused on those situations where compensation consultants and their clients are not evaluating and considering the relative performance of the executive team and the company as a whole. For example, a company that consistently performs in the 25th percentile of its peer group in critical areas should not consistently be providing executive compensation at the 75th percentile of its peer group. In these situations, not only can the overall benchmark pay levels be unduly impacted, but the alignment between pay and performance can be derailed.

## 14.5   ESTABLISHING A CONSULTING FOUNDATION: CONSTRUCTING THE FACT PATTERN

### (a) Understanding the Business Strategy and Key Performance Drivers

The first step in establishing a consulting foundation is to understand the business strategy and key performance drivers. In other words, how has the organization chosen to compete and how will it measure its success? Without this fundamental understanding, it is impossible to provide sound advice and counsel that will drive business results. For example, a mature company in a stable industry with few significant competitors will have very different executive compensation needs and challenges compared to an emerging company in a growth industry with limited barriers to entry. Similarly, a company focused on operational efficiency and cost optimization would select very different performance measures and compensation program designs compared to a company focused on capturing market share and growing the business. These issues are discussed in Chapters 1 and 2.

### (b) Identifying a Peer Company Group and Pay Practices

The next step in the building process is to identify appropriate peer companies and their pay practices. Peer companies often reflect organizations within the same industry and of similar size to the client. However, it is also important to consider companies that may better represent the true market for talent or companies that are performing at a comparable level. For example, a large transportation company may want to evaluate its pay practices against other similar transportation companies (industry peer group) and to a collection of large nationally dispersed organizations that have similar key positions responsible for capital-intensive logistics and related technology infrastructure (talent peer group). Another example would be a life sciences company that may want to evaluate its pay practices relative to an industry peer group as well as a group of companies that have achieved double-digit revenue growth and earnings per share over the last three years (performance peer group). See Chapter 9 for a detailed discussion of peer group selection.

Once the peer companies have been identified, pay data and practices can be collected, cleaned, and compiled. Compensation data typically are gathered for base salaries, annual incentives, and long-term incentives (including both cash and equity-based incentives). Data also can be gathered for beneficial ownership, stock option overhang (shares granted and reserved for future compensation grants compared to shares outstanding), annual stock option grant rates, and other compensation-related information. It is often important to review multiple years of compensation data to smooth any anomalies that may exist from one year to the next with respect to the variable elements of the total compensation package. For example, a single-year analysis may be distorted if one of the peer companies has an every-other-year stock option grant strategy or had an isolated year when an extremely large or mega stock option grant was made.

### (c) Establishing the Compensation Philosophy

In order to make use of the competitive market compensation data, the company must first agree on a compensation philosophy or strategy. In addition to addressing the definition of the relevant labor market (e.g., the selection of peer companies and the rationale for their selection), the compensation philosophy should articulate how the organization desires to position pay relative to the labor market. For example, the company may want to target base salaries at the 50th percentile, total cash compensation (salary plus incentive) at the 60th percentile, and total direct compensation (total cash compensation plus the annualized value of long-term incentives) at the 75th percentile. This would be considered a leveraged pay strategy because it relies heavily on the variable pay elements to drive the overall competitiveness of the pay package.

### (d) Comparing Current versus Desired Practice

Once the pay philosophy has been set or validated, variance analysis can be performed to assess how current pay practices align with the company's desired positioning. For example, based on the fact pattern just described, it may be revealed that actual base salary levels are positioned above the 50th percentile while total cash compensation is below the 60th percentile. This suggests that salary increases should be evaluated carefully and that incentive compensation levels are not providing the desired level of total cash compensation.

There are many elements in a typical total compensation program, and care must be taken to avoid making isolated decisions on individual elements without regard for the impact on the total program. For example, since many annual and long-term incentive plans have award opportunities tied to participants' base salaries, changes to base salaries cannot be made without considering the impact on total cash compensation and total direct compensation. A major responsibility of the compensation consultant is to bring this holistic perspective to bear on analysis and recommendations.

## (e) Testing Pay and Performance Linkage

An often overlooked but critical component of any compensation analysis is an internal and external test of the pay and performance linkage. Internally, the targeted compensation mix and variable pay plan designs should be reviewed and modified to ensure an appropriate mix between fixed and variable award opportunities and an appropriate alignment of pay and performance. Externally, variable compensation levels should be compared to companies that have performed similarly over the performance period on critical measures. For example, absent extenuating circumstances, there should be alignment between the competitiveness of annual incentive awards (e.g., 60th percentile) and the relative performance of the company compared to its peers (60th percentile).

## 14.6   COMPENSATION CONSULTANT AS A TRUSTED ADVISOR

## (a) Business Advisor versus Data Provider

Compensation consultants typically collect, clean, and compile a significant amount of compensation data in providing their services. These data provide a critical reference point from which to review and assess a company's current compensation arrangements relative to competitive market practices. However, the compensation consultant needs to be more than a data provider. Highly effective consultants need to function and be perceived as business advisors.

In the past, many compensation consultants focused exclusively on providing data. Today, compensation data often are automated and regarded as a commodity. Also, many companies have become dissatisfied with this approach and the quality of the advice it yields. Compensation consultants must get beyond the data and provide sound advice and counsel based on a broad understanding of their client business strategy, industry dynamics, competitive positioning, relative performance level, and other facts and circumstances. Collecting, cleaning, and compiling compensation data is the beginning, not the end, of the compensation consultant's responsibilities to the client.

To become a business advisor, the consultant needs to provide insight in addition to information. The ability to develop and provide insight is the by-product of combining the compensation consultant's expertise and experience with the deep knowledge and continuous learning that comes from lasting consulting relationships. In this role, compensation consultants rely more on personal trust than professional certifications and will add the most value by asking pointed and probing questions rather than providing additional pay data.

## (b) Guide to Best Practices

Most companies have some firsthand knowledge of best practices, among their board members, their executive team, or their human resource professionals. Also, most compensation consultants have access to and knowledge of best practices, and some helpful in-depth research exists on this topic. However, in order to be highly effective, the compensation consultant must serve as a guide to best practices. The difference between being knowledgeable regarding best practices and serving as a guide to best practices is the ability to filter the vast array of ideas, approaches, and solutions to arrive at the specific best practices that make the most sense for the company and that have the greatest potential for creating sustainable shareholder value.

This filter is not a tool, a technique, or even a process. Instead, it is an ability that a business advisor can obtain only through experience, intellectual curiosity, deep knowledge of the client, and enduring relationships. For example, the ability quickly to identify passing fads, myopic thinking, inconsistencies with core strategy, and hidden implementation obstacles can save valuable time and money. Being able to map, modify, and apply best practices from other industries and situations can create the greatest opportunity for competitive advantage and is therefore another invaluable competency of a business advisor.

## (c) Shareholder Perspective

The hallmark of a true business advisor is the ability to review and analyze information and decisions from multiple perspectives. Only through thoughtful and deliberate consideration of all relevant constituencies can a consultant truly provide sound advice and counsel. In the executive compensation arena, one of the most critical perspectives to review thoroughly is that of shareholders.

Much of what is done in executive compensation is focused on shareholders. For example, when setting executive compensation strategy, alignment with shareholder interests is of paramount concern. When developing restricted stock or stock option grant levels, shareholder dilution is reviewed carefully. However, these are simply the direct and tangible areas in which the shareholder perspective needs to be considered; many other components need to be taken into account.

The significant rise of institutional ownership and shareholder activism has changed dramatically the concerns and considerations of compensation consultants. It also has changed the roles, responsibilities, and in some cases attitudes of the compensation consultant's most visible customer—the board's compensation committee. Although these issues are explored more thoroughly in other chapters, the importance of completely understanding the shareholder perspective and acting on this knowledge cannot be overstated.

In theory, shareholders are most concerned with long-tem value creation as evidenced by increases in total shareholder return. Therefore, everything the compensation consultant reviews, analyzes, and recommends needs to be viewed through this lens of long-term value creation. Whether it is attracting the right talent to the company, providing the right reward structure to drive high performance, or retaining the organization's key talent, the impact on shareholder value needs to be understood, analyzed, and documented. Finally, in today's environment, shareholder communications need to be complete, clear, timely, and accurate in order to meet fully the needs of this important constituency.

# Index